Received from O D...
26 Ju

MW00637278

REV MATT...
GRANDMA PEARL &
GRANDPA JOE!

MARRIED AUNT MARY AND
UNCLE JACK
BAPTISED MOM

The Reverend Mark Matthews

An Activist in the Progressive Era

The Reverend Mark Matthews

An Activist in the Progressive Era

Dale E. Soden

[signature: Dale E. Soden]

University of Washington Press

Seattle and London

Library of Congress Cataloging-in-Publication Data
Soden, Dale Edward.
The Reverend Mark Matthews : an activist in the progressive era /
Dale E. Soden.
p. cm.
Includes bibliographical references and index.
ISBN 0-295-98021-4 (alk. paper)
1. Matthews, Mark A. (Mark Allison), 1867-1940.
2. Presbyterian Church—United States—Clergy—Biography.
I. Title.
BX9225.M38 S63 2000
285'1.'092—DC21
[B] 00-064823

For my parents and in memory of my grandmother,
who first told me stories of Mark Matthews

Contents

Acknowledgments

This book is the result of the work and encouragement of many people throughout the past twenty years. I am particularly indebted to my mentor at the University of Washington, Lewis O. Saum, for his many insightful comments and suggestions. I am also very appreciative of the encouragement and criticism from the late Robert Burke, who inspired so many historians of the Pacific Northwest. Charles LeWarne and Tom Edwards have been especially supportive of this project, and I am very grateful. In many ways my intellectual companion has been Howard Berger, whose friendship and thought-provoking conversations since our days as graduate students at the University of Washington have sustained and inspired me in inestimable ways.

I wish also to thank two of my professors from my undergraduate days at Pacific Lutheran University—David Johnson and Philip Nordquist. Without their teaching and inspiration, I surely never would have attempted to pursue history as a profession. Similarly, my many friends and colleagues at Oklahoma Baptist University supported my efforts; in particular, Marc Billson provided encouragement for my research and writing on this and other subjects. Over the past fifteen years, I have benefited greatly from the friendships and support from my colleagues not only in the History and Political Studies Department but from people throughout Whitworth College. In particular, Jerry Sittser, Arlin Migliazzo, Jim Hunt, and Jim Waller have offered helpful comments regarding Matthews and his significance in the Pacific Northwest. President Bill Robinson and Dean Tammy Reid have been particularly supportive of this project.

Many people have contributed significantly in other ways. Karyl Winn and her staff at the archives and manuscripts division at the

University of Washington have been particularly helpful. Julidta Tarver and especially Kim McKaig have offered invaluable assistance. Robert Welsh has been most helpful in providing additional research, and Dick Finch has been exceptionally supportive. And at Whitworth, Anna Kenney and Arvita Mott have been most helpful in the preparation of the manuscript.

And finally, I wish to acknowledge my debt to five of my life-long friends from Pacific Lutheran days. These individuals have always prompted me to think in new and better ways, but more important, they have demonstrated the power of true friendship—John Beck, Bruce Bjerke, Mark Houglum, Steve Lansing, and Bruce Willis. And lastly, I wish to acknowledge the patience, love, and support of my family— my wife, Peggy, who has demonstrated her own courage, and our two children, Joel and Marta, whom I love dearly.

Preface

On February 8, 1940, Seattle residents by the thousands and people from around the country paid their last respects to the pastor of the largest Presbyterian church in the world, Mark Allison Matthews. Three days earlier, the seventy-two-year-old pastor had died from pneumonia complications; with his death, a remarkable era in the history of Seattle ended. On the day of Matthews's funeral, hundreds of men and women stood outside First Presbyterian Church in a chilly wind and winter rain for hours in order to acknowledge silently the life of this man who had exerted so much religious influence in the Pacific Northwest. An estimated 5,000 people passed by his casket; many barely knew him, while others had worked intimately with him during his thirty-eight years in Seattle. The funeral service itself reflected the broad reach of this Southerner who came to the Pacific Northwest shortly after the Klondike gold rush at the turn of the century and soon went to work with mayors, governors, and presidents to realize his vision of a righteous urban community. Washington Governor Clarence Martin and Seattle Mayor Arthur Langlie joined members of the church session at the head of the procession, and elders of First Presbyterian served as honorary pallbearers. The Reverend Frank Warren, chair of the religion department at Seattle Pacific College, gave the opening prayer, and the Very Reverend John D. McLauchlan, dean of St. Mark's Episcopal Cathedral, closed the service. Seattle newspapers published tributes from around the state and across the nation that praised Mark Matthews's impact on the many people whose lives he had touched. But there surely were others in the city who did not mourn the cleric's passing. His life had been filled with controversy and criticism of his method and manner. Yet without doubt, he left an imprint on the city and the region that has not been fully analyzed or understood.

No other clergyman wielded greater influence either socially or politically in the Pacific Northwest during the first half of the twentieth century. Matthews built the First Presbyterian Church of Seattle into a remarkably complex organization. A few Seattle residents can still recall the rabid prohibitionist's attacks on police corruption and his charges of political graft and his public feuds with Colonel Alden Blethen, publisher of the *Seattle Times*, and Mayor Hiram Gill. The preacher was an imposing figure at six feet, five inches tall; he wore his hair longer than was the custom in Seattle and could exert a commanding presence in almost any gathering. He could be charming in the tradition of a Southern gentleman, but he also could be vicious in his attacks upon his enemies.

Matthews's ministerial career was remarkable. From the beginning of his pastorate in Georgia to the end of his life in Seattle, Matthews immersed himself in the political issues of his day. Attracted to a number of the reform issues associated with Populism and Progressivism, Matthews embraced many tenets of the Social Gospel movement, which attempted to address the ills associated with urbanization and industrialization. Famous for its fight against tuberculosis and its innovative kindergarten, Matthews's church in Seattle also organized day nurseries to assist working mothers and unemployment bureaus for the downtrodden. Matthews helped establish the first juvenile court in Seattle, and his work with Japanese and Chinese immigrants—at a time when Asian prejudice ran high on the Pacific Coast—was a significant contribution. Late in his career he led the drive to build Harborview hospital and served on countless social service boards. As the head of a congregation that numbered nearly 9,000 at its peak, Matthews exercised considerable political influence over numerous mayors, and many Seattleites benefited from his friendship with President Woodrow Wilson. In many ways, his approach could be considered progressive and innovative. At the same time, Matthews harbored an anxiety about the state of American society that manifested itself in fundamentalist religious views and extremely conservative political positions. He became a central figure in the battle between fundamentalism and modernism within the Presbyterian church.

Yet little has been written and virtually no analysis offered about this cleric who was born in the hills of Georgia. Several historians of the Pacific Northwest have mentioned him briefly in the context of certain events. Perhaps most notably, Murray Morgan, in his book *Skid*

Road (1951), described Matthews as someone who could have stepped out of a seventeenth-century Puritan New England village. In general, Matthews has attracted the attention of historians for the way in which he seemingly ran against the tide of historical change. From his diatribes against alcohol to his opposition to women in the pulpit, Matthews has appeared to many to be the symbol of a male-dominated religious world that increasingly found itself out of place in a modern society. Often thought of as conservative or reactionary by historians or local commentators, Matthews perhaps has seemed uninteresting as a window into the world in which he lived. However, Mark Matthews is an excellent lens through which to view American society from the Civil War to the beginning of the Second World War. Although at times he did indeed attempt to live in opposition to a number of historical forces, far more of his life is a product of the broader intellectual, religious, social, and political currents of his day.

Yet if Matthews's life is best understood as a result of many of the forces of his day, it is nevertheless a complex prism through which to view his times. He was no simple-minded preacher or one-dimensional thinker. He blended social reform with conservative theology in a way that distinguished him from the majority of his colleagues. His Southern religion, peculiar intellectual training, and early political experiences created a potent and complex combination of ideas and values for a minister coming to the Pacific Northwest—the least-churched region of the country. Matthews attempted to make Christianity relevant and compelling to the modern person without falling prey to the temptation to abandon orthodox evangelical Christianity. At his most confident, he believed that the Bible could provide a solution for every problem facing American society; his sermons reflect a remarkable breadth of topic and concern. He never wavered in his conviction that Christianity provided the one true path for all who cared to believe. At his most anxious, however, Matthews felt that Christianity as well as traditional American values were vulnerable to conspiracy, heresy, and an emerging secular and hedonistic popular culture.

The complexity of that tension between his vision of a more socially just and humane society and his fears and anxieties that resulted in bitter conflict with those with whom he differed provides a major theme of this book. In the end, Matthews is best understood as largely the product of his time and place rather than as a person who lived simply in opposition to his era. And yet there are surprising moments of unpredictability in Matthews's life that make any effort to explain confidently the reasons behind all of his actions a difficult challenge.

To attempt to understand the vision and direction of Mark Matthews's ministry, one must start with his religious and political experiences in the South. Born two years after the Civil War in a small town north of Atlanta, Matthews grew up in the milieu of Southern evangelicalism. Trained in Old School Presbyterian theology, which tended to reinforce intellectual rigidity and helped lead him toward fundamentalism, he grew up in a part of Georgia that experienced the unrest of the farmers' movements and nascent Populism. From an early age he witnessed religion and politics being intertwined in such a way that he found them inseparable for the rest of his life. His basic set of intellectual assumptions, his fundamental political worldview, and his foundational religious outlook originated during his years in the South. This combination of influences led him to the basic conclusion that his primary duty as a minister was to help create righteous communities whether they were in Calhoun, Georgia, Jackson, Tennessee, or Seattle, Washington.

Like thousands of religious leaders of his day, Matthews expressed confidence that America would be the New Israel and that urban communities would play a vital role in the spread of Christianity. He embraced political reform in order to create a more socially just society and to cleanse the community of evil forces. Matthews believed, like a good Calvinist, that he should transform the communities in which he lived according to Biblical principles. Like thousands of Protestant ministers, Matthews believed that the sick and needy should receive adequate care; he believed that cities should exemplify the best of democratic traditions; and he believed that the future depended on Americans embracing appropriate moral values. Women, children, and the common laborer should all be protected from the exploitative nature of free-market capitalism. At the heart of his dream was a belief that people must share a common commitment to the well-being of the community. He assumed that homogeneity was superior to heterogeneity, and moral absolutism superior to cultural relativism. But if those assumptions help explain his zeal for reform, they also help explain his religious fundamentalism and tendency to repress his political enemies. His commitment to a common set of truths and values led him to attack vigorously political, intellectual, and religious ideas that seemed to threaten that unity. For Matthews, producing a righteous community required both reform and vigilance; it required both persuasion and coercion. His urge to shape the social ethos of the city and his determination to dominate Seattle's religious life earned him both admiration and enmity.

Organized in a roughly chronological fashion, this book identifies the principal religious, intellectual, and political forces that shaped his early ministries in Georgia and Tennessee. Significant attention is paid to the way in which Matthews embarked on a ministry that reflected the influence of social Christianity in the late nineteenth century. Once in Seattle, Matthews rapidly increased membership in the First Presbyterian Church and attempted to impart a complex worldview to his parishioners. From attitudes toward gender, the home, and the workplace to issues of cultural authority and the role of the church in the larger society, Matthews attempted to shape the nature of his congregation's understanding. Chapters four and five explore the ways in which his quest for urban righteousness led him to embrace the strategies of the Social Gospel and most of the reforms associated with the Progressive movement. Chapters six and seven analyze his well-publicized battles with Mayor Hiram Gill and the publisher of the *Seattle Times*, Alden Blethen. Chapter eight details Matthews's response to the First World War and the impact of nationalism on his political values. An overwhelming fear of communism and radical politics influenced his views of the Seattle General Strike and the activities of the Industrial Workers of the World (Wobblies). Matthews's drive for righteousness made him particularly vulnerable to the patriotic tenor of the times. The Red Scare exacerbated his natural intolerance of religious and political differences. And yet, far from being out of step with his times, Matthews reflected the general views of the majority of Seattle residents during this period.

Chapter nine explores Mark Matthews's role within the national Presbyterian church. Elected moderator of the General Assembly, the largest governing body of the church, in 1912, Matthews emerged as a major figure at precisely the point at which Presbyterians began to split over fundamentalism and modernism. By the 1920s, he could be identified with the extreme conservatives, and yet he came to play a critical role on the Special Commission of 1925, which helped to avoid a major schism within the church. He also wielded influence in the debate within the national Presbyterian church over the role that women should play. His career and his sermons provide evidence of the complexity of the fundamentalist movement.

The final two chapters analyze Matthews in the context of the 1920s and '30s. Like many Americans, he experienced considerable anxiety over everything from the "amusement mania" of the period, as he liked to call it, to the changing nature of Seattle politics. Through his radio station and other means, he continued to attempt to influence the ways in which people experienced the modern world. During the last decade of his life, Matthews remained engaged by the events of his day. He tried desperately to mitigate the effect of the Great Depression on hundreds of people, he warned his parishioners and anyone who would listen about the dangers of communism, and perhaps most notably, he spoke out vigorously against the rising tide of Nazism and Jewish persecution.

Mark Matthews was a man of enormous energy and vision. He was clearly shaped by the times in which he lived, and yet he struggled mightily to gain control over the forces at work within American life. He attempted to move thousands of people to believe in a transcendent God and hoped that a righteous society would be the result. He was not universally liked in his own time, and certainly some of his activities appear to be the result of poor choices, his own quest for personal power, or bad judgment. Yet Matthews touched a tremendous number of lives and proved unusually influential not only in the Pacific Northwest but throughout the country. His dream of a righteous urban community seems naïve to most Americans in the late twentieth century, but Mark Matthews's vision empowered him to become the Pacific Northwest's most prominent religious figure of the twentieth century. This is the story of how he was shaped by the times in which he lived, drew upon every resource at his command, and attempted to redeem the world around him.

The Reverend Mark Matthews

An Activist in the Progressive Era

CHAPTER 1

The Hills of Georgia

You say you love God and your fellow man who is your brother. Now prove that love by entering the field and working for the salvation and elevation of your city and country at large.

—Mark Matthews (1893)

Mark Matthews loved the Pacific Northwest with a great passion. Few people voiced their support for the region more frequently than did he. Boosterism permeated his soul; he never turned down an opportunity to praise Seattle's climate, economic resources, and hospitality. Yet throughout his life, the preacher retained a deep affection for the region of his birth—the South. Because Matthews spent his first thirty-four years in Georgia and Tennessee, his approach to problems, his patterns of work and thought, as well as his vision for a righteous society were nurtured in the South. Born only two years after the end of the Civil War, he grew to maturity in Georgia during Reconstruction. He, like many fellow Southerners in those years, faced the problem of survival. The experience of poverty seared Matthews's childhood memory in a way that helped develop his compassion for the downtrodden. But in addition to his experience with poverty, Matthews grew to maturity in a region steeped in the religious values of Southern revivalism and evangelical Presbyterianism. This Southern religious background would greatly shape his attitudes toward church growth and congregational mission.

Matthews's formal education also took place in the South. Limited to a great extent by the economic and social upheaval after the Civil War, his schooling nevertheless provided him with an intellectual

3

framework grounded in Southern Presbyterian theology. It was this brand of Presbyterianism and this specific intellectual orientation that he took with him to the Pacific Northwest.

Matthews could not help being influenced too by the political climate of his native region. Growing up in the hills of northern Georgia, he experienced the frustrations and hardships that encouraged farmers to attempt political change. The Farmers' Alliance movement and subsequently the Populist movement helped shape his political views and pushed him toward reform efforts. These movements clearly helped him develop the perception that politics provided the key to shaping the social ethos of a community. Matthews became convinced that religion and politics could be effectively intertwined. Throughout his life, he responded to forces for change in American society and specifically within the Presbyterian church. But his basic assumptions and his commitment to taking an active part in shaping the affairs of his community and country were established in the tiny communities of Calhoun and Dalton, Georgia, at the southern tip of the Appalachian Mountains.

Few details about Matthews's childhood have survived. His father, Mark Lafayette Matthews, was born near Raleigh, North Carolina, in 1826; his paternal grandfather, Frank C. Matthews, was a prominent planter. For some reason, most probably financial, Mark Lafayette migrated to Macon, Georgia, where he established himself as a carriage maker in approximately 1840.[1] Tall, handsome, and ambitious, Mark Lafayette aspired to respectability in Southern circles. Later in life he sported a distinguished white beard, and his granddaughter remembered him as an inveterate chewer of tobacco. In Macon, Mark Lafayette met Melinda Rebecca Clemmons, the daughter of a hat manufacturer. Clemmons, a Methodist, had been born in Dandridge, Tennessee, in 1837. In 1850, Mark Lafayette and Melinda Rebecca married and, shortly thereafter, moved to Calhoun, a small community of fewer than 1,000 people on the railroad line between Chattanooga and Atlanta. Surrounded by hills and pine forests, Calhoun served as a small commercial and business hub for area farmers. Mark and Melinda Matthews became respected members of the community and apparently rose to relative prosperity, as indicated by their ownership of two slaves. However, the family suffered a number of tragedies. Melinda Matthews was pregnant as many as ten times between 1850 and 1867, but until September 24, 1867, when Mark Allison was born, not one child survived infancy.[2]

The Hills of Georgia

With the onset of the Civil War, prior to the birth of their son, the Matthewses' lives changed dramatically. Matthews enlisted as part of Georgia's Fifth Regiment, but ill health forced him to return home prematurely, and he turned his carriage business into a repair shop for the Confederate army. By May 1864, General Sherman had begun his march to Atlanta, and Calhoun stood directly in his path. On or about the sixteenth of May, Sherman's troops burned Matthews's shop to the ground, though Matthews and his wife escaped. They later returned to Calhoun and attempted to begin their lives anew.[3]

The Matthews family suffered deeply from the economic dislocation after the war. Typical of many businesses in the South, Matthews's carriage enterprise never regained the level of prosperity it had reached prior to the war. A proud man, Matthews failed to develop a new trade or move into a new line of business. As a consequence, Mark Allison came into a financially impoverished world, and his family eventually needed his help to survive. As soon as he was able, young Matthews went to work at a variety of odd jobs to supplement his father's income. Later in life, Mark Allison Matthews liked to tell people of his work at J. M. Harlin's dry goods store, where he learned the art of salesmanship in the shoe department, and of his service as county treasurer. For a short time he worked at a local printing press, where he learned not only the power of newspapers in shaping local opinion but also a healthy respect for machines. On one occasion a piece of iron flew off the press and narrowly missed decapitating him. Even after he began to preach, Matthews still advertised himself as a salesman of pianos, organs, violins, and guitars. In his adult life, Matthews often told people that his experiences as a young boy helped him learn about the business world, meet different people, and discover that he had the power to persuade others.[4]

We know very little about Mark Allison Matthews's life inside his home. His dress and mannerisms bore the imprint of his Southern upbringing and suggest that his parents desired to fashion him into a gentleman. In the Southern family, the gentleman exercised firm control. He was a commanding presence, well educated, finely formed: in short, the perfect patriarch. "Women, along with children," according to the Southern historian Anne Firor Scott, "were expected to recognize their proper and subordinate place and to be obedient to the head of the family."[5] However, in the Southern mind, the woman was much more than a subservient creature: the ideal Southern woman possessed innocence, beauty, keen perception, grace, and modesty. Revered as the person who gave society its meaning, the Southern belle conveyed the essence of civilization to her children. Little is known about the Matthewses' home life, but it is likely that his parents expected Mark and his sister, Laura, who was born two years after he was, to fulfill these roles. Mark respected his father but venerated his mother; in his eyes, she was the ideal woman. In his sermons, Matthews would hold to this Southern model when addressing problems of the family and, more specifically, when dealing with the role of women in society.

Young Matthews may also have been influenced by what recent historians have identified as the blend of values associated with the "Lost Cause of the Confederacy" and late Victorianism. One historian has argued that in the South "things spiritual ranked higher than things material," and the Southerner tended to equate things spiritual with the chivalry of the Old South.[6] Historians have argued that this sense of spirituality distinguished Southern culture from Yankee civilization. Northern capitalism, industrialism, and urbanization manifested a crass materialism in the minds of Southern writers and clergy, whereas Southern society reflected more genteel and spiritual values. Many Southerners argued that the Civil War centered on a constitutional principle involving civil liberty and states' rights. After their defeat on the battlefield, the former Confederates still believed that true civilization and true religion flourished below the Mason-Dixon line. This postwar environment encouraged young men like Matthews to value the role of religion in society.

Religion provided the most immediate influence on Mark Matthews's life. Years later the preacher recalled, "I was regenerated when thirteen years of age. The call to preach was as clear and as definite as it could possibly be. I announced to my parents and friends that my life was directed to God's ministry."[7] Apparently, he did not record the details of his conversion, but one can assume that the event for him was similar to that experienced by so many others. It may have happened in the midst of a Sunday morning service as part of a regular altar call, or it might have taken place during a tent revival led by an itinerant evangelist. Whatever the details, the thirteen-year-old Matthews committed his life to Christ; he would later say that he could not get into the pulpit fast enough. "I would go to the church before the hour for the services; gather up hymn books and give them to the people as they entered the building for worship; ring the bell or do any kind of work."[8]

The Hills of Georgia

Matthews grew up in America's evangelical subculture—a subculture that transmitted a specific set of values and attitudes for dealing with the secular world. His initial encounter with the evangelical world came with the guidance of his father. The elder Matthews actively participated in the most evangelical wing of the Presbyterian church in the South, the Cumberland church. The Matthews family regularly attended the Liberty Cumberland Presbyterian Church, located just south of Calhoun in a tiny community called Lily Pond. It was in that church that Mark Allison and his sister, Laura, were raised. In 1875, the Reverend Z. M. McGhee organized the Calhoun Cumberland Presbyterian Church, and the Matthews family switched its membership and attended for four years until the struggling church folded. Then the family moved back to the Liberty Cumberland church in Lily Pond.[9]

The Cumberland branch of Presbyterians came into existence in 1813 in Kentucky as a result of the breach between Old Side antirevivalists and New Side revivalists. The Old Side emphasized confessional doctrine whereas the New Side, which grew out of the Great Awakening of the 1730s and 1740s, emphasized spiritual conversion. With the Second Great Awakening at the beginning of the nineteenth century, the schism widened. Presbyterians faced significant difficulties in developing congregations on the frontier because, unlike their Methodist and Baptist colleagues, Presbyterians required their clergy to be college educated and to have a seminary degree. As a consequence, many Presbyterian churches did not have pastors. In response, the Cumberland presbytery in Kentucky, with the support of New Side advocates, began in 1837 to ordain and license pastors who had no seminary education. However, the General Assembly and presbytery, the representative body that governed a number of congregations in a geographic region, refused to recognize these pastors as legitimate clergy.

The Cumberland presbytery also made it clear that the concept of election (God's choice of who would be saved) need not be emphasized as strongly as it had been among Old Side proponents who stressed the omnipotence of God in regard to personal salvation. Cumberland preachers tended to place greater responsibility for salvation on the believer. Preachers invited individuals to accept Christ as their Savior; rejection was thought to condemn one to eternal damnation. The resulting controversy ended with a formal schism in 1810

The Hills of Georgia

in which the Cumberland presbytery left the main branch of the Presbyterian church. Matthews accepted Old Side or Old School theology, but he never abandoned the evangelical emphasis on conversion and personal commitment to Christ.[10]

One other Cumberland emphasis that may have played a part in shaping Matthews's worldview was the stress on the mission of America. One historian of the Cumberland church asserts that Cumberland Presbyterians believed that "the future of the world depended on the future of America, and the future of America depended on the triumph of the evangelical message."[11] Primarily rural in background, Cumberland Presbyterians believed that cities were dens of iniquity. Cumberland preachers attacked gambling, liquor, tobacco, dancing, card-playing, Sabbath "desecration," and the Roman Catholic church.[12] Another Presbyterian historian concluded that Cumberland members believed that "the blessings God had bestowed on Christian America made the export of its civilization as well as its religion a divine imperative."[13] This missionary zeal, this confidence in American history, and the assumed responsibility for converting the nonbeliever would prove to be rock-solid foundations for the rest of Matthews's career.

A contemporary of Mark Matthews's who was influenced to some degree by the Cumberland experience was William Jennings Bryan. Several of Bryan's biographers assert that the Cumberland experience made the "Great Commoner" much more sympathetic to revivalism, as well as more disposed to seeing politics as a realm in which religious vision should be a driving force. In this respect, Matthews and Bryan, who came to know one another fairly well, had much in common.[14]

The Cumberland experience fostered an atmosphere in which theological discussion focused on the battle between the forces of good and evil. Most evangelicals held that the devil was very much alive and well. The proponents of freedom were matched against tyrannical oppressors, and the children of light fought valiantly against the children of darkness. This worldview had no place for neutrality, complexity, or bystanders. To what extent young Matthews was conscious of these issues is difficult to say. Certainly, it would have been unusual if he had worked out these issues in any systematic form. Yet the vocabulary would have been familiar; *sin, grace, salvation, devil, good,* and *evil* emerged as words and concepts that shaped his thinking and his belief system at an early age. Religious experience, for young Matthews,

The Hills of Georgia

meant a heart-felt conversion, a simple piety, and a belief that one lived in the midst of a cosmic struggle between good and evil.

If his father's disposition toward Cumberland Presbyterianism influenced Matthews's early religious inclinations, the development of his more formal theology came largely under the tutoring of Joseph B. Hillhouse. More than any other person, Hillhouse schooled Matthews in the peculiarities of Presbyterian theology and served as his single most important intellectual influence. Born in 1820, Hillhouse graduated from the Presbyterian seminary in Columbia, South Carolina, in 1845 and began preaching the same year. As a student and later as a teacher, Hillhouse earned a reputation as a fine scholar of Latin, Greek, and Hebrew classics.[15]

Residing in South Carolina for nearly thirty years after entering the ministry, Hillhouse decided in 1873 to move to Gordon County, Georgia, where he proceeded to organize the Calhoun Presbyterian Church. By 1879, Hillhouse added to his duties by developing Calhoun's educational institutions. He became principal of the Calhoun Academy, which during the war had served as a horse stable for the Union army. Under Hillhouse's direction, the academy emerged in the 1880s as the most respected educational institution in the county. Hillhouse directed a curriculum that emphasized a classical education. In 1883, townsfolk built a two-story annex to accommodate an increased number of students, and in the following year, the Calhoun Academy officially became the Gordon County University. Shortly thereafter, Mark Matthews attended the institution and began to receive the guidance of Hillhouse's tutorials, with a specific emphasis on theology.[16] Years later, Matthews wrote, "The name [Gordon County University] was only prophetic and pathetic because it was not a university but had a good college curriculum."[17]

Nevertheless, for Matthews, this was the sum of his formal education. Hillhouse introduced him to the formal theological underpinnings not of the Cumberland church but of the Princeton theology, commonly referred to as Old School Presbyterianism, as practiced in the Presbyterian Church in the United States (PCUS), the formal name for the Southern Presbyterian church.

At Columbia Seminary in South Carolina, founded by graduates of Princeton, Joseph Hillhouse had learned the basics of orthodox Calvinism. Years later, Matthews told an interviewer that Hillhouse "never lost an opportunity to teach me the truth and beauty of Calvinism."[18]

Old School Presbyterians emphasized the omnipotence of God and his divine election as articulated in the Westminster Confession of 1643. The key philosophical underpinnings for Old School Presbyterianism were found in the principles of Scottish common-sense realism. Articulated primarily by Thomas Reid (1710-1796) and Dugald Stewart (1753-1828), common-sense realism attempted to refute the idealism of George Berkeley and the skepticism of David Hume. It supported several key theological conclusions, and, unquestionably, Hillhouse bequeathed this intellectual legacy to Matthews.[19]

Old School Presbyterians appealed to proponents of common-sense realism to affirm the notion that the existence of God could be intuited. Old School Presbyterians found common-sense realism helpful in supporting the belief that the natural world could be studied by the scientific method of observation. They believed that the Bible was a repository of facts that corresponded with the natural world. Scholars at Princeton embraced a Baconian method of induction in order to convince themselves that the Bible was an objective reflection of reality. Princeton theologians consciously embraced a scientific method for studying both the natural and the transcendent world. They asserted that religion and science did not conflict; scientific discoveries, believed Old School Presbyterians, only confirmed the majesty of God's creation. Mark Matthews retained this confidence in Biblical authority throughout his life. He never expressed a doubt that science done properly would always correspond with Biblical truth.[20]

Common-sense realism also helped reinforce for young Matthews the necessity of Biblical revelation for all people. Reid and Stewart had asserted that the mind had finite capabilities and therefore was limited in its ability to understand God. Princeton theologians believed Scripture was necessary to help inform the mind more fully of the nature of God. Armed with the methodology of induction, confident in their defense of revelation and moral precepts, Hillhouse and other Old School Presbyterians attempted to fend off challenges from all sides. They worked assiduously to refute opponents who tried to use reason to dismiss religion, as well as rivals who tried to reduce Christianity to nothing but reason. Children of the moderate wing of the Enlightenment, Princeton Presbyterians were also deeply aware of a more radically skeptical strain of thinking, particularly among the French. Extremely hostile to religion, this radical skepticism sought to juxtapose free inquiry and science against religion and metaphysics. Princeton-trained scholars fervently sought to avoid such a dichotomy and re-

The Hills of Georgia

lied heavily on Scottish common-sense assumptions to affirm the compatibility of religion and science.

Perhaps a little more difficult for Matthews to accept was the way in which Old School Presbyterians used common-sense realism to temper excessive evangelism and piety. Princeton Presbyterians often argued that Methodists, Baptists, and many other denominations emphasized the heart at the expense of the head. The pervasive anti-intellectualism of the antebellum period moved Presbyterians to bolster their stated preference for a balance between heart and head by affirming the complementary relationship between religion and science.

By far the most influential effort to integrate the assumptions of Scottish common-sense realism into Protestant theology was that made by Charles Hodge. Teaching at Princeton beginning in 1822, Hodge became the institution's most respected spokesman throughout the nineteenth century by editing the powerful *Princeton Review* and by publishing in 1871 his *Systematic Theology*. Required reading for Matthews, Hodge's works shaped the doctrinal understanding of the young Southerner.

Quite strikingly, Charles Hodge's introduction to his *Systematic Theology* made clear his emphasis on science as the important model for theology.

> The Bible is no more a system of theology, than nature is a system of chemistry or of mechanics. We find in nature the facts which the chemist or the mechanical philosopher has to examine, and from them to ascertain the laws by which they are determined. So the Bible contains the truths which the theologian has to collect, authenticate, arrange, and exhibit in their internal relation to each other.[21]

From the very outset, Hodge emphasized induction as the principal means of scrutinizing the Holy Scriptures. "The Bible is to the theologian what nature is to the man of science," he argued. "It is his storehouse of facts; and his method of ascertaining what the Bible teaches, is the same as that which the natural philosopher adopts to ascertain what nature teaches."[22] The theology of Charles Hodge, conveyed through Joseph Hillhouse, formed the intellectual foundation for young Matthews.[23] Hodge's approach also provided a basis for Matthews's eventual shift toward fundamentalism when he was in Seattle.

The combination of Princeton theology and his parents' frontier religious influence provided Matthews with his intellectual roots and his pietistic vision. Reared in the American evangelical tradition, Matthews embraced revivalism and appealed to simple piety as the best means to increase the flock. Yet when necessary, he could rely on Old School theology and common-sense realism.

In addition to teaching Princeton theology, Hillhouse helped develop Matthews's approach to pulpit ministry. Hillhouse worked incessantly with Matthews on his speaking style; the older pastor had his young colleague practice enunciating with gravel in his mouth to perfect the projection of his voice. Thus, it was with apparently great confidence that Matthews began preaching in local churches shortly after he graduated. In the spring of 1887 he looked forward to his first major public address: speaking before the graduating class of the university. Tragically, Hillhouse never saw his protégé make his debut. Two weeks prior to Matthews's speech, Hillhouse fell ill and died. Undaunted, Matthews made the address to much acclaim. The local newspapers reported that he spoke in "a masterly way, beautifully illustrating [and] . . . making the thread of connection strikingly visible to the eye of the imagination."[24]

Licensed to preach in 1886 by the Cumberland church, the nineteen-year-old Matthews filled a succession of Presbyterian and Methodist pulpits. Churches in small towns like Calhoun frequently could not pay one minister a full salary, and young pastors like Matthews often "rode the circuit," serving two or three different congregations by alternating Sundays. In October 1887, the Cumberland Presbyterian Church officially ordained Matthews as a minister, since the church did not require seminary training for its pastors. But following the death of Hillhouse, the Calhoun Presbyterian Church, affiliated with the main branch of the Presbyterian church in the South—the Presbyterian Church in the United States (PCUS)—needed a pastor. Unlike the Cumberland branch, the PCUS did require seminary training for its pastors. But perhaps because Matthews had been so close to Hillhouse and the congregation so familiar with the young preacher, he seemed like the natural choice to replace his mentor. The church arranged to circumvent the seminary requirement by having Matthews take an examination, which he passed in January 1890.[25] From the beginning, the young cleric's remarkable energy and his organizational skill impressed the Calhoun congregation. Hillhouse, though greatly beloved, had unsuccessfully attempted for five years to raise enough money to construct a new church. In less than two years, Matthews directed the completion of the building and steadily increased the membership.[26]

The Hills of Georgia

From the outset, Matthews possessed a certain flair that caught the attention of both parishioners and the press. He cultivated a sense of distinction at the same time that he exuded an affinity for the common man. He seemed at ease with everyone, from the wealthiest and most powerful to the poorest and the youngest. One of the best contemporary descriptions of Matthews comes from someone who observed him in Chattanooga.

> In appearance, Mr. Matthews is very striking. . . . His face is small, devoid of beard or mustache, and exceptionally strong. His forehead is very high, and as the hair is worn long and very curly, and combed well back, this feature appears very prominent. In his dress, Mr. Matthews, as a minister, is also quite out of the ordinary run. His clothing is of the very latest cut, and fits him to perfection. He wears a high standing collar, white lawn tie, low-cut vest, and in the midst of a broad expanse of immaculate white shirt bosom there glitters and glistens a magnificent diamond stud.[27]

In contrast to Matthews's rather imposing image in the pulpit, Calhoun residents saw him invite all of the town children to go fishing with him at a nearby creek. Telling them to bring biscuit, worm, and pole, the young preacher found his favorite fishing hole and undoubtedly entertained youngsters with stories containing a moral lesson. All through his life, Matthews developed warm relationships with children.[28]

Matthews's early ministry in Georgia during the 1880s and 1890s established most of the fundamental patterns that would endure for the rest of his career. Matthews did not emphasize the finer points of theology but stressed the importance of the church as a place where one committed to serving Christ, studied the Bible, learned the appropriate Christian lifestyle, and served the social needs of the community. Most of his early sermons, in fact, are noteworthy for the absence of theology and the stress on common sense and simple piety. Matthews preached a simple straightforward message to his flock; he exhorted them to believe in Christ as their personal savior, to love their fellow human beings, and to apply Christian principles to the social and political problems of the community.

Matthews's methods and approach remained remarkably consistent throughout his ministry. He built church membership through a combination of local revivals and consistently stimulating preaching. He organized the membership into a variety of groups and worked interdenominationally to cultivate a sense of Christian unity in the community. And, finally, he used the pulpit and the local press to make moral arguments about social issues and to influence public policy. Matthews would soon gain regional attention for the success and the intensity with which he applied these strategies.

Matthews's reputation as an evangelist grew very rapidly in northwestern Georgia, southeastern Tennessee, and northeastern Alabama. He frequently led local revivals and spoke about prohibition. "Mark is one of the most popular men of this section," reported the *Calhoun Times* as early as 1889, "and attracts large congregations wherever he is called upon to speak or teach."[29] As an evangelist, Matthews did not believe in exhorting emotional frenzy, but he did want his listeners to confront their sins and consider an immediate commitment to Christ.

But Matthews was interested in more than simply bringing people to adopt Christ as their personal savior. He became fascinated with politics. Surely some of his zeal for political involvement developed because of his awareness of the activities of three fellow Georgians: Samuel P. Jones, William Felton, and Tom Watson. Samuel Jones emerged as the most popular itinerant evangelist not only in Georgia but throughout the South. Beginning in the 1880s, Jones led large-scale revivals in Memphis, Chattanooga, Jackson, Knoxville, and, most notably, Nashville, in 1885. Matthews never adopted Jones's penchant for slang, coarseness, or vulgarity, yet Jones must have impressed Matthews with his emphasis on social issues, which was unusual for an itinerant evangelist. Jones developed a reputation for being as committed to civic reform as any evangelist in the South. He even demanded that his listeners become involved in efforts to legislate card-playing and other forms of gambling, billiards, baseball, circuses, prostitution, and, most of all, alcohol. Matthews's early sermons reflected this convergence of revival and social issues, though his focus was primarily on prohibition.[30]

Matthews could hardly escape politics, since he lived in Georgia's seventh congressional district. Known as the "Bloody Seventh," the district proved to be a hotbed of independent and agrarian movements. As early as the 1870s, a Methodist minister, country doctor, and farmer by the name of William Felton began to raise objections to the Atlanta political machine that gained power after Reconstruction. Described as the "arch-insurgent of the era," Felton was elected to Congress in 1876 and 1878, where he pushed for Populist reforms.[31] He urged greater power for the railroad commission, advocated abolition of the convict-lease system, fought for the restriction of liquor, and sought improvements in the public school system. For twenty years, Felton pricked the consciences of people within Matthews's district and proved to be a significant thorn in the side of the Atlanta machine. Like Sam Jones, Felton provided another role model for Matthews. Both clearly believed that religion and politics mixed quite naturally. Young Matthews became well acquainted with the Felton family. He considered their son a good friend and occasionally invited Mrs. Felton to speak before the Gordon County Sunday School Association.[32]

Although the extent of his support for Felton is difficult to determine, Matthews participated in the Farmers' Alliance movement in the late 1880s and early 1890s. The alliance had emerged as an important political force in the South and West, primarily because its platform included the abolition of national banks, free coinage of silver, a federal income tax, a reduction of tariffs, and rigid control of the railroad and telegraph companies.

But the alliance also had a religious flavor. Historians have shown how "Alliance men adopted the language of Zion to explain the depression of southern agriculture and to clothe their movement with the legitimacy of culturally sanctioned symbols."[33] Many of the most active alliance leaders were preachers or ministers, and their rhetoric frequently utilized Old Testament imagery. "Men of Israel," summoned the alliance spokesperson, S. K. McGowan, "gird on the whole armour and unsheathe the shining sword of God's eternal truth and fell these traitors to the earth."[34] The alliance often used a revival style for its meetings. Orators attacked those who exploited the farmer, and organizers integrated song, food, and fellowship. According to one historian, "Alliance political theology rested in this neat division of society into the oppressed and the oppressor, the godly and the sinful."[35] "The Lord's side is the side of the oppressed," wrote an alliance spokesman from Virginia, T. J. Stone, "and the other side is the side of the oppressor."[36]

Alliance lecturers frequently used Biblical imagery to address the problem of poverty and the sanctity of labor. One popular alliance speaker, Isom Langley, an Arkansas Baptist minister, wrote, "It is God's plan that men and women who are able to work must live by their industry." The working men and women "are not the poor that 'we have with us always' who are spoken of by Christ . . . he meant that those who are disabled should be cared for by alms or charity, and not those who are able to work."[37] Langley further wrote that it was "the duty of all [Christian] governments to eradicate the evils of extreme poverty and vice, restrain the strong and vicious, and strengthen the weak and helpless."[38] Alliance speakers frequently attacked usury and, more specifically the "robber barons" of the late nineteenth century, Jay Gould, John D. Rockefeller, and Cornelius Vanderbilt.

Matthews's first exposure to politics came in the context of the Farmers' Alliance movement. The *Calhoun Times*, like hundreds of local weeklies in the South, became an official organ for the movement. According to one local historian, by 1890, residents made the alliance the most prominent organization in Calhoun. Matthews caught the fever and actively supported the alliance cause, becoming a regular spokesman for it in his native region. One newspaper from a neighboring town, the *Ringgold New South*, indicated how favorably Matthews was received. "We have been complimented on our report of the alliance sermon, as preached by Rev. Mr. Matthews," the newspaper said. "The eloquent young divine never appeared more advantageously as an orator and theologian."[39] It is difficult to determine with absolute certainty the impact of the alliance movement on Matthews, but it seems most likely that the political agenda and, more important, the use of religious imagery in political activities significantly influenced the young preacher.

The impact of the alliance on Matthews was probably reinforced by the work of Tom Watson, the most famous of Georgia's Populists. We know that Matthews retained for himself a copy of a Watson speech originally delivered in the 1890s. Heavily underlining certain passages, Matthews wrote "excellent" in the margins. Watson's speech emphasized that each person should "seek the truth and live it." With evangelical fervor, Watson proclaimed oppression and discrimination to be rampant in Southern society—he compared it to France prior to the 1789 revolution. "The unequal treatment of classes, the unequal levying of taxes, the unequal distribution of wealth," argued the red-headed Populist, "have been three of the main causes which have peopled the cemeteries of the past with dead empires."[40]

Further applauding the spirit of the French Revolution, Watson attacked not only the nobility but the church, for holding so much untaxed wealth as to create an inordinate burden on the peasants. Matthews found this notion of taxing the church so compelling that he would later espouse it in both Jackson and Seattle. "Every dollar's worth of church property, bonds and securities ought to be taxed," he argued in 1900. "It is unconstitutional and unchristian not to tax said property."[41]

Matthews agreed with Watson on other issues than criticism of the nobility and the church. In his own address on the French Revolution, delivered at the turn of the century, Matthews echoed Watson's sentiments concerning the right to revolution itself in what was perhaps the most radical statement the preacher ever uttered. "We have capitalistic feudalism—the tools are owned by the few, and the many work by their consent," Matthews said. "There is an innate principle in man, guaranteeing the safety of government, that demands the repudiation and death of corrupt executives."[42] Praising Voltaire, Rousseau, and others, Matthews further urged his audience to recover the spirit of the French Revolution and to effect change throughout the political system.

Attracted to Populism for a variety of reasons, Matthews frequently expressed his sympathy for the plight of the farmer. Perhaps most important, Populist rhetoric, like alliance imagery, fit very nicely into the categories of the evangelical mind. Populists portrayed America's survival as contingent on social reform; they pictured the world in stark terms and often utilized Biblical imagery to communicate their vision of the problems. William Jennings Bryan's "Cross of Gold" speech, delivered in 1896, reflected the religious tone. "The humblest citizen in all the land, when clad in the armor of a righteous cause," asserted Bryan, "is stronger than all the hosts of error. I come to speak to you in defense of a cause as holy as the cause of liberty—the cause of humanity."[43]

Jones, Felton, and Watson reinforced Matthews's sense of the importance of a unified community and active civic involvement. His Sunday School activities began to reflect this larger sense of community involvement. Early in his career, Matthews paid little heed to denominational differences. His notion of Christianity focused on the importance of making an impact on the secular world. Minor disagreements over doctrine and liturgy invariably irritated him. As a result, he set out to shape the Gordon County Sunday School Association into a model of interdenominational cooperation. As president of the association in 1891, he set a clear tone.

> I hope if there is a school which has any of this infamous sectarian prejudice about it that it will lay that aside and send delegates. This idea that "We" are right and others are wrong is a child of infamy and gross ignorance. Come and let us exchange views on this grand subject, and be broad-minded and show a Christian spirit which

makes us recognize and fraternize all as equals to ourselves, and you will go back home a wiser and better person.[44]

The idea of interdenominational cooperation continued to excite Matthews throughout his life; even during his later years, when he became an advocate of fundamentalism, he never totally abandoned the belief that Christians have much common ground. For many years, he hoped that this cooperation would allow ministers to speak collectively on a variety of issues. But in Calhoun, Matthews felt increasingly compelled to speak out alone concerning particular problems.

The political movements in Georgia helped Matthews to see more clearly the problems of his own community. Convinced that local governments could be reformed only by an informed public, Matthews became more vocal in urging civic consciousness.

I am tired of the ignorant spirit that abuses our beloved town. You simpleton you, the town is what you make it! Calhoun has produced more noble sons and daughters than any town her size. Her intellectual, musical, artistical, and moral talent is great. He is the basest of base who does not love and work for his own home, his native town.[45]

Matthews practiced what he preached. He helped establish the town debating society for discussing rationally the lively political and social issues of the day. He regularly visited local prisoners at the town jail. And on Thanksgiving and Christmas, Matthews brought them dinner. On at least one occasion, the prisoners responded with a letter of thanks in the *Calhoun Times*. More pointed and controversial were his admonitions to Calhoun residents to eliminate local corruption. Specifically, he told them to keep that institution of local government, the courthouse, clean.[46]

The opportunity to work in a slightly larger town and with a larger congregation arose in May 1893, and Matthews decided to move from Calhoun to Dalton, Georgia. At first glance, Dalton would appear to be a rather small step up for Matthews. With slightly fewer than 5,000 residents (Calhoun had 2,000), it was hardly a great metropolis. Nevertheless, Dalton appeared to be headed for substantial growth in 1893, when Matthews arrived. The Crown Cotton Mills provided significant employment, and the town also had a flour mill, meat-packing plant, axe-handle plant, hub and spoke factory, planing mill, furniture factory, cotton press, gin mills, sawmills, and a tannery. In 1885, Dalton built an opera house, and in 1890 the Hotel Dalton opened and soon became the social hub.[47]

Mark Matthews came to Dalton confident that he could make an immediate impact on the social and political life. Emboldened by his successes in Calhoun, the twenty-five-year-old Matthews set about almost immediately to voice his political opinions. Growing more sophisticated in his attacks, he began to propose solutions to the problems of local government. He maintained the pattern that he had established in Calhoun: build the congregation and educate the parishioners to work to solve community problems. An early sermon to his Dalton congregation reflects his energy and zeal.

> The enemy is upon us. Awake and polish your sword of peace. . . .
> You say you love God and your fellow man who is your brother.
> Now prove that love by entering the field and working for the salvation and elevation of your city and country at large. . . . Make it a point to be in your pew every service and bring someone with you.
> . . . God and your pastor expect you to do your duty. It is NOT the men who STAGNATE, but who CIRCULATE, who PULSATE, that are LIFE and POWER.[48]

The Dalton congregation grew rapidly to more than 200 active members. The gangly pastor made a strong impression on his congregation; a member recalled how Matthews, on one occasion, rode a donkey, and the preacher's legs were so long that his shoes dragged on the ground.[49]

Matthews characterized his vision for the church in the phrase "My church is my force and not my field."[50] He organized a fifteen-member committee for the relief of the poor and an industrial bureau in charge of securing jobs for the unemployed. "Day after day, in winter," one of his parishioners later recalled, "did the citizens . . . see Dr. Matthews—regardless of his own comfort—tramping through sleet, ice and snow, or rain and wind to minister to the wants of the poor and needy."[51] At one point, Matthews described his Dalton congregation as "growing and doing grand work. It has three fine Sunday schools; the missions are growing nicely. . . . In the pastoral work, I want to do less of the social and more work for the sick and poor."[52]

During his second year in Dalton, Matthews boldly criticized city officials. Citing one of his favorite passages, 2 Sam. 23, he offered: "He that ruleth over men must be just, ruling in fear of God." He then proceeded to excoriate city officials not only for lacking the vision to solve certain problems but also for benefiting financially at the expense of the public. Speaking before a packed church from which many were turned away, Matthews drew the attention of the *Dalton Argus.*

> Mr. Matthews' sermon was very severe on city officials. . . . Mr. Matthews spoke of the filthy condition of the city, and the fact that although there was an ordinance against pig pens in the city, those in high authority in the city and county had stinking hog pens on their premises, and similar deeds of law-breaking, permitted through favoritism or because the party had "political pull."[53]

Immediately after the congressional elections in the fall of 1894, Matthews expressed his outrage at how the Democratic party unfairly controlled that election. "So today men buy votes; not with a kiss," preached Matthews. "The scoundrel would promise to kiss a dog before the election, to get his vote, but afterwards would kick him out the door if he applied for bread. . . . This last primary and election remind me of Absalom and his crowd. . . . It was a disgrace. . . . But thank God parties may rise and fall; . . . but God and His kingdom shall outlast them all."[54] The defeat of Tom Watson and William Felton in the elections of 1894 surely discouraged Matthews and other reformers; many observers charged that corruption pervaded Georgia politics and would end only when the people stood up to party bosses at all levels.[55]

But Matthews was nothing if not resilient; less than a year later, he made his most direct appeal for the citizens to drive the "old gang" of Dalton politicians from office. In an open letter to the Dalton community, Matthews provided a blueprint for a more righteous community. He argued that for Dalton to be healthy it had to be united on the basic questions. It could not be run by special interests; it had to emphasize education, and the churches had to work together. "This town should grow and prosper, but [it] is impossible for this or any other town to prosper where selfishness is the motive power," he told Dalton residents. "You take a town where every man is for 'self' and self alone, and you necessarily give it the name of grabbers-ville, and littleness will always mark its confines." Matthews lobbied for tax reform that would encourage new business to come to town. "Build up home enterprises; patronize them regardless of cost. A home paper, home plow,

The Hills of Georgia

pot, hat or suit is the best." There is something quite quaint but also fairly sophisticated about Matthews's urgings to buy locally produced goods. Throughout his life he recognized the importance of economic well-being to community health. Above all, however, he maintained that a moral community is achieved only by developing a fundamental consensus on key issues.

> Pull and pull together for Dalton. You can afford to differ on many questions, but when it is a question affecting the interest, moral, social, financial, or religion of Dalton you cannot afford; you must not attempt to differ. It must be one voice, one head, one heart, one hand and one plan and that for Dalton's advancement. This little narrow-minded, infamous, backbiting, throat-cutting, cross-firing spirit will ruin any town or city in the world.[56]

Matthews always believed that one set of values would eventually dominate. The concept of a community that encouraged pluralism or different lifestyles within it was simply unacceptable to him.

Proper health care was also a key ingredient in Matthews's vision of a holy city, and it would remain so throughout his life. "The town must be cleansed and kept so. Make the citizens clean their yards and wells. . . . Who ever heard of a town of this size and no 'board of health.' It is a disgrace; it is a criminal shame not to have one and make them inspect the town every month."[57]

In that same letter, Matthews once again attacked the Democratic machine that had run Dalton politics since the end of Reconstruction. He picked up where he had started a year earlier. "Destroy the little corrupt, political ring in this town," he urged. "Let the people understand your public offices do not go by 'rotation,' and that purity must mark the man and office." But Matthews called for more than simply the elimination of the old guard. "We should float bonds and sewer the town and decently 'light the streets,' and run the town more economically. Pave the side-walks, they are a disgrace."[58]

Matthews's prescription for Dalton residents offered a much broader and more sophisticated vision of civic consciousness and urban reform than that put forward by the Georgian evangelist Sam Jones and many other ministers who worked on behalf of social reform. Matthews exhorted not just his congregation but the entire community to work for institutional and political change, not simply regeneration of the soul.

The Hills of Georgia

And finally in the Dalton city election of December 1895, Matthews's efforts (and those of many other civic reformers) paid dividends. In the most dramatic shift in local power in twenty-five years, the old guard was ousted from office. Much of this collapse could be attributed to the general upheaval in politics during the Populist period, but at the very least Matthews seemed to be on the cutting edge of political change in his native state.[59]

Matthews's star had risen rapidly in the hills of northern Georgia. Like many in that first generation born in the aftermath of the Civil War, Matthews had to overcome difficult circumstances. From poverty and family tragedy to the general disruption of Southern society, Matthews faced a number of obstacles as he grew into adulthood. Yet his early religious conviction that he go into the ministry was nurtured by the steady hand of J. B. Hillhouse. Raised in the more evangelical Cumberland Presbyterian church, Matthews found his theological moorings in Hillhouse's tutorials in Old School Presbyterianism. As Matthews matured, he seemed to gravitate to the political and social world around him. Soaking in the political conflict of his region and era, he confidently applied his Calvinist theology to issues of his day. Heartened by the positive response he received in Calhoun, Matthews began to dream of larger venues for his ministry. He fully believed that cities could be shaped in ways that would manifest the Kingdom of God.

Mark Matthews's achievements in northern Georgia during his early ministry set him on a trajectory toward greater recognition. On at least one occasion, Matthews turned down a call to a much larger church—the First Presbyterian Church of San Antonio, Texas.[60] However, on December 26, 1895, the *North Georgia Citizen* announced that Matthews was leaving Dalton for the First Presbyterian Church in Jackson, Tennessee. According to the editor, "He is a young man of brilliant attainments, which deserve a larger field and wider scope. It is his duty to go, and in going we most heartily recommend him to the whole people of his new home, and in addition, we confidently expect to hear most flattering news of his abilities."[61] Preaching his last sermon to a packed church, Matthews told his audience that he would someday like to be a missionary in Japan. This is the first indication of the motivation that would lead him to the "Gateway to the Orient"— Seattle. But for the time being, he would remain in the South. Matthews clearly had ambitions; he wanted to be in a larger city and serve a larger congregation where he could wield broader influence. And clearly his ambitions and his talents were attracting the attention of many people who believed that he would sooner or later leave the region for even larger venues. *"The Citizen* predicts he will finally go to New York or Boston and we shall watch his course with eager anticipation. We, in common with the majority here, hate to give him up. May God bless him and his forever."[62] For the rest of his ministry, Matthews mixed evangelism with social Christianity in an attempt to build a righteous community. Very few people ever suspected, however, that the roots for this unusual combination came from the hills of northern Georgia.

CHAPTER 2

Social Gospel in Tennessee

Rev. M. A. Matthews never misses an opportunity to do something for the moral and material advancement of Jackson. A man of quick perception, philanthropic impulses and of dynamic force, he is ever enlisted in enterprises of a worthy character.
— *Jackson Sun* (1901)

The political ferment in northern Georgia had made a deep impression on Mark Matthews. Convinced that religion and politics made appropriate bedfellows, he believed that he could be an important force in shaping the public policy of his community. He attacked a variety of problems from the pulpit, including everything from alcohol abuse and gambling to courthouse corruption and business monopoly. Sam Jones, William Felton, and Tom Watson had all seemed to confirm the importance of fighting for one's political views. These men's influence, combined with Matthews's evangelical background and energetic personality, helped make him one of the most exciting young preachers in the South.

But Matthews's ministry in Jackson, Tennessee, from 1896 to 1902 reflected far more than mere political influence. As Matthews moved to a larger community, he became increasingly aware of efforts of ministers in the Northeast and Midwest to make Christianity relevant to the poor and to the numerous social problems associated with urbanization. In fact, he modeled many of his initiatives after those strategies identified with the Social Gospel. And in doing so, he carved out a relatively unusual niche in the South. Few Southern ministers from any denomination embraced as many tenets of the Social Gospel as did Matthews.

Until very recently, most scholars have described the South as a region that was little influenced by the Social Gospel reform movement. A number of historians of American religion have documented American Protestantism's growing concern with the problems of industrialization and urbanization, but most have focused almost exclusively on the Northeast and Midwest. Emphasizing the conservative role that religion historically played in Southern culture and the resistance of Southern clergy to abolitionism, scholars have suggested that very little social reform took place in cities below the Mason-Dixon line. Likewise, it generally has been believed that evangelical religion was hostile to social reform. Too often, scholars have assumed that the 1920s battles over evolution reflected deep-seated patterns of resistance against any idea associated with social reform or liberal theology.

More recently, however, many scholars of Southern religion have identified several ministers and, in particular, women's organizations that actively participated in social reform movements in urban areas. Southern Baptists worked on behalf of prohibition, and the Woman's Home Mission movement in the Methodist Episcopal church worked on behalf of many reform efforts. Women in many denominations organized boarding schools, day schools, kindergartens, hospitals, and other social services. A limited number of Southern clergymen, including Matthews, pushed for a variety of social reforms. In addition to the previously mentioned Sam Jones, the Southern Presbyterian and North Carolinian Alexander McKelway was perhaps the most prominent as well as the most influential through his religious journalism. The Episcopalian Edgar G. Murphy, in Alabama, fought on behalf of child labor and improved working conditions, as did Edward O. Guerrant in eastern Kentucky. Perhaps Matthews can be more closely compared with Frank Barnett, editor of the *Alabama Baptist*. Barnett spoke out on a wide range of issues from convict abuse and child labor to prohibition. At the very least, Matthews's early career provides additional evidence of the greater influence of social Christianity in the South than most historians have allowed. And in general, Matthews's utilization of a number of Social Gospel strategies made his ministry more the exception than the rule in the South. He boldly directed his church and community to address social and political issues in ways that most

Southern ministers did not, and his success in his native region provided a base for his rise to prominence within national Presbyterian circles.[1]

Certain features of the Social Gospel appealed to Matthews from the outset. Perhaps because of his own experience with poverty, he reached out in many ways to the urban poor. His ministry in Georgia and Tennessee was marked by a desire to help the unemployed, the undereducated, and those who could not afford good health care. While deeply concerned with the state of his parishioners' souls, he embraced the Social Gospel's emphasis on the importance of the social and political environment. Matthews believed that Christianity required one to change structures as well as hearts. He accepted without question the assertion that poor living conditions were unjust and that Christians had a responsibility to work for social justice. Matthews's preaching had clearly reflected these assumptions during his ministries in Calhoun and Dalton, Georgia, and now he set about the task of implementing this vision in Tennessee.

The First Presbyterian Church extended its call to Mark Matthews in the fall of 1895. Although Matthews had certainly envisioned leaving Dalton one day, it still must have been a difficult decision for him and his family. His father was seventy-one and his mother was sixty-three; one can imagine that there might have been some painful family discussions, for it seems likely that either all or none would go. Perhaps it was easier for Matthews's mother, since she had been born and raised in Tennessee. Whatever the reason, the family made the decision to move to Jackson, a city of nearly 15,000 located approximately 80 miles east of Memphis. Dalton residents bid the Matthews clan a tearful farewell at the train station.[2]

Jackson's economic development blossomed in the late 1880s, when a railroad line connected the city to Memphis. By the 1890s, developers had constructed several large lumber and woodworking plants.[3] However, Jackson's political climate provided a few uncertainties for a young preacher with Populist or alliance inclinations interested in shaping debate on public policy. Certainly, most people in western Tennessee would have been suspicious of anyone who dared challenge the existing order. Since 1870, Tennessee had been a political battleground for small farmers, Whig industrialists, and states' rights planters. However, regardless of what faction happened to be in power, Democrats recognized that they must unite before a general election or risk losing

Social Gospel in Tennessee

to the Republicans, who held majorities in many counties in the hills of eastern Tennessee.

The threat of Republicanism contributed to the weakness of Populist candidates in the 1890s. Democrats feared that Populists would create division and thus provide an opening for Republicans. Populists "threatened the *status quo*," according to Roger Hart, a scholar on Tennessee politics, "by seeking access to power."[4] This threat united the ruling elites in an effort to smash Populism, just as they had earlier driven the Farmers' Alliance from the Democratic party. Ironically, the Populists' problems were exacerbated by the presidential candidacy of William Jennings Bryan in 1896. By running as both a Populist and a Democrat, Bryan created a dilemma: those Populists who were left in Tennessee never knew whether to concentrate their efforts on their state-wide enemies, the Democrats, or on their national enemies, the Republicans. As a result, Populists at the state level suffered many defeats.

How careful Matthews had to be about expressing his Populist inclinations is difficult to say. He identified himself as a Democrat with reform sympathies. In general, Matthews seemed to possess an intuitive sense that allowed him to avoid a variety of problems when it came to politics; however, there were times when people found his outspokenness and even his idealism unacceptable.

Beginning his work in Jackson in January 1896, Matthews followed the same strategy there that he had used in Dalton: building membership in the congregation, organizing the church at the denominational level, and immersing himself in the social and political life of the community. Within a few months, he became a familiar sight on Jackson's downtown streets and his sermons became the talk of the town. He certainly did not soften his rhetoric; on religious matters, he continued to express clear expectations for his congregation. "You have not attended Church regularly, especially at night," stated Matthews to the whole congregation in a questionnaire. "This we will not submit to, you must attend every service."[5] He further asked for responses to forty-six items ranging from the strength of one's prayer life and the "secret" sins against one's neighbors to the particular committee on which one would like to serve. His sermon "Why Women Should Not Remove Their Hats" caught the attention of more than just his parishioners. Matthews argued that the Apostle Paul urged good women to wear hats in order to distinguish themselves from the wicked. Dismissing that reason as insufficient in the nineteenth century, Matthews launched into a satire on the wearing of hats, mocking a tradition that had long been a part of the Southern culture of churchgoers. The following extended passage illustrates Matthews's style and why so many people took notice of him, whether they agreed or disagreed with what he said.

To remove their hats would destroy the most resourceful, pleasant and profitable medium of advertisement for the millinery shops. The keepers of these shops are poor merchants; they are unable to advertise through the only legitimate channel—our papers—and therefore must have the benefit of a church exhibit every Sunday. . . . To remove their hats would give a clearer view of all things. Even their bald heads or wigs could be seen. It would grant you the right and opportunity of seeing all things, including the speaker, and of hearing the performance of music, all of which is wrong. You have no right to see or hear—that is not what you go to church to do. You go to church to look and admire and covet the fine dresses and bonnets. You have only a right to see that mountainous hat. To remove their hats would make each lady comfortable. It is unlawful for a woman to be comfortable, especially in congregations. It is one of the fiats of the eternal curse that women should dress fine and wear hats and thereby be uncomfortable at church. To remove their hats and wear simple, plain clothes at church would make each and all comfortable, happy, and worshipful, all of which would be sinful and wrong. In order to be good, religious, fashionable, pious, sensible and to be beneficial to the church and respectful to the feelings of the poor and to regard the wishes and pains of suffering man, women should dress most elaborately and wear the largest and most expensive hats when attending divine services in our churches.[6]

His biting criticisms found marks beyond just his own congregation. He again created controversy by openly berating the work done by other ministers. "It is a fact that the ministry, the clergy are responsible for the perpetuation of wickedness," Matthews argued, "for the reign of vice, lethargy, indifference and hypocrisy in the church. . . . The minister of today is deficient in personal purity, piety and godliness."[7] If he was somewhat disposed to sensation, he was relatively evenhanded in its use against his own denomination as well as others. He constantly attacked the materialism and selfishness of most every

Social Gospel in Tennessee

Protestant and Catholic church. "The Methodist Church is a ponderous ecclesiastical drop-a-nickel-in-the-slot machine. The Presbyterian Church is a beaver hat historical society," proclaimed Matthews. "The Baptist Church is an individual plumbing shop. The Episcopal Church is a ritualistic club of would do, do not, would not, I do people, with a 'spring opening' attachment."[8]

However, Matthews's criticism of various denominations did not sway him from his belief in interdenominational efforts. His vision of holiness, at least early in his career, was not confined to a particular denomination. In fact, he vigorously supported cooperative activity among denominations and worked regularly on behalf of ecumenical efforts. The stimulus for this vision of unity may have come from Matthews's tutor, J. B. Hillhouse. Hillhouse had been well known in Georgia for his opposition to the Northern and Southern split in the Presbyterian church just prior to the Civil War. Most likely, he had urged young Matthews to seek reconciliation rather than further separation. Matthews's ordination in the Cumberland church and then his move to the Presbyterian Church U.S. might also have made him more tolerant of differences. "Why can't we have denominational tolerance? A ridiculous spectacle is presented to this world," Matthews stated, "in that of the northern and southern division of our representative denominations. . . . Let me say to the bigoted northern Presbyterians and to the bigoted southern Presbyterians, put up thy sword into its scabbard."[9]

Matthews fought for more than just Presbyterian unity; he engaged in a variety of ecumenical projects and interdenominational activities. In April 1898, he delivered the keynote address at the dedication of the temple B'nai Israel in Jackson.[10] In September 1900, he presided over a Sunday School convention, which had representatives from ten Methodist, six Baptist, two Cumberland, one Presbyterian, one Christian, and two Union churches, among others.[11]

However, it was neither his ecumenical work nor his denominational activity that brought him the most attention. In the end, residents of the city would remember Matthews for the remarkable number of civic projects that he helped develop. Thus, his career in Jackson sheds light on the impact of social Christianity in the South during the late nineteenth century.

The roots of Matthews's social concern can be found in the political environment of northern Georgia and the emphasis of Cumberland Presbyterianism on reforming America. We have previously seen the importance of role models such as Sam Jones and William Felton on Matthews's view of politics and institutional reform. By the time he started serving the Jackson congregation, however, Matthews was increasingly aware of the efforts of Northern clergy who were directly addressing the problems of slums and poverty.

More than any other individual, the Presbyterian minister Thomas DeWitt Talmage, from New York, seems to have provided a role model for Matthews during his days both in Dalton and in Jackson. Matthews's scrapbooks contain numerous sermons from Talmage and a number of articles documenting his travel and activities. Talmage became the editor of the *Christian Herald* in 1890, and Matthews frequently clipped its articles. The thoroughly evangelical Talmage gained attention by personally exploring the slums of New York City and preaching sermons that supported the poor and criticized landlords. Matthews met Talmage and traveled with him to Chattanooga, where Talmage brought his message of social concern to Tennessee. Talmage invited Matthews to speak at his Brooklyn church; however, the church caught fire and Matthews failed to make the trip.[12]

Matthews also clipped articles concerning Charles Sheldon, who published one of the best-selling books of his era, *In His Steps*, in 1897. Like Talmage, Sheldon urged that Christians fight poverty and social injustice. Sheldon recognized the growing gap between the rich and the poor, and he persuasively argued that religion was irrelevant to those people whose basic needs for housing, food, and clothing remained unmet. His famous question to the urban dweller, "What would Jesus do?" surely reinforced Matthews's tendencies to see religion and social issues as intertwined.[13]

Matthews's message resonated with those ministers throughout the country who expressed great concern over whether the church could appeal to the growing working class in American society. In his effort to make the church more responsive, Matthews embraced the concept of the "institutional church," which was becoming very popular among Social Gospel advocates in the urban North. Modeled to some extent after the Young Men's Christian Association and the Salvation Army, the institutional church attempted to meet almost every social need of an individual. Kindergartens, gymnasiums, classes, libraries, employment services, loan funds, game rooms, soup kitchens, and many other programs were developed by congregations throughout the country. Matthews had begun to develop this concept of an institutional church back in Dalton. But it was during his ministries in Jackson and later in

Seattle that he began to earn praise throughout Presbyterian circles. It was through the institutional church that Matthews tried to attract both the middle and the working classes. In a number of sermons, he discussed the relationship between wealth and poverty as it related to the church's identity. The following excerpt expresses his concern:

> Is the church a club where wealth is a qualification of membership? No wonder the masses are drifting away from you, because the masses are poor people. Why is it that your churches all over the land are empty while the streets and hovels are crowded? Because of your unsympathetic, unfellow-shipping, cold-grab-all-heart.[14]

In another sermon in Jackson, Matthews preached that "every one knows that the laborer is being forced to the wall. Show me the church that is demanding an increase in wages for the poor. Show me the church that is trying before its courts those infamous kings who thus grind to powder our poor."[15]

Matthews began to implement his concern for the working class by developing a number of projects, but few were more highly praised than the night school at First Presbyterian. He announced that his church would provide facilities and teachers for those who were unable to attend school during the day. Opening in the fall of 1897, the school attracted more than 150 students during its first year. Books were purchased with money collected from an interdenominational women's Bible class. Matthews organized the faculty by persuading twenty people to teach courses ranging from reading and writing to stenography and typing. Within four years, the number of teachers had risen to thirty-five, and more than 650 students had passed through the school.[16]

Very well received by the community, the school was attended mostly by Baptists, Methodists, and non-Christians. "Rev. M. A. Matthews has done a noble work," wrote the *Jackson Sun*, "and that self sacrificing and assiduous corps of teachers who have proffered their services are also due an unstinted meed of praise."[17] The reputation of the school grew impressively, and by 1901 Matthews was receiving inquiries from people in other states concerning its operation and organization.[18]

Another of Matthews's projects began shortly after his arrival in Jackson, when he initiated work on establishing a public library. Here again, Matthews believed that the church had a responsibility to promote the overall education of the community. In 1898, he started to seek funding. He finally persuaded Andrew Carnegie to donate $30,000, contingent on Jackson securing a proper location and the necessary funding for the maintenance of the facility. Matthews pled his case before the city council in January 1900, but he encountered significant opposition. Not to be denied, he took his case to the people by writing articles for the local newspapers. Finally, fifteen months later, the city council approved the purchase of a lot and appropriated the maintenance funds. When the library finally opened in March 1903, Matthews received high praise from the town fathers for his persistence and vision.[19]

In addition to his interest in the intellectual well-being of the city, Matthews, like other Social Gospel ministers, believed that his church had an important role to play in providing health-care facilities as well. In 1896, Matthews started campaigning for a hospital. He had hoped to raise the funds exclusively from within the Presbyterian church but was forced to go outside and seek individual contributions. By the end of the year, he had secured enough capital to purchase a building that had served first as the county jail and then as a tenement house. Matthews appointed an advisory board consisting of members from every Protestant denomination in the city; he served as the hospital's initial president.[20] The following year, he turned over the daily operations to Ambrose M'Coy, although Matthews continued to support the hospital in a number of ways. Always the entrepreneur, he contacted the major railroad companies that operated through Jackson and succeeded in persuading them to donate not only money to the hospital but also carloads of coal for the poor. In addition, he convinced railroad management to support a minimal health insurance program through the hospital for the company's workers.[21]

By 1899, Matthews had found that the work of the hospital was becoming burdensome, and he decided to sell it. He, however, continued to express interest in health care, specifically the problem of drug abuse. In 1900, he lobbied for a city ordinance that would prohibit cocaine prescriptions and severely limit the medical use of morphine. Though he fought for treatment centers, he always believed that an individual's will had to be emphasized. "Those who are addicted to the habit can quit," Matthews believed, "and if you want to reform you will do it."[22]

His interest in drug abuse certainly was related to his desire to prohibit alcohol, but more subtly it revealed his paternalism in regard to race relations. "The cocaine fiend is an insane and dangerous negro,"

Social Gospel in Tennessee

argued Matthews as he cited a rise in the drug's use by blacks.[23] He pointed to reports of blacks, reputedly under the influence of the drug, assaulting whites, and then suggested that the solution was to fine and punish the sellers. "The South is the natural home of the negro," voiced Matthews. "Southern people love the negro and are doing great things for his elevation. He will ever be the trusted servant of the white man."[24]

But Matthews never seemed quite comfortable with his position on race. He fully believed that slavery had been wrong and the Civil War necessary. Eventually, in the 1920s, he wrote extensive criticisms of the racial discrimination exhibited against the Japanese. However, in regard to blacks, Matthews rarely spoke. Two black servants came with him to Seattle, but otherwise we know very little of his views. When once asked by a Seattle reporter what his views on the "Negro Problem" were, Matthews emphasized his benevolent paternalism and support for Booker T. Washington's position on vocational training. "I have worked for the negro. His salvation will be industrial education," argued Matthews. "Teach the women to sew, cook and keep house; teach the men to farm, instruct them in the mechanical arts and in various lines of industry. That will solve the problem."[25]

Matthews's concern for the plight of blacks was somewhat limited because of his paternalism, but his desire to aid the white poor and unemployed was much stronger. It was estimated that 1,200 of the white poor were wards of the city, and as in most municipalities there was almost no effort to treat the problem. Matthews can be credited with organizing a group, the Ladies Bible Training School, that began to make the first serious efforts in Jackson to help the impoverished. The group discovered the cases, and Matthews reviewed each one to determine what exactly was needed. By 1901, the group was meeting the clothing, food, and fuel needs of up to 750 people a year. Matthews became increasingly identified with social causes. "The chill of winter drove many a destitute one to seek his aid," observed a local newspaper, "and no hungry person was turned away unfed. The larger part of his salary was spent annually to feed the hungry, clothe the naked and to educate boys and girls who toiled for their sustenance."[26] At Thanksgiving and Christmas each year, Matthews delivered food, coal, and wood to Jackson's needy.[27] In conjunction with his church's industrial bureau, he secured jobs for as many as twenty people a month. "Rev. Matthews has no complaint of his burden," attested the *Jackson Sun*. "He glories in this self-imposed task, holding that it is part of the duty of a minister of God to labor amongst the poor and relieve their sufferings."[28] Another Jackson paper urged the city council to create a "Provident Association" based on the model provided by the Ladies Bible Training School so that the city might assist Matthews's group in a task that should be jointly shared.[29]

Matthews's sermons in Jackson often blended evangelism and social concern. "Employment must be provided for the unemployed; church farms opened, soup houses and cheap lodgings erected, in order that the tramp and homeless may be provided with the physical comforts and Christianity at the time."[30] Two other civic efforts by Matthews reflected the influence of social Christianity on his ministry in Jackson. Concerned about the mistreatment of animals and children, Matthews organized the Jackson Humane Society in 1897. Later described as the "best organized society in the South," the organization provided protection and publicized the problems of animal and child abuse.[31] During his last year in Jackson, Matthews spearheaded the drive to establish a branch of the Young Men's Christian Association. Opening December 25, 1901, the Y.M.C.A. housed a parlor and reception room, reading and writing rooms, an auditorium capable of seating 250 people, and a gymnasium. "Rev. M. A. Matthews never misses an opportunity to do something for the moral and material advancement of Jackson," noted the local newspaper. "A man of quick perception, of philanthropic impulses and of dynamic force, he is ever enlisted in enterprises of a worthy character."[32]

Matthews does not fit easily into the categories outlined by historians of social Christianity and the Social Gospel. His emphasis on revivalism and the conversion of the sinner places him clearly in the tradition of someone like Charles Finney, the great evangelist of the early nineteenth century. Focusing on changing the heart of the individual rather than the institutions themselves, Finney influenced other reform movements, albeit indirectly. Matthews likewise stressed the heart of his listeners in many of his sermons during the late nineteenth and early twentieth centuries. "The human heart is not a fertile soil, unless it is made fertile by the Holy Ghost," preached Matthews. "He must prepare the soil before the divine life, which Christ came to give to every man who is prepared to receive it, is planted."[33] Yet Matthews clearly went well beyond Finney. His work with hospitals, unemployment bureaus, and night schools as well as his political concerns place Matthews within what the historian Henry May described as "Progressive Social Christianity." May asserted that this brand of social

Christianity emphasized institutional reform rather than either the creation of new institutions, as argued by more radical social Christians, or simply an emphasis on the heart, as urged by more conservative social Christians.[34]

By 1896, Matthews had distinguished himself as a regionally popular, evangelical preacher with a penchant for involvement in political and social affairs. Without question Matthews matured and gained great self-confidence during his years in Tennessee. Taking Jackson by storm, he became one of the most discussed figures in the city. "Dr. Matthews," wrote one newspaper, "has a reputation as a pulpit orator second to but few if any in the state."[35] In 1900, Southern Normal University in Huntington, Tennessee, acknowledged Matthews's accomplishments by bestowing upon him an honorary doctorate.[36] His newly awarded degree and his overall success encouraged Matthews to become more involved in the political issues of the day. "Do you know that through the avenue known as the political sphere," asked Matthews of his Jackson congregation, ". . . the greatest opportunity is offered to the church to do more good than through, perhaps, any other avenue in the world?"[37]

Matthews's commitment to working in the political sphere was further exemplified by his study of the law. He began his education in Dalton by reading legal works. Continuing this individual study, he passed the Tennessee state bar exam in March 1897. A source of great pride for Matthews, his legal status gave him further confidence with which to debate the political questions of the day, as well as the expertise to assist his parishioners, though he rarely appeared in court.[38]

Perhaps Matthews's most controversial political statements during his tenure in Jackson involved the Spanish-American War. Matthews had to be careful not to alienate people in Jackson by identifying himself too closely with critics of the Democratic party. Nevertheless, while claiming to be a Democrat in 1898, he openly criticized both Republicans and Democrats for their support of the war. This action did not go unnoticed within Jackson's political circles, and Matthews was openly criticized in the local press.[39] His position on the armed conflict reflected the Georgian Populist Tom Watson's views almost precisely. "What are we going to get out of this war as a nation?" asked Watson. "Endless trouble, complications, expense. Republics cannot go into the conquering business and remain republics. Militarism leads to military domination, military despotism. Imperialism smooths the way for the emperor."[40] Matthews also condemned what he believed was the imperialistic direction of the war. He not only blasted William McKinley and Mark Hanna for their actions, but he also argued that the Democrats in Congress were almost as culpable. "Imperialism is undemocratic and invites from external forces, inevitable disaster," he argued before the Jackson Conversational Club. "A standing army of party leeches and military canteens, an ever increasing pension roll, for the services of rum shot soldiers and heroic substitutes, produces a parallel condition in America."[41] He further claimed that "there are strong circumstances pointing to the moral certainty that the war was brought on by the cooperation of traitors to the Spanish government and the republican administration."[42] Apparently criticized by editorialists from the *Nashville Banner* and the *Memphis Commercial Appeal*, Matthews responded by saying, "The fact that I am a democrat from principle and Southerner by birth does not prevent me from seeing faults in the democratic party. This age demands practical righteousness in every department of life. It is a duty to expose and condemn unrighteousness wherever found, regardless of party or creed."[43]

Matthews actively tried to shape the nature of Jackson politics. In April 1898, he submitted a "Municipal Platform" to the city. It illustrated his lifelong assumption that morals could be regulated and vice controlled. The seven planks of the platform emphasized issues that would be associated with the Progressive reform movement. Honest government, a clean city, regulated saloons, and strict law enforcement were the cornerstones of Matthews's approach to municipal government in the late nineteenth century.[44]

Encouraged by the spirit of Progressivism, Matthews optimistically believed that a clean city government was not only possible but the key to solving most urban ills. "It is true that evil men are in power," wrote Matthews while in Jackson. "It is true that government is recognized as evil and unrighteous, but the evil is dying and its last battles are being fought. It will be completely overturned, and by the citizenship which will be the direct product of the larger purer and truer Christ."[45]

The power and influence that Matthews gained in his six years in Jackson were indeed remarkable. Consequently, he came to believe that he was different from most men, and he cultivated this sense of distinctiveness. Indeed, Matthews was a striking individual. Standing about six feet, five inches tall, Matthews weighed at most 160 pounds. He wore his curly hair rather long, and he always appeared in a long black frock coat. The issue of Matthews's height actually made the news-

Social Gospel in Tennessee

paper in September 1901, when it was reported that a native of Michigan was the tallest Knight Templar in the United States at six feet, four inches tall. However, one of Matthews's friends quickly responded with the claim that the preacher, then serving as the Eminent Commander of the Jackson Commandery, was the tallest Mason in the land at six feet six inches tall.[46]

Matthews did nothing to discourage commentary about his height or appearance; he certainly did not mind standing head and shoulders above most of his contemporaries. But his style extended well beyond his appearance. His pulpit manner always attracted press attention. As a writer for the *Southwestern Presbyterian* observed concerning one of Matthews's sermons, "The lecture abounds in wit, humor, ridicule, sarcasm, pleasantry, indignation, denunciation, pathos, poetry, and the most fearless rebuke of the sins of our time. . . . Dr. Matthews is a prince of popular platform speakers."[47] The power that Matthews possessed in the pulpit was indeed impressive, and it certainly accounted for a great deal of his following. "A stranger always feels at home in this church the moment he crosses the threshold," observed one church visitor. "It is safe to say that every one in the large audience, men, women, and children, when they left the church carried with them the conviction that it was their individual duty to find and bring some one to Christ."[48]

The overall effect on Matthews's personality of this rapid rise to success is not entirely clear. Surely it provided him with the confidence necessary to extend his involvement into other arenas. However, being called "Doctor" (after he received the honorary degree) and being praised by much of the town were heady experiences. Matthews grew up as a poor Georgia boy with only a minimal formal education; thus, it was difficult for him to maintain his humility.

Matthews certainly loved power; on occasion, he seemed to enjoy manipulating his congregation's feelings. During his Jackson years, he developed a technique for responding to a formal call that he knew he would turn down. In the midst of a sermon, he would read the terms of another church's call, which usually included high praise for Matthews. He would indicate that the need was so great that he felt that he should accept the new opportunity. Then, just at the height of the suspense, he would suggest why his present call was the most important, and he would "decide" to stay. He first did this in response to a call from a Presbyterian church in Knoxville, Tennessee, in April 1899; he repeated this technique on numerous occasions in Seattle. Matthews justified this approach on the grounds that it stimulated his congregation to greater action. Yet it cannot be doubted that it was also a very ego-satisfying experience to have his parishioners pour out their affections in an effort to convince him to stay where he was.[49]

On the face of it, the reasons why Matthews left Tennessee and the South in 1902 for a remote corner of the Pacific Northwest seem difficult to understand. He always had a great love for the South, and any traveling he had done seems to have been on the East Coast. Obviously, Jackson residents admired him, and he openly admitted that he knew very little about the northwest region of the United States. However, beneath the surface, there appear to have been several factors that directed him westward. A major reason, which would continue to exercise a powerful impact on Matthews for the rest of his life, was his interest in China and Japan. Long before he became interested in Seattle, he began to study aspects of the Orient. He was apparently genuinely interested in becoming a missionary even while he was in Georgia. How much he pictured Seattle as a missionary gateway to the Orient is not entirely clear; yet shortly after he arrived in the Northwest, he began to articulate publicly his interest in sending missionaries to China.[50]

Matthews's decision to go to Seattle may have been made slightly easier with the death of his mother in March 1899.[51] Melinda Matthews had been seriously ill with the grippe since January of that year, and most of her last thirty years had been fraught with suffering. Born in Tennessee, Melinda probably would not have wanted to leave the South. Matthews always felt close to his mother, and it seems unlikely that he would have made a major move without her approval. His father, on the other hand, seemed willing to move wherever his son was called.

The First Presbyterian Church of Seattle first heard of Mark Matthews sometime during 1901. Charles Crane, a member of the Seattle congregation, let his brother, Will Crane, a commercial traveler in Tennessee, know that the church was seeking a minister. A frequent traveler through Jackson, Crane was acquainted with Matthews and was much impressed by him; he recommended him highly to the Seattle church. Matthews at first refused an invitation to Seattle. He changed his mind, however, and visited in September 1901. Matthews was impressed with the possibilities of new ministries, in terms of both missions to the Far East and the vexing moral problems associated with this port town that had just experienced the Alaskan gold rush.[52]

In turn, Seattle First Presbyterian, upon hearing Matthews preach, was quite impressed with this striking young Southerner. The session decided to call Matthews and offered him a salary of $5,000 per year, a significant increase from the $1,700 paid to the previous pastor. Pondering the decision for nearly two months, Matthews finally agreed to accept the call under certain conditions. He stipulated that every elder and officer of the church must resign so that new officials could be elected after he had identified the specifics of his program. In order to emphasize the style and intensity of his ministry, Matthews also required that the church pass a resolution recognizing that the congregation is "the minister's force and not his field."[53] He wanted to make it clear that First Presbyterian would be involved in the Seattle community.

Matthews's Jackson congregation and much of the city pleaded with him to remain and continue his work. The *Jackson Sun* glowingly summarized his contributions in an attempt to persuade him to stay.

> Rev. M. A. Matthews has done more for Jackson than any other man ever did, and should he see fit to accept the call to a larger field, his loss would be mourned by every man, woman, and child in Jackson. To him we will largely credit the great Carnegie Library. It was he who established the first sanitarium, and organized a humane society. He has fought evil sometimes alone, and always with a courage undaunted. Let us hope that he will return to Jackson and resume his great and noble work.[54]

Despite such pleas, Matthews planned his departure from Jackson. For Matthews's final two sermons, the church was filled to capacity in demonstration of the great affection his congregation had for him. "The occasion was like the spread of a funeral pall, but it was a splendid tribute to the man," observed one witness. "There is something extraordinary in the personality of an individual who can so deeply touch the natures of the people among whom he has performed his mission."[55]

Though the Seattleites of First Presbyterian Church had seen and heard this thirty-four-year-old preacher from Tennessee, they were probably not quite prepared for Mark Matthews. Few Seattle residents understood how deeply he had been influenced by the impassioned political climate of his native region. Most did not understand that his religious background included a combination of frontier evangelical revivalism, Old School Presbyterian theology, and modern Social Gospel strategies. This amalgam produced an individual who was extremely self-confident about his ability to change the very nature of the communities in which he lived. Few Seattleites understood the intensity of that confidence or the clarity of his vision for a righteous city. Undoubtedly, what the members of First Presbyterian did sense was that a striking individual with a reputation for being an outstanding preacher and an active minister was entering their midst. Shortly thereafter, they would begin to realize, mostly to their approval but sometimes to their chagrin, what a Southern preacher could do in a city in the Pacific Northwest.

CHAPTER 3

Building Seattle's First Church

There is no place for drones, meddlers, pets or chronic grumblers in a live church. Love one another, forgive your enemies, hate sin and live righteously. Be considerate of the poor, support the feeble and help the struggling.

—Mark Matthews (1902)

On Monday evening, January 27, 1902, the Matthews family—Mark, his father, and his sister, Laura—boarded a train to Seattle. Traveling across the mostly snow-covered plains of the western United States, they arrived four nights later, and a small group from First Presbyterian Church whisked them off to the Occidental Hotel.[1] Matthews had little time to recuperate from the extended trip. On Sunday, February 2, he ascended the pulpit at the church on Fourth Avenue and Spring Street to preach his first sermon. According to the *Seattle Post-Intelligencer*, there was more than the usual hoopla surrounding the arrival of a new preacher; indeed, Matthews's reputation had preceded him, and the atmosphere was electric. In that first sermon, entitled "The Gospel of Soup, Soap, Salve, and Salvation," he called for unity in the congregation and liquidation of all debts. Matthews established a no-nonsense tone by telling his congregation that he expected them to be punctual and regular in their church attendance. Time was of the essence, responsibility was the requirement, and duty was the watchword. This Southern preacher did not come to the Pacific Northwest with the idea that he would go slowly and carefully assess the strengths and weaknesses of his flock. On the contrary,

41

Matthews arrived in Seattle with a precise idea of how he wanted to organize his church and of the specific objectives he wanted to accomplish. He fully believed that the church was a tool, or force, as he liked to put it, by which Christianity could be spread and the outside community redeemed. In short, Matthews came to Seattle and immediately set about the task of redefining the mission and identity of First Presbyterian. And for him, this meant developing a church that would attract leaders from the emerging middle class in order to embark on the larger enterprise of making Seattle a righteous city and a model of what a Christian community should be in the twentieth century.

At first glance, Matthews's strategy for building Seattle's First Presbyterian Church into one of the country's premier congregations appeared simple: he came with a clear vision and mission; he vigorously promoted his preaching and church activity through the press; he developed a plan for a new facility, and he developed a superb organizational structure that enabled thousands of his members to minister to the broader community. On a more subtle level however, Matthews attempted to attract significant numbers of the middle class by providing clear answers to the pressing social issues, economic questions, and political debates of the day. Matthews came to Seattle at a time when many Americans in the middle class seemed to be caught in the great transition from small towns to the urban metropolis. A robust business and professional culture was emerging in the midst of the advance of the industrial revolution and its accompanying urbanization. Organizational culture was quickly changing, and a consumer society began to develop rapidly. Artisans and craftsmen gave way to factory owners and workers; small-town proprietors gradually disappeared in favor of salesmen and office workers. Similarily, the Victorian culture of the nineteenth century found itself under siege as younger Americans, in particular, claimed increasing moral autonomy and greater personal freedom. Modern America was in the process of being born at the time Matthews moved to the Pacific Northwest.

Many Protestant Americans expressed anxiety over a rapidly changing world in which familiar moorings seemed threatened by industrialization and immigration on the one hand, and Darwinian theories and Biblical criticism on the other. Historians have identified a discernable cultural reaction to the emergence of modernism, and they broadly define that response as antimodern. Matthews did his best to sort through these complex forces and persuade his audiences that he could provide them with compelling answers. At moments he clearly embraced modern society's affection for the values of organization, efficiency, and hierarchy. On the other hand, Matthews fiercely held on to a number of Victorian values; he resisted the increasing tendency in contemporary society to pursue pleasure for its own sake, to crave a rootless individualism, and to challenge traditional social roles. Once in Seattle, he attempted on a weekly basis to shape the worldview of his middle-class parishioners. He regularly preached on issues of wealth and luxury, gender roles, family values, and cultural authority. More so than when he was in Georgia and Tennessee, Matthews was forced to confront American middle-class culture as it was emerging in the twentieth century. Much was at stake. Cultural hegemony rested with those opinion makers who could win the hearts and minds of the middle class. Protestantism had carefully positioned itself to assume prominence in the lives of this burgeoning class in urban America, but Matthews instinctively sensed that all was not well. He hoped that his charisma, in conjunction with his patterns of ministry established in the South, would enable him to lead the middle class into the twentieth century. He believed that the combination of modern organizational structures and methods, tempered with evangelical zeal, Victorian values, and a vision for social justice could be a successful formula for building Seattle's First Presbyterian Church into one of the great congregations in America.

Mark Matthews attracted more attention than was usually given to a new preacher, but it is doubtful that anyone sitting in the pews predicted that he, in a few short years, would build the church into the largest Presbyterian congregation in the world. He would soon command national attention. Perhaps even more remarkable, his success in building church membership would come in the least-churched region of the country. The Pacific Northwest might be said to be a most inhospitable ground for the development of institutional religious activity, and yet Matthews set about building a church that he hoped would transform Seattle into the ideal Christian community he had always envisioned.

Founded in 1853, Seattle had emerged as a significant port on Puget Sound by the time of the great Seattle fire in 1889. In the aftermath of the disaster, city residents built a more modern city, complete with its own water supply, electrical power, and a commitment to carve out more physical space for commercial development by leveling some of the many hills. With the extension of the Great Northern railroad into the city in 1893, Seattle could effectively compete with Tacoma, which

Building Seattle's First Church

had been the terminus of the Northern Pacific railroad since 1883. Increasingly, economic leaders looked to the Far East and the extension of trade with China and Japan as the source of future prosperity. In addition to the completion of the railroad, the discovery of gold in Alaska in 1897 provided a much-needed economic boost. Entrepreneurs of all stripes flocked to the Pacific Northwest for fame and fortune, and Seattle caught the fancy of more than one individual who believed that future wealth might be just around the corner.[3]

For a young minister looking to create an urban community based on Christian principles, the environment created by the Alaska gold rush was hardly promising. More saloons than retail stores existed in downtown Seattle. With the burgeoning population, the "mechanisms for maintaining law and order broke down. . . . The police department," according to one historian, "when not directly in league with the 'vice lords,' simply found itself outnumbered."[4] Seattle had become an entertainment mecca for miners, sailors, and loggers. One writer described the city as "a crude, somewhat primitive place . . . nonetheless a very exciting place" in 1897.[5] Exciting port and frontier towns on the West Coast generally were not the most fertile ground for religious growth, and Seattle was no exception. Many town fathers believed that, if the city hoped to survive economically, it would have to embrace the pursuit of pleasure. To many, embracing this pursuit meant being tolerant of gambling, alcohol, and prostitution.

Beneath the surface, Seattle had certain features that worked to Matthews's advantage, although one should never underestimate his ability to take advantage of any circumstances that might have been present. In terms of the size of the town, it would be difficult to imagine a more propitious moment for Matthews to arrive on the scene. The boom in Seattle's population that had begun by 1902 eventually would provide him the numbers of people and the important resources necessary to build a major church. Yet in 1902, the city was still small enough that Matthews was able to move easily into a position of civic as well as religious leadership. The table shows Seattle's population growth from 1880 to 1910, illustrating the enormous growth that occurred during the minister's first few years in Seattle.

1880	1890	1900	1910
3,553	42,837	80,671	237,174

Equally important in the creation of an agreeable climate for Matthews was the tendency among many groups in the city to dimin-

Building Seattle's First Church

ish class differences and agree on a basic set of middle-class values. There seemed to be a constant mixing of people and activities. "The boarding houses accommodated not only transients like salesmen and sailors," according to the historian Roger Sale, "but also jewelers, engineers, teachers of anything from violin to penmanship, clairvoyants, midwives, and retired couples."[6] There was a significant group of professionals who did not have to live downtown but chose to do so, according to Sale. First, Second, and Third Avenues included a healthy mix of hotels, businesses, newspapers, retail stores, and churches. The diversity encouraged Matthews's belief that Seattle could be an attractive place to live if, in fact, it embraced middle-class values and a Protestant ethic. The town had survived the panic of 1893 by pooling its resources; it had not gone into depression when the gold rush ended, because of both its economic diversity and its ability to take advantage of Jim Hill's transcontinental railroad. By 1902, many Seattleites expressed both pride in their young city and expectations of further growth and development.[7]

Even before Matthews arrived, this growing middle class began to express its discontent with those who believed that Seattle had to cater to the miner and the logger. Beginning in the 1890s, there was a certain anxiety among the more consciously middle class over just how tolerant the town should be of gambling and prostitution. Two weeks after Matthews arrived, a local newspaper lamented the problems of the open town. Three months after the preacher's arrival, the *Seattle Times* ran an extensive article describing the problems of the "Tenderloin," or red-light district. It is clear that from the beginning, Matthews felt encouraged to work for moral reform because he believed that Seattle's middle class desired just such efforts.[8]

The demographic makeup of the city also contributed to Matthews's success as a leader of public opinion. One historian has argued that, unlike Boston's or Chicago's, "Seattle's population was homogeneous, or at least homogenized." Seattle did not have the large immigrant populations that "led to the formation of distinctive ethnic neighborhoods and institutions and, often, the clustering of certain ethnicities in particular jobs and job levels." At least through 1910, this absence of ethnic diversity "kept Seattle from developing the sense of an urban mosaic found elsewhere."[9] Travel costs and distance from immigrant ports of entry on the East Coast prevented Seattle from being inundated with large numbers of the poorest immigrants, particularly when compared with other metropolitan areas. Those who held blue-collar jobs, such as loggers, fishermen, mine hands, and cannery workers, tended to work and live outside the city. As a result, Matthews walked into a surprisingly fertile ground for proselytizing new Christians. The structural elements facilitated the growth of a strong middle class; the moral and ideological climate seemed ripe for leadership from those who were sensitive to middle-class values. The size of the city and its middle-class nature proved to be crucial to Matthews's early success. The time seemed right for someone with a vision of righteous reform to come and take charge.

When Mark Matthews arrived in Seattle in 1902, he believed that God had called him to transform the city into a place where Christian principles informed public policy and Christianity defined the social ethos. If he had any second thoughts about his decision to leave his native region for the hinterlands of the Northwest, he revealed not a hint. At age thirty-four, he presented an imposing physical presence and commanded full attention when he spoke from the pulpit. Perhaps most impressive, Matthews exuded boundless energy and enthusiasm virtually twenty-four hours a day for all that he did. Clearly, he believed that his success depended on his ability to build a dynamic and powerful congregation. Just as he had done in Calhoun, Dalton, and Jackson, he set about establishing a vibrant, well-organized, and socially active church that would enable him to raise civic consciousness and influence public policy.

First Presbyterian Church in Seattle had been established in 1869 by the "Father of Presbyterianism" in Washington Territory, George Whitworth.[10] Whitworth had come west on the Oregon Trail and had ended up establishing as many as twenty churches in Oregon and Washington. He represented a generation of Christians who migrated to the region with the intent of bringing western-style government, schools, churches, and hospitals to a region populated by Native Americans.[11] Whitworth had taken the post of president of the fledgling University of Washington in 1866. Three years later, he established the First Presbyterian Church. However, life on the frontier was never easy; First Presbyterian in Seattle struggled for survival until A. L. Lindsley moved from the First Presbyterian Church in Portland to become the first regular pastor in 1880. Shortly thereafter, the church's first building was constructed at Third Avenue and Madison Street. More pastors followed; by 1887 membership reached 130, and the church reported that it was now self-supporting. First Presbyterian continued to grow modestly relative to the overall growth in Seattle's population. A second church building was constructed in the 1890s on the corner of Fourth Avenue and Spring Street. And by 1902, when Matthews began his ministry at First Presbyterian, the congregation was in generally stable condition, though it was burdened with a $25,000 debt.

The 400 members surely hoped that Matthews could lead them over the financial hurdles and build a dynamic congregation. But few, in fact, expected the rapid success that he achieved in attracting new members. Within a month, the pews were filled to near capacity. After six weeks, eighty-seven new members joined First Presbyterian, a growth so rapid that it unsettled some of the older members, who were accustomed to arriving no more than five minutes prior to the beginning of the service to find their favorite pew still available. "The immense crowds which we are now having in constant attendance at church make it necessary from my point of view," one old-timer wrote Matthews, "that some action be taken toward the securing of seats to the regular congregation."[12] But Matthews refused to change the seating arrangements.

In the beginning, Matthews attracted people with his sheer energy, and perhaps many simply were fascinated by this unfamiliar preacher. By the first of June 1902, First Presbyterian had grown by 230 members, and one local newspaper had described Matthews as "without question the best orator in the city."[13] At the end of the month, Matthews delivered what was to be his inaugural annual report at First Presbyterian, and though brief, it still captures much of the energy and vision of that first year.

My dear Parishioners: Your pastor expects every man to do his duty. The church is his force. Loving obedience should characterize the congregation. There is no place for drones, meddlers, pets or chronic grumblers in a live church. Love one another, forgive your enemies, hate sin and live righteously. Be considerate of the poor, support the feeble and help the struggling. Read the Bible daily, establish a family altar and in secret pray often. Be kind, hospitable, and unselfish. Live for others. Give liberally, support the Cause willingly. Pray for the pastor.
Be a faithful soldier. I am,
Respectfully,
M. A. Matthews[14]

As he did in Jackson, Matthews purposefully cultivated an image of distinction. His six-and-a-half-foot frame was accentuated by his long black waistcoat. Perceived to be skinny as a rail, he made an excellent subject for editorialists' one-liners and local cartoonists' drawings. Matthews never objected; he probably found that such attention made people take even greater notice of his ideas, and this was exactly what he wanted. He consciously strove to arouse public interest. He instinctively understood the dictum that virtually any publicity was good publicity. He sought the limelight and succeeded in a way that any public relations expert in the late twentieth century would envy.

In his first year in Seattle, Matthews drew attention by claiming that churches should not be exempt from taxation. "I am disgusted with the people who go around the country pauperizing the church, by holding it up as an object of charity and asking people to render it gratuitous service," he said. "The bride of Christ is not an orphan . . . and she is willing and able to pay her taxes to all governments."[15] This was the same position that he had expressed in Jackson, but few Seattle residents had ever heard a preacher take such a stand. The press loved this type of issue, and Matthews possessed a flair for controversy that always made good newspaper copy. Reporters found his bluntness to be a breath of fresh air on the religious scene. "His philosophy is broader than most ministers of the gospel are willing to admit into their pulpits," said a reporter for the *Seattle Mail and Herald*. "He has advocated among other things the taxation of church property; and has said that the clapping of hands in response to a point well taken in a sermon is not, in his opinion, a desecration of the house of God."[16] Another eye-opener for Seattle residents was Matthews's sermon against wearing hats in church. Just as effective as it was in Jackson, the sermon served the purpose of attracting community attention and helped build the image of Matthews as someone unique. The *Seattle Times* commented that his position reflected a "decided innovation," for the custom of wearing hats had existed as long as anyone could remember.[17]

During Matthews's first thirty-six months at First Presbyterian, membership grew very rapidly. In the year prior to his arrival, the church budget amounted to $3,500. The receipts during 1902 climbed to $12,500. By January 1903, membership had reached 1,100—a gain of 700 during the first year. Within three years, Matthews had established a financial base that enabled him to push for the construction of a new church building. The project gained an unexpected boost when, in 1905, a serious fire destroyed much of the sanctuary. Investigators discovered that the chimney had cracked when the building settled due to construction of the Great Northern railroad tunnel underneath the church. The congregation temporarily met in Seattle's Grand Opera House while repairs were made, and the experience convinced members that a new building was needed.[18]

Under Matthews's direction, church leaders sold property to raise $200,000 and subsequently purchased three lots on the block bordered by Seventh Avenue and Spring Street. Matthews led groundbreaking ceremonies on July 4, 1906, and the church's cornerstone was laid on Thanksgiving Day, November 29, 1906. Designed by the firm of Crapsey and Lamm from Cincinnati, Ohio, the building covered 21,600 square feet, seated 3,000 people, and included a new $30,000 pipe organ. It was reportedly the largest auditorium used for orthodox preaching in the United States at that time. Matthews was particularly proud of the fact that six rows of pews, seating approximately sixty people, were equipped with special apparatus for the hearing impaired. He also liked to point out the 125 intercom connections throughout the church.[19] The design attracted national attention for an oval configuration that was compared with the Coliseum at Rome. Architecturally, two domes dominated the building. Most impressively, Matthews helped design this building to become what Social Gospel advocates called an institutional church. As he had in Jackson, he believed that his church should meet as many of his parishioners' needs as possible. He desired space for seven basic departments: education, industrial, physical, philanthropic, social, sociological, and religious. A room designed to hold 250 people was designated for the young men's Bible class. The church included a running track, and the basement contained a gymnasium and kitchen, while the third floor held an art gallery. Matthews's office and library were built in the dome over the foyer, allowing him to gaze out over the harbor and most of the city. Matthews believed that the church should be open seven days a week and used nearly twenty-four hours a day.[20]

With the new building completed in 1907, First Presbyterian grew very rapidly. In Matthews's first decade, the church averaged growth of between 400 and 500 members per year, which outstripped every other congregation in the denomination. By 1910, membership had increased to more than 4,000. In January 1911, the church claimed to be the largest Presbyterian congregation in the United States with 4,576 members. By 1915, First Presbyterian counted nearly 5,700 in membership, and that total continued to climb throughout Matthews's ministry. In 1920, Matthews reported a membership of 6,599; in 1925, 7,533; in 1930, 7,886; in 1935, 8,192; and in his last year as pastor (1939), 8,818.[21]

Matthews succeeded in attracting great numbers of Presbyterians for a variety of reasons, not the least of which was the power of his personality. He possessed an excellent memory for names and faces. "To meet him is to like him," said a reporter for a local newspaper, "and to know him is to become his friend."[22] Most people first encountered Matthews through his preaching, and those who still remember him consistently remark upon his commanding presence in the pulpit. He projected his voice exceptionally well and of course spoke with great conviction. Typically he spoke for forty to forty-five minutes. Although not overly emotional in tone, Matthews delivered his sermons with inflection and effectively utilized broad gestures.[23]

Matthews loved attention; he had the rare gift of being able to dominate a room simply by his presence. He fascinated Seattle residents as did few, if any, other public figures. Why the local press treated Matthews differently is difficult to say, but it did. "He has revived the lost art of self-advertising," said the *Argus*, "until today he is known as a living, breathing character from Belfast to Bombay."[24] Repeatedly, stories about his "unusual height, his striking face and his great slouch hat" appeared in the local papers as journalists kidded the preacher about the rarefied air in the "upper strata of the atmosphere."[25] Matthews could laugh at himself in a way that many found ingratiating. For example, when he was asked to umpire a charity baseball game between the police and fire departments, the newspapers gave more attention to the antics of his arbitration than to the game itself. "'Play Ball,' shouted the divine. This familiarity with baseball procedure made a great hit with the fans," reported one newspaper. "They did not know that Dr. Matthews had spent twenty-four hours preceding the game in reading up on Robert's Rules of Order."[26] Shortly thereafter, Matthews again made the newspapers in a folksy manner. The article was introduced with two markedly different cartoon drawings of Matthews.

> Another Seattle landmark is gone. . . . It is expected that when the public general awakes to a full and complete realization that, indeed, the worst is true. . . . [C]ivic organizations will draft resolutions and

the Pioneers Association will address a memorial to the extraordinary session of the legislature asking for relief. Dr. Matthews has cut his hair.[27]

Newspapers often portrayed Matthews in terms that remind the reader more of Paul Bunyan than of Paul the Apostle. "There was nothing of the wishing business about Dr. Matthews," according to one newspaper. "He proposed to take hold of a man and cram him so full of goodness that he would yell for more."[28] Matthews fascinated observers because he exuded so much energy. "He comes nearer to being a perpetual motion machine than anything which has yet appeared on the horizon," wrote one reporter.[29]

The press enjoyed a good joke at Matthews's expense, and one such instance occurred in November 1908. As a member of the executive committee of the Ministerial Federation, Matthews recommended a speaker named Reverend H. C. Killen, a former Presbyterian from Port Townsend, who now was without denominational affiliation. Apparently Matthews had never heard Killen speak, because when the itinerant preacher began his address, he commenced to attack virtually everyone in the audience. Killen told the ministers that "denominationalism is in league with vice and sin and God will not tolerate it much longer. The man who teaches and practices infant baptism is doomed and will occupy a place with other sinners in the world beneath." The preacher exhorted the ministers to revitalize "feet washing ceremonies, love feasts, and holy kissing bees." As Killen proceeded, "laughter became uproarious," according to the *Seattle Times*. And when it was over, the ministers mercilessly chided Matthews, and he sheepishly promised that "no crank will be permitted to address the ministers as long as we are on the executive committee."[30]

Although Matthews could take a joke at his expense, he never left any doubt that he was in charge of most meetings and of his organization. Without question, he wielded enormous influence. One of the conditions for his accepting the call to First Presbyterian required that every elder and officer of the church resign upon his arrival, giving him the right to appoint his own cabinet, boards, auxiliaries, and committees. On the evening of February 3, 1902, the day following his first sermon, the session (church council) met to carry out the terms of the agreement. A congregational meeting was called, and on February 17 new officers were elected at Matthews's recommendation.

Matthews embraced a modern business model of organization. Historians of the late nineteenth and early twentieth century have noted the widespread acceptance of cultural values in the business community that focused on efficiency, order, bureaucracy, and hierarchy.[31] Burton Bledstein in his study of middle-class values during the late nineteenth century argued that this concept of organization was crucial.

> In his head, however, the middle-class person attempted to eliminate wasteful competition and to establish universal standards for moral and civil behavior. He was the world's organizer: punctual, industrious, mathematical, and impersonal. He sharpened his mind into an analytic knife. He sought accurate information, acted with the "coldest prudence," and built a more perfect institutional order than had ever been known, an order that permitted meritorious middle-class persons to realize their inner selves by means of publicly recognized status, power, and wealth.[32]

Models of incorporation flourished throughout American society during this era, and Matthews wanted First Presbyterian to embody business principles. The new minister's energy, combined with superb organizational and managerial abilities, helped him build an extraordinary congregation by any standard. He characterized First Presbyterian as the "best-organized church in the United States."[33] The church evolved into a complex web of groups that handled everything from library books to Sunday school transportation. A new member could participate in a number of activities specifically designed to nurture his or her Christian faith, centering on Bible classes and Sunday school. Matthews organized women into a variety of groups that helped him meet the individual needs of parishioners. The Pastor's Aid Society kept Matthews informed of crises among members and responded with clothing and food. Visitation groups focused on the needs of the sick, elderly, and imprisoned.[34] Matthews exhorted his male parishioners to address specific political and social concerns. The First Presbyterian sociological society, men's brotherhood, and debating club were all highly developed organizations.[35] The Industrial Department at First Presbyterian had responsibility for finding jobs for unemployed church members.

Ten rules governed the various church departments. Most important, all appointments theoretically came from Matthews, and he stipulated that he would preside at all meetings unless he directed the executive chairman to take his place. Rule Ten underscored his zeal for order: "No Elder will be allowed to speak more than twice on the same subject. All debates must be confined to the subject under consideration. No debater will be allowed to use personalities, personal references, or in any way, shape, form, or manner become acrimonious during the debate."[36] Matthews made clear his commitment to organization and tangible accomplishments. "You should not expect men to come to a meeting and listen to reports that are empty, addresses that are unprepared, or complaints of brethren whose pessimism has reached the cholera stage," he told a church group. He believed that people wanted to be part of something well organized and successful. "Men want good, strong, aggressive, optimistic work, reports, and speeches," he claimed. "In other words, the work of men and by men must have a definite plan, a business method, and sure encouraging results."[37]

Matthews installed a board of elders who helped organize a network of committees and departments, including the Departments of Executives, Finance, Purchase and Repair, Branch Sunday Schools, Members, Men's Work Evangelism, Bible Conference, Extension and Pulpit Supply, Young People, Main Sunday School Stewardship, Publicity, Oriental and Filipino Work, Colleges, Hospitality, Sympathy, Books, Visitation, Transportation, Special Service, Communion, Labor, and Relief. Pairs of elders were assigned to twenty-four "circles" that coincided with the different neighborhoods in the city. These pairs called on all new members and helped integrate them into the life of the church.

In addition, the customary group of deacons tended to the special needs of parishioners. At its height, First Presbyterian claimed a board of sixty-two deacons that looked after widows and orphans as well as the fatherless and other wanting individuals. Eighty-eight deaconesses worked collaboratively with the deacons. At church on Sunday, scores of ushers were on duty; they were assisted by twenty-nine women who were stationed at various places throughout the church in order to greet visitors.[38]

Matthews seemed tireless. He often worked twelve to sixteen hours a day, seven days a week. He employed as many as ten assistant pastors to help him with his work, keeping them on a tight rein. Assistant pastors were always under his close scrutiny. Matthews appointed all of his assistants and quickly removed them if they were not performing up to his standards. Some assistants served for as short a time as one month and some for as long as seven or eight years. Those who succeeded as assistants were "humble, obedient and industrious."[39] The one assistant who seemed to win Matthews's complete confidence was Dr. Frederick L. Forbes. He served as Matthews's assistant for more than thirty years, and he died in 1940, only two months after Matthews had passed away. Throughout his ministry at First Presbyterian, Matthews required assistant pastors to report to him in writing once a week. They were instructed to detail the calls that they had made to parishioners and the nature of the conversations held with members of the congregation. The assistant was "expected to follow as punctiliously as a soldier does his orders from a general in time of war."[40] Even the janitor was given exacting instructions about what needed to be done for each day of the week and each hour of the day.[41]

Matthews's leadership and organization of the church session bears mention. Within the organizational structure of the Presbyterian church, the session was the key decision-making body. In 1902, when Matthews came, the session consisted of twelve members, but through the years he kept increasing the membership through appointment until it reached 107, a staggering size compared with other churches throughout the country. The session met regularly for dinner and business on the first Tuesday of every month, and they also met every Sunday. Responsible for interviewing prospective members and gathering data for church records, the session played a key administrative role in facilitating the growth of the church. In this way, new members could be received on confession of faith and letters of transfer every week. Matthews himself appealed to nonmembers to make a profession of faith, and he invited them to join the church at the close of every service. When a person made it known that he or she wanted to join First Presbyterian, the prospective member was required to meet with the pastor and the session and answer the following questions in the affirmative:

Do you believe in God the Father, God the Son, and God the Holy Spirit?

Do you accept Jesus Christ to be your personal Savior?

Do you believe God has for Christ's sake pardoned your sins?

Do you wish to join the Church because you love God and His Church?

Do you promise to live a Christian life as you are aided and led by the Holy Spirit?

Will you do what you can to bring others to Christ and into the Church?

Building Seattle's First Church

Will you give of your time and money for the advancement of His
   Kingdom?
Will you read your Bible, which is God's infallible Word, daily?
Will you pray for the Pastor and officers of the Church, and study
   the peace, unity and harmony of the Church?[42]

Over a period of thirty-eight years, only two men held the office
of clerk (leader) of the session: the attorneys A. C. Dresbach and
Walter A. McClure. And though one should not overestimate their
influence, mainly because the pastor never removed himself from
the management of the operation, Matthews valued highly their
consistency and loyalty.[43]

First Presbyterian became known throughout the country for its
ability both to spawn new churches and to build a branch system that
allowed it to surpass every other congregation in the denomination in
membership. The case of Boulevard Park, located just south of Seattle
in the community of Des Moines, provides a good example of how the
branch system worked. In this instance the community had grown to
about a thousand people, and a group of Christians had found a school
building in which to meet. They contacted First Presbyterian and an
assistant pastor worked with a real estate agent to find a suitable lot. A
Sunday school was first organized, and eventually a church was constructed. For several years the assistants at First Presbyterian minis-
tered to the branch church while receiving their salary from the main
church. The parishioners focused on raising money to pay for the building and its maintenance. During the first year of his tenure, Matthews
encouraged the development of church properties throughout the city,
and over the next few years, churches in different parts of the city, including West Seattle, South Park, the University District, Georgetown,
Green Lake, and Interbay, were established. The branch concept was
simple: wherever the need existed, land would be secured and a building constructed. The membership would be recorded at First Presbyterian (one of the reasons its total membership figures were so high),
and the new church would be supported financially by the main congregation. Eventually, twenty-eight branch Sunday schools were created, and in large part they helped account for the stupendous growth
of the church.[44]

The Sunday school at First Presbyterian became a major feature of
the church. By 1910, 2,400 young people participated in the various
classes. The "Cradle Roll," Beginners Department, Primary School,

Junior Division, Intermediate Branch, and Senior Department constituted the principal divisions. Matthews often spoke with pride about
the fact that teachers graded the performances of their students; teachers stressed the memorization of Bible texts, and students advanced to
the next classes on the basis of their proficiency. Awards of diplomas,
Bibles, and special marks recognized work well done. By 1910, much
of the adult congregation participated in one of ten different Bible
classes. The Young Men's Bible Club claimed 300 men, and the Young
Ladies' Bible Club had 125 members.[45]

Sunday morning began with Matthews and the teachers meeting
from 9:00 to 10:00 A.M., for Bible study. Instructors then held class for
various age groups from 10:00 to 11:00 A.M. One of Matthews's associates usually taught a post-sermon Bible class from 12:30 to 1:30 P.M. At
7:00 P.M., Matthews delivered the sermon during the evening worship
service. Teachers took a three-year course that included several exami-
nations, and Matthews required that every teacher and officer sign a
statement of faith. "No one is permitted to teach who is not sound in
faith. Every one must know and teach the Deity of Christ, and His
vicarious death and blood atonement," Matthews wrote. "No teacher
is permitted to utter an uncertain note."[46]

The Sunday school at First Presbyterian included more than just
Bible study. Matthews periodically required all students to seek other
children needing medical attention or surgery so that the church could
assist their families. In addition, the Sunday school had its own or-
chestra, with as many as fifty musical instruments.[47] The annual Sunday school picnic was virtually a citywide event, attracting up to 1,500
people. Mark Matthews relished occasions like these when he could
stroll among the families and acknowledge the work of his people and
create a sense of community in an extraordinarily large congregation.
An annual song contest generated spirited competition, with branch
Sunday schools selecting a song to perform before a panel of judges.
The students sat in the main auditorium of the church, their schools
identified by banners, and the winners received trophies for their
performance.[48]

Without question, Matthews embraced modernism's zeal for efficiency and an economy of scale. He relished the notion that First Presbyterian embodied the most up-to-date thinking about the ways to
run successful organizations. However, like hundreds of other Protestant ministers and thousands of middle-class parishioners through-

Building Seattle's First Church

out the country, Matthews resisted other tendencies associated with modernism.

The Seattle minister, along with numerous voices on both sides of the Atlantic, expressed a fear that modern culture was morally impotent and spiritually sterile. For some critics, as the westward movement and the frontier experience diminished, the modern world that was emerging in the twentieth century was vulnerable to becoming "overcivilized."[49] While critics focused on a number of issues, one of the most common concerns focused on gender roles. According to some commentators, the obsession with science and the pursuit of material progress had led to a form of urban "effeminacy" that had to be rooted out if the modern world were truly to advance.[50] The concern about an effeminate influence on American culture was even more pronounced in religious circles. The historian Ann Douglas has argued that religion in the nineteenth century assumed more feminine characteristics as Americans abandoned Calvinism and embraced more sentimental notions.[51] Many men in the burgeoning middle class seemed to need to reassert their hegemonic role in the culture as a whole and specifically reassert their masculine identity in all aspects of life.

Matthews, himself, was clearly concerned about these issues and forces in late-nineteenth- and early-twentieth-century America. He attempted to counter the modern cultural forces that seemed to undermine the role for men within the context of American religion by looking for ways that he might appeal to men's deepest needs. Matthews often stated that the key to attracting men into the church was to preach a clear, evangelical Gospel and to challenge them to become involved in their community. "This age needs doctrinal preaching," he said. "Men will crowd the churches to listen to doctrinal evangelistic preaching, but when the minister is in doubt or turns his attention to the watered-down, unscriptural vagaries of the new theology, he will preach to empty pews or to a few effeminate, sentimental hearers."[52] But Matthews also believed that men needed to be convinced that religion was compatible with masculine values. He exemplified what historians of American religion have described as "muscular Christianity." Along with preachers such as Billy Sunday, he attacked any notion that Christianity consisted of unmanly virtues. Matthews believed that men could be convinced of the importance of infusing Christianity into the great social and political problems of their day. Far from being passive and sentimental, Christianity fostered strength and even

Building Seattle's First Church

virility. "A man should pass from the child state of Christian life to the strong, robust, muscular period of Christian manhood," preached Matthews in a sermon entitled "Wanted: More Man in Men." He further stressed that the "physical powers of man should be trained to express truth, to embody cleanliness and to manifest a purpose and design for God's glory, and the elevation of the human race." He warned his audience that "the bloody football grounds of prominent colleges are not monuments to righteousness, or to intellectual genius," but that the true Christian man embodies the virtue of sympathy for others while being bold and courageous. "The greatest evil this country has to combat is the lack of boldness born of righteousness. Therefore, we want in men a righteous, masculine boldness."[53] As they sat week after week and month after month in First Presbyterian, men found themselves inundated with sermons that stressed "manly" virtues. Matthews challenged his male audiences repeatedly to "be real, independent, courageous Christian men, in the church, in business, in politics, at the family altar, and at the ballot-box."[54] In fact, Matthews achieved remarkable success in attracting men. Contrary to the national pattern of church attendance—women dominating Sunday morning services—First Presbyterian had a majority of men. Matthews estimated in 1911 that on a typical Sunday morning approximately fifty-five percent of the audience members were men. On a typical Sunday evening, as many as eighty percent were men.[55]

Matthews preached a fairly typical series of sermons during the late winter and early spring of 1909 that was directed at men. All delivered on Sunday evenings, the sermons focused on specific vices to eliminate and virtues to develop. In the first sermon, "Homeless Man," Matthews preached, "Idleness is a crime. If it is a voluntary idleness, the idle man is the criminal. If it is forced idleness, those who are responsible for the condition producing the idleness, are the criminals."[56] In the second sermon, entitled "Friendless Man," he urged each man to take up some great task or cause. "The man who represents, stands for and is the embodiment of a great cause, a controlling principle and an all-absorbing idea, makes friends who would die for him though they never saw him."[57] In "Penniless Man," a week later, Matthews excoriated verbosity, laziness, prodigality, extravagance, sin, and stinginess. He then moved on to behavioral and social responsibility. In "Heartless Man," he berated any man who mistreated women and children, but in particular he focused on horse beaters and those who were otherwise cruel to animals. In "Conscienceless Man," he attacked

Building Seattle's First Church

greed and exploitation. "Do you suppose landlords who are systematically and persistently raising rents on office buildings, stores, restaurants, bakeries, barber shops, hotels, flats and residences are controlled by the dictates of a righteous conscience? No." The next-to-last sermon, "Childless Man," emphasized the importance of family and stressed Matthews's belief that every man ought to produce a family. And, finally, the series culminated with an emphasis on conversion to Christianity in the "Christless Man."[58]

The men of First Presbyterian, with Matthews's encouragement, participated in a nationwide movement known as the Brotherhood. Formally endorsed by the Presbyterian Church U.S.A. General Assembly in 1906, the Brotherhood attempted to train men for positions of church leadership, to enhance Bible study, and to encourage participation in civic affairs. For the next decade, Matthews worked closely with the Brotherhood at First Presbyterian, and this organization proved to be one of the strongest in the entire church.[59]

Matthews, in fact, seemed to be slightly ahead of many of his peers in his efforts to masculinize religion and specifically middle-class Protestantism. In 1911 and 1912, a major interdenominational religious revival took place across the country. Over a million people attended events associated with the Men and Religion Forward Movement (M&RFM). As Matthews had tried to do at First Presbyterian, the M&RFM hoped to revitalize churches around the country by bringing more men into the church. It was estimated in 1911 that there were approximately 3,000,000 more women than men in churches. Much as Matthews had been preaching for the previous four to five years, organizers of the campaign consistently stressed "virile hymns," "strong men," and the pursuit of "Christian manliness." Real Christianity, according to most of the speakers, did not have "feminine" traits but exhibited "masculine" virtues.[60]

Matthews clearly needs to be understood in the larger context of a complex effort not only to attract more men into the church but also to counter what was perceived to be a deterioration of Christianity because of its association with feminine values. His views reflected a series of complex forces and developments in late-nineteenth- and early-twentieth-century America. From his assertion about the proper role of males and females in the family to his desire to exert the church's influence over American culture in general, Matthews worked to establish male hegemony in all aspects of American culture.

At the same time that Matthews consistently preached the virtues of a manly Christianity, he articulated what he believed was the proper role that a woman should play in contemporary society. The "new" woman of the twentieth century posed extraordinary challenges to the "true" woman of Victorian America. Without question, his Southern background reinforced his notion that a woman's place was in the home and that her responsibility lay primarily with insuring the moral sanctity of American life. But concerns about the role of women in the new century spread far beyond the South. Victorian thinkers clearly saw the family as a "haven in the heartless world of capitalist competition."[61] Victorian women were encouraged to provide a refuge for their children from the perversions of the marketplace and to provide comfort and encouragement to overworked husbands. Matthews found himself in complete agreement with these ideas. He vigorously opposed woman's suffrage and repeatedly defended a Victorian perspective on gender roles. "The purity of woman is essential to the establishment of society, the sacredness of home and the perpetuation of the nation," he preached in 1907.[62]

In a sermon entitled "The Evolution of the Model Girl," Matthews reflected the swirl of ideas surrounding gender issues in the early twentieth century and in many ways what must have been his own agonized thinking about the subject. He began with a clear statement that, from "an intellectual standpoint, [a woman] is the equal of man." But then Matthews quickly stated that intellectual equality did not imply social equality or the necessity of social change. "Woman's position in society is definitely fixed. It is not possible to make a change in her position without wrecking society. She is an essential factor in the world, and in the world's development." He argued that her place had been determined by "custom, by education, by religious and non-religious influences" and therefore should never be changed. Here, Matthews sounds remarkably conservative for a person who was so quick to challenge social, economic, and political traditions from the time he first stepped into the pulpit. But Matthews's views were not completely predictable: he boldly asserted that a woman should have the right to hold property in her own name and that she should be treated equally to men on the job. He further argued that it was hypocritical to place more social restrictions on women than men as if one should not trust women: "She can in fact withstand more temptations than her brother." And yet he could not relinquish the idea that woman's place was in the home.

Building Seattle's First Church

She is the controlling character in the evolution of domestic life, and, to her has been committed the trust of preserving in absolute purity the domestic influence. Her sphere is distinctively the domestic sphere, and whenever she steps beyond its confines, in order to retain her eternal position, her controlling motive for going out into the world must be the interest of the domestic sphere from which she has gone.

Matthews admitted that some women might develop professional interests in medicine, education, and business, but then he would quickly insist that "any system of education that drives a woman away from home or drives the home idea out of her mind is a curse to her, to her se[x], and to society. No woman's education is complete until she has graduate[d] from Pie School."[63] During the first two decades of the twentieth century, Matthews vigorously opposed woman's suffrage and did so with the conviction that social stability hung in the balance. "Your niche in life must be essentially female and no encroachment on man's because his is also essentially male. This gives and guarantees to woman an essential place in the universe and if understood by these 'freaks' who are clamoring for the right of suffrage, they would at once cease their disgraceful babbling."[64]

Of course Matthews's pronouncements on gender-related issues extended into the realm of marriage relationships. He loved to advise both men and women about what they should look for in a spouse. He thought that men should seek women who did not nag or lack womanly affection. He once said that "man wants a lover, not a monstrosity."[65] In another sermon he advised young women to get ten hours of sleep on a regular basis, adopt a proper diet, wash their faces regularly with cold water, and avoid wine and the card table.[66] He also stated, "A woman cannot be a man's friend. She must be his acquaintance, his fiancee, his wife, his daughter, his sister, or his mother. She can be nothing else."[67] At First Presbyterian, women were encouraged to teach Sunday school and to take responsibility for many of the social ministries of the church. But serving as an elder or deacon was certainly out of the question. Throughout his career, Matthews consistently spoke out against women occupying the pulpit. As late as 1930, he was still haranguing against female preaching.

There may be a few masculinely minded women who want to project themselves, but there are not many. Those within our knowledge do not belong to the Presbyterian Church. They belong to the freak class and are usually found in denominations that are heretically inclined or mentally unsound.[68]

From the perspective of the end of the twentieth century, it is clear that Matthews was not alone in his concern over the role of the family in modern America. Historians now find the period at the end of the nineteenth century to be one of great change and ferment in the basic structure and orientation of the family in American society. The historian Susan Curtis found that "middle-class Protestants' lack of certainty, identity, and purpose in industrial America caused them to suffer in the unappealing separate spheres of home and work, not entirely sure of alternatives."[69] She and other historians have described a set of shifting role models for men and women and numerous conflicts over cultural expectations. Curtis argued that Social Gospel ministers did not intend to make a radical break with the past. They wanted to adapt Victorian expectations to modern reality. Accordingly, they continued to insist on individual regeneration as well as social responsibility, and they accepted the values of domesticity even though they chose to carry them out in different ways.[70]

Matthews clearly felt anxiety about the role of the family and did all that he could to bolster a rather idyllic picture of the middle-class home: "Hearth-stones are always warm and the fire-side circle is made up of obedient children and happy parents." He always stressed the importance of the family altar, Bible study, and using the hymn book daily. "Loyalty to God, to the state and to the church is the rule in every household," he said. "Frugality and economy are the laws binding upon every member of the domestic class." His confidence in the middle class as the savior of society seemed almost unbounded at times. "There is practically no rottenness in the domestic class proper. All the rottenness that may develop in it will settle down to the submerged class or rise as froth to the upper ten or nude class."[71]

Matthews emphasized in sermon after sermon the importance of the home. Again not alone in his generation, he virtually demanded that the middle class accept its responsibility to build a healthy home in order to ensure the future of western civilization. To the contemporary reader this may appear to be nothing more than the rhetoric of "family values" associated with conservative politics. But at the beginning of the twentieth century, both liberals and conservatives in the middle class seemed to accept the necessity of strengthening the home and the family as the key foundation for a healthy society. Typically, Matthews would excoriate his congregation for not being vigilant enough against even the mildest forms of vice that might find their way into family life.

> The average home is not the child's friend. Parents are engrossed in cards, wines and frivolity to the neglect of the highest interest in children. The children ought to be indoctrinated at home. Who at the home is going to do the teaching? The father is at some lodge, and the mother is at some social function. If this is not changed and changed speedily, the next generation will be so intellectually puny it will have to be kept in the nursery and fed on milk.[72]

He frequently berated parents for not providing enough intellectual stimulation for their families and argued that too many homes had "no amusement, no pleasure, no sunshine, no life and no happiness in them."[73] Aghast at the increasing divorce rate in the twentieth century, Matthews blamed a variety of social maladies, from gambling and alcohol to parental lenience and woman's suffrage. On one occasion after his own marriage, his frustration with the health of the family unit reached such proportions that he suggested bachelors be taxed and the revenues distributed to large families.[74]

Matthews's own marital status was a topic that generated considerable discussion in the Seattle press during his first few years in the Pacific Northwest. "Dr. Matthews is opposed to divorce," one newspaper reported. "It would appear that he is also opposed to marriage."[75] Newspapers kidded him about his advice on marriage and child rearing since he had no actual experience. But during the winter of 1903 and 1904, Matthews became attracted to Grace Jones, the church secretary and the daughter of one of his assistant pastors, the Reverend Owen Jones. Jones had come to Seattle from Wales in 1887, where he had been well educated. Matthews first met Grace when he caught her wearing his overcoat at her secretarial desk in the church in an attempt to stay warm. On August 24, 1904, the two married, much to the tongue-in-cheek enjoyment of the newspaper commentators. "Dr. Matthews is making a grave mistake in getting married," wrote the Seattle Argus. "When he has a little practical experience along certain lines on which he has been lecturing and preaching, he will be under the humiliating necessity of writing a new set of lectures and sermons."[76]

Building Seattle's First Church

Just over a year after his wedding, on August 26, 1905, Matthews became a father for the first time when Grace-Gwladys (called Gwladys and sometimes spelled Gladys) was born. Four years later, Matthews's son, Mark, Jr., was born, on April 14, 1909. The family was exceptionally close. Throughout their thirty-five years of marriage, Mark and Grace continued to express deep affection and support for one another. Grace believed her role as a pastor's wife required her to be active in the church, to be the most gracious of hostesses, and to be a credit to her husband always; by all accounts she excelled in these areas and was deeply admired by many people. Any list of women's organizations at First Presbyterian usually featured Grace Matthews's name. She was particularly well known for her work with the Red Cross.

The Seattle minister's concern over the state of American society extended beyond the state of the family and gender roles into a number of other areas. One of his more persistent issues centered on the debilitating effects of extravagant wealth on the soul. Again, he was not alone in this concern. Historians have found that *luxury* was a word frequently used to disparage those who had abused the benefits derived from economic prosperity.[77] Matthews and many of his colleagues excoriated the symbols of upper-class life as a reflection of the moral deterioration in modern culture. In 1904, he gave a sermon entitled "Luxury: The Enemy of Character, Personal, and National." "Men are killed by excesses, and not moderation," preached Matthews. "Luxury, then, is necessarily an enemy of character. No man has grown spiritually, who has reveled in it; who has tried to satisfy the desires and passions of life."[78] In a sermon entitled "Extravagance is Criminal," he argued that Americans were the most wasteful people in the world.[79] In "Making a Life, Making a Living, or Making a Failure," Matthews again condemned extravagance and selfishness.[80] Perhaps the best example of his attempt to distinguish virtuous wealth from wealth improperly attained was in a 1906 sermon entitled "Are There More Kinds of Blood Money than Mr. Rockefeller's?" Matthews accused John D. Rockefeller of perverting legitimate avenues of trade and immorally destroying competition. Matthews argued that Rockefeller's "philanthropy cannot purify the motive of the company nor regenerate the souls of its officers."[81]

Beyond simply affirming basic middle-class values, Matthews often attempted to develop a very specific middle-class consciousness among his congregation. In a 1906 sermon entitled "Are the Foundations of Society Rotten?" Matthews divided society into three classes. He defined the lower class, or "submerged class," as he liked to call it, as the "under-developed, under-protected and under-loved person." He spoke paternalistically about the need to help such people. When he turned his attention to the upper class, he expressed nothing but disdain. He called them "the nude or 'upper ten' class composed of rich, educated, vulgar persons. Their stomach is their god. The gratification of their passions is their supreme purpose in life." When it came to the middle class, however, Matthews had nothing but praise. The domestic class, as he called it, was "composed of the sound, sane, sober, common people. They give the world homes, children and domestic governments."[82]

Matthews and other spokespersons for Victorian America contrasted the evils of luxury with the merits of wealth achieved by virtuous behavior. In "Three Essentials to Success," he stressed the rewards of knowledge, industry, and sobriety.[83] In a sermon entitled "Digging up Business' Skeleton," Matthews reiterated that one's business and professional life could not be separated from one's personal character.[84] And in one other sermon, entitled "The Young Man in Business, in Society, and in Church," he linked moral virtue to success.

Matthews as well as many other Victorian males repeatedly asserted their cultural authority in a variety of contexts. What set of ideas would come to inform the middle-class perspective on reality and who would be responsible for purveying those ideas were critical questions at the turn of the century. Matthews believed that it was his calling and duty to direct his church and his community on issues of moral and political significance. He was not alone in this. Opinion makers throughout American society jockeyed for positions of influence over a middle class that has been described by historians as morally and spiritually adrift. Protestants seemed particularly fearful that their beliefs were being obliterated by myriad other voices, worldviews, and cultures in an ever more diverse American society.[85] Matthews himself was often self-conscious about the issue of authority. He must have sensed that, even if his regular parishioners seemed compliant to his preachings, he needed to remind his audience of how they should view authority at various levels. He loved to reiterate the authority of God, the authority of the pastor, the authority of men, and the authority of husbands. As a Calvinist, he found it easy to emphasize God's sovereignty, but he often ended with an assertion of the authority of the church or the pastor. In countless sermons, he reminded his audience that "the clergyman was the expounder of *truth* and . . . his voice should be heard on all questions involving the existence and perpetuity of government."[86]

Historians have noted that through most of the nineteenth century the minister served as one of the key intellectual and civic leaders—if not *the* key leader—in his community. The clergyman was heeded on a variety of subjects, primarily because his education was respected, his oratorical powers persuasive, and his moral orientation clear. Small-town America responded favorably to the urgings of its local pastor whether those urgings had to do with politics or religion.

However, as Americans moved to larger metropolitan areas and the economy became more industrialized, the minister began to lose authority in the public arena. The clergyman retained the right to speak on issues of faith, or clear-cut issues of morality, but the ability to lead his community in political discussions waned rather rapidly. The trained professional in city government or public policy began to replace the minister. The desire for expertise and the move toward specialization dominated middle-class thinking beginning in the early twentieth century. In large part, this change was the result of the middle class becoming increasingly well educated and acquiring additional authority in the society as the result of that specialized education.[87]

Matthews's own cultural authority had to survive in this climate of middle-class thinking. If Matthews found himself too much at odds with the worldview of the middle class, he risked becoming marginalized, particularly in the area of public policy. Yet his genius seems to have been his ability to tap into the underlying anxieties of the middle class in such a way as to gain the attention of significant numbers of Seattleites. And clearly, as we shall see, he never pandered to his audience; he repeatedly challenged them to examine their lives, their unstated assumptions, and their personal behaviors. He exhorted them to move outside of their comfort level and engage the world around them with their Christian ideals.

During his first five years in Seattle, Mark Matthews attracted the attention of the city's top leaders. He built a church that appealed to a great many of the local elite. The list of deacons and elders during the early years generally read like *Who's Who*. People such as the civic leader Austin Griffiths, the former governor John McGraw, and, a little later, J. D. Ross, head of Seattle City Light, the major utility company, headed a list of doctors, lawyers, judges, and businessmen. A member of

Building Seattle's First Church

Seattle's prestigious Rainier Club, a private men's club, Matthews could converse about virtually the entire spectrum of Seattle public issues. He did, however, have many critics. There were leaders in Seattle who opposed his positions and resented his influence. But, particularly in the first decade of the twentieth century, Matthews seemed well on his way to creating a role for himself and his church that would allow him to help shape public policy for years to come. As yet, professionalization had not become so entrenched in the middle class that its members would not listen to a person like Mark Matthews—at least as long as he seemed to be thinking and acting in ways with which they generally agreed. Clearly, the force of his personality and the manner in which he reflected middle-class values provided him with a platform for his vision of a righteous city.

Matthews had come not only to a strange land in 1902 when he moved to the Pacific Northwest, but he had come to a culture in flux if not crisis. Mark Matthews was typical of many opinion makers at the turn of the century who attempted to shape and lead that culture into the future. In several ways he can be seen as a person who embraced certain tenets of the modern world, and he certainly developed his church into an organization that reflected many of those underlying assumptions. And yet, ironically, Matthews reflected distinctly antimodern notions in his weekly critique of the cultural values of modern society. He worked at a tremendous pace to establish his authority over his flock and in the community with the clear hope that he could make a lasting impact on the city of Seattle and the world beyond by redeeming it from its wayward pursuits.

∼ CHAPTER 4 ∼

The Church Is My Force, the City My Field

The correct solution of the political, economic, and social
evils of this country is to be found in Christian Socialism.

—Mark Matthews (1906)

Mark Matthews's first sermon in Seattle, on February 2, 1902, "The Gospel of Soup, Soap, Salve, and Salvation," not only articulated what he expected from his parishioners, but also made clear his vision for his role as pastor. "Under the 'directings' of the Holy Spirit, I am to be your leader. The First Presbyterian Church of Seattle is to be my force and the whole city my field." The church, according to Matthews, "must be kept open every day during the year to be used by anyone who desires to enter, read, or meditate. The church building must be a kind of workshop and some kind of work for the elevation of humanity must be in progress every day." Matthews preached that his congregation would be "simply one of the many companies of a big regiment of which Jesus Christ is the commander-in-chief."[1]

If the members of First Presbyterian were aware of what Matthews had done in Calhoun, Dalton, and Jackson, they surely should have anticipated that this tall Southern preacher could not be more serious about trying to use religion for what he called the "elevation of humanity." Matthews repeated the phrase "The church is my force and the city my field" throughout the years of his ministry. As a good Calvinist, he believed that Christianity must be the means by which the social life of a community is transformed. And though he was not unique among religious leaders in Seattle, he quickly emerged as the most important religious voice in the city when it came to social reform.[2]

The years following the Civil War had transformed the face of America: the industrial revolution created economic opportunities that attracted millions of new immigrants to the cities of the East and Midwest. Capitalism thrived and the overall standard of living began to rise, but competition also created circumstances that produced hardship on an unparalleled level. Industrial accidents skyrocketed; in 1889, for example, nearly 2,000 railway men were killed on the job, and more than 20,000 were injured. Until the 1890s, courts considered employer negligence a normal risk to be borne by the employee. Children and young immigrant women worked long hours in terribly unsafe and unhealthy environments. The financial panic that gripped the nation beginning in 1893 produced the worst depression in American history next to the Great Depression of the 1930s. The Pacific Northwest was particularly beset by labor problems associated with timber and mining industries. Millions of Americans were thrown out of work with no safety net of social services. Long before 1906, when Upton Sinclair wrote *The Jungle*, in which he described the horrible conditions in the meatpacking industry in Chicago, Americans knew of the difficult conditions facing workers. Throughout the country, problems associated with urbanization challenged city governments, churches, and other voluntary organizations.[3]

Mark Matthews was part of a much larger movement among Protestants who attempted to meet the challenges of urbanization and industrialization in the late nineteenth and early twentieth century. While the historian Paul Boyer in his *Urban Masses and Moral Order in America* has shown that church leaders expressed concern about urban problems from the early part of the nineteenth century, nevertheless, momentum increased in the 1880s and 1890s when clergy began to articulate more forcefully the need to apply Christian principles to the problems of the worker and the city.[4] One of the most famous in this Social Gospel movement was a Congregationalist minister from Columbus, Ohio, Washington Gladden, who began to call for his church to stand with striking railroad workers on behalf of social justice. In 1886, he wrote *Applied Christianity* in an attempt to appeal to the consciences of the nation's business leaders. The depression of the 1890s stimulated other efforts to bring Christian principles to bear on the industrial revolution and rapid urbanization. The British journalist W. T. Stead wrote the very popular *If Christ Came to Chicago* in 1894, urging readers to contemplate the "ugly sight" of a city with 200 millionaires and 200,000 unemployed workers. In the same year, Edward Everett Hale wrote a similar tract entitled *If Jesus Came to Boston,* and in 1897, Charles Sheldon defined the genre with a work, *In His Steps,* that sold 23 million copies by 1933. Matthews read Sheldon's book, which asked the simple question, What would Jesus do if he were faced with the conditions of the day?[5]

Protestant ministers, particularly in the North and Midwest, but also in the Pacific Northwest, hoped to redefine the ways in which Christianity attempted to address the major social problems of the era. Dissatisfied with the emphasis that the previous generation of Protestants had placed on changing individuals' hearts in order to improve social behavior, this newer generation focused on structural and environmental change as well. Ministers throughout North America as well as in England were concerned that the working class would abandon Christianity if the church were not seen to be interested in the tremendous social problems of the poor. The historian Paul Phillips wrote, "Americans were not slow to realize that the adverse social environment could work against the rehabilitation of the masses no matter what their individual attitudes were."[6]

In many cities across the country, women's groups, men's organizations, and church leaders in general devoted themselves increasingly to the needs of working men and women. Fundamental to the vision of most of these Protestants was the belief that their efforts were part of a larger process of bringing God's kingdom into being on earth. Mark Matthews nurtured this idea within his congregation at First Presbyterian; he proclaimed in sermon after sermon the obligation of his flock to work on behalf of God's kingdom. Matthews worked tirelessly on issues associated with the working class and frequently preached about the evils of unrestricted capitalism. His efforts on behalf of the poor, the sick, and the jobless became known throughout the community. Soup kitchens, unemployment bureaus, night schools, day care, and other services became part of the mission of First Presbyterian and many other churches during the first decade of the twentieth century.

Determining the degree to which Matthews accepted and was influenced by the Social Gospel movement during his Seattle years is somewhat challenging. He never identified himself as a pure advocate of the Social Gospel, because he believed that his emphasis on regeneration of the soul and the importance of sinfulness separated him from some of the more liberal religious spokesmen, such as Walter Rauschenbusch and Washington Gladden. Matthews often expressed concern that too many ministers were neglecting the issue of salvation.

The Church Is My Force, the City My Field

There was a time when the first and only thought of the individual Christian, and of the church, was the salvation of the soul. That time has passed. The salvation of the soul is secondary. In fact it is the last thing accomplished by the church. . . . The sole business of the individual Christian, and of the church, is to live and teach Christ, to thereby bring sinners to him, that he may save them with everlasting salvation.[7]

But as his efforts in Georgia and Tennessee indicate, Matthews was clearly influenced by the desire to make Christianity socially relevant.

In Seattle, Matthews seemed even more energized by the prospect of bringing God's kingdom to the Pacific Northwest. He was obsessed with the idea that he could redeem Seattle and make it a righteous community. The Seattle pastor envisioned the possibility of God's kingdom being virtually centered in the city. "The kingdom of God in men is daily developing them into perfection," he preached in 1906. "The leaven is leavening the whole man. The separation between righteousness and unrighteousness is more distinct today than ever before."[8]

The notion that the world was improving and that the righteous would ultimately triumph over the unrighteous reflected Matthews's general acceptance of a postmillennial view of Christ's second coming. Widely held by advocates of the Social Gospel, the postmillennial view, in its purest form, held that Christ would come after 1,000 years of peace and harmony on earth. Theologians such as Charles Finney, early in the nineteenth century, and Jonathan Edwards, in the eighteenth, had articulated the idea that the universe operated under the moral government of the Creator. Ultimately, the righteous would prevail over the unrighteous. But every Christian still needed to find his or her individual role in bringing about this victory. And more specifically, Finney and others believed, America would be the place in which this triumph would occur.[9]

Although Matthews's papers do not reveal any direct influence by Finney, Finney's optimism is clearly evident in many of the Seattle pastor's sermons. "The next false statement, namely, 'the world is growing worse,' is easily answered. The righteous are growing better every day, and in so far as their power and influence over the general affairs of mankind can be exerted, the world, in its entirety, is growing better."[10] There is some evidence that Matthews adopted a postmillennial outlook during his very early days within the Cumberland Presbyterian Church in Georgia. Postmillennialism was very popular among the Cumberland preachers of that period and was clearly evident in the teaching of Reverend Z. M. McGhee and others that Matthews surely heard as a boy.[11] But it was far from peculiar to Cumberland ministers; postmillennialism was widely held in nineteenth-century America and provided an important intellectual foundation for many within the Social Gospel movement.[12]

If Matthews expressed optimism regarding the ultimate triumph of righteousness, he always put it in the context of a great struggle. He believed that Christianity was locked in a battle with the forces of evil. His parishioners repeatedly heard from their preacher how important it was for them to take up the fight and press on to victory. For Matthews, this victory would mean civic righteousness and Christ's triumphant return.

> Soldiers are needed. The battle is on; the conflict is fierce; the victory is sure to come to [the] forces of Christ and to the Kingdom of God. The fact we are engaged in a successful warfare ought to induce men to enlist and make courageous and determined those who are already in the thick of the fight. We are fighting at the present time the fight of fights; we are engaged in the battle of battles. When we press through this period now upon the church, the world will have peace and the millennium will dawn. Following this conflict in which we are now engaged, Christ will make his second advent into the world.[13]

Although Matthews, in this period, never expressed much precision about when Christ would return or when the kingdom would be instituted, he did frequently preach that Seattle would play an extremely important role in the destiny of the American experiment and in the ultimate triumph of Christendom throughout the world. "Our republic was predestined," stated Matthews. "It is the natural evolution of forces that have been working for 6,000 years."[14] Suggesting that America's mission was one of political altruism and the "civilizing" of Asia, Matthews believed that the key geographic region was the Pacific Northwest.

> We are the descendants of Japheth who moved northward and westward from Babylon through Asia, Europe and America and on westward until we have arrived at Seattle, and our feet have touched the shores of the Pacific in our tramp of the ages back to Asia from Babylon

The Church Is My Force, the City My Field

to Seattle. . . . We, his descendants, . . . have arrived at the Pacific Coast in our last march back to Asia in the work of saving the world. During the last 100 years the progress of the world has surpassed all other ages because of the power of Christianity.[15]

Matthews's belief that Seattle would play an important role in the larger history of the world encouraged his tendency to combine civic boosterism with his interpretation of God's grand design. He hoped to motivate his audience to work for civic righteousness, and he seems sincerely to have believed that the march of history had come to the West Coast, where he might serve as a commanding general. "The Pacific slope must necessarily take a prominent part in this great work— in fact, it will eventually become the controlling factor," argued the native Georgian. "Seattle will be the dominant city of the Pacific. . . . Seattle will be known as the queen city, and will be known and referred to throughout the world as the Imperial Gate."[16] However, economic and political possibilities could only be realized, according to Matthews, if the region dedicated itself to God's will. "If Christianity continues to dominate, grow and prosper," he preached, "this city will, when it reaches a population of two or three millions, be, from a religious standpoint, the greatest city in the world."[17] He repeatedly told his congregation that the world would come to see Seattle in the most idealized terms.

This town is destined by Almighty God to be the center of world events. It will be the ground of arbitration between great nations. It will be the gate for the golden commerce of the world. It will be the hospital for the world's discouraged and sick. It will be the world's school and college for the ignorant and uninstructed. . . . From this church's pulpit the gospel will be preached to Asia, and Asia will come to Christ and be saved.[18]

Ultimately, Matthews perceived Seattle as being connected to the great Calvinist experiments of the past. He revived Biblical imagery that was used by his seventeenth-century Puritan forefather from Boston, John Winthrop. "We are truly a city set upon a hill; we cannot be hid," Matthews claimed. "We should not try to hide nor should we conceal our resources nor withhold the fact of our future glory from others."[19] It would be a mistake, however, to assume that Matthews was voicing some romantic notion about the past. Matthews clearly belongs in a generation of Social Gospel ministers who believed fully that their efforts would result in God's kingdom being manifested on earth. On one occasion, he preached that "the Christian ought to be in the world, because it is through the Christian in the world that the Kingdom of God will dominate the world. . . . The Kingdom of God is practical [and] its methods are practical. Therefore, when we pray for the coming of the Kingdom of God, we are not praying for some ideal conception of government, but we are praying for the most practical and most successful government that could possibly be established in the world."[20] At times, Matthews could be extraordinarily concrete with his vision of what Christians and Christianity should be doing in the world. He once preached that Christianity would "end child labor" and "change the whole economic system of this country." He boldly asserted that Christianity would make prisons more humane and that it would establish a compulsory court of arbitration that would settle the disputes between the oppressors and oppressed. In simple, powerful terms he stated to his congregation that "the life of service is the life of Christianity, and, all suffering humanity are subjects of Christ's love. Therefore, if we would serve Him we must administer to them. . . . Practical Christianity administers to those in need. Are you a Christian?" Matthews asked his parishioners.[21]

Matthews's commitment to God's kingdom led him and others to one of the most critical issues of his day—the problem of the maldistribution of wealth in American society. As he did in Georgia and Tennessee, Matthews challenged the members of his congregation to raise their level of consciousness about the social needs of the working class. He, like most proponents of the Social Gospel, questioned the pervasive acceptance of classical economics and specifically the dogma of unrestricted competition. Though many clergy found pure socialism unacceptable, significant numbers agreed with some of its criticisms of capitalism. During his first decade in Seattle, Matthews frequently preached on the evils of unrestricted capitalism. In at least one sermon, he talked about the merits of Christian socialism as a solution to the exploitation that he witnessed among certain industrialists. He clearly stated, "The Socialist Party will never be able to answer the question, because it rejects Divine authority, severs its connection with the church and denounces all who do not think as it thinks."[22] According to him, "The correct solution of the political, economic, and social evils of this country is to be found in Christian Socialism, as taught by Jesus Christ."[23] Matthews believed that through Christian socialism the problems inherent in a system devoted exclusively to the satisfaction of the individual could be resolved. "Christian Socialism hates the doctrine expressed by selfishness," he argued. "The man who lives to himself, or for himself, is an enemy to society; . . . Christian Socialism believes in consecrated individualism, devoted to the highest interest and to the greatest good of the community, and as a means to a wholesome collectivism."[24]

Matthews often preached on the tension between labor and capital, a topic that historians have found to be prevalent among Social Gospel clergy.[25] And he certainly expressed progressive or liberal views on the subject during the first decade of the twentieth century. "Capital," he argued, "has no right to accumulate wealth until it crushes to death those who seek the right to live and the right to toil."[26] In another sermon he stated, "I do not know that there is anywhere promised a reward for the man who sits down and takes advantage of the labor of others to fill his coffers. The man who has grown wealthy by the unearned increments is nothing more or less than a parasite."[27]

Matthews believed that laborers needed protection from the acquisitive ethic that seemed to pervade the capitalistic system. Although he did not favor strikes as the best means of securing these safeguards, he acknowledged their necessity as the only recourse available to workers. "We deplore the existence of strikes. They injure everybody concerned," he preached. "Capital is injured, labor is hurt and the general public suffers, but, the strike is the only weapon in the hands of defenseless labor."[28] Matthews, from a very early point, hoped that the church could offer help and protection for an unprotected laboring class. "Everyone knows that the laborer is being forced to the wall. Show me the church that is demanding an increase in wages for the poor. Show me the church that is trying before its courts those infamous kings thus grinding to powder our poor."[29] He fully believed that Christians should assume moral and political leadership in this area of public policy. Fully confident that applied Christianity could solve any social problem, he frequently exhorted the larger church to become proactive in societal matters. "The great sociological problems properly belong to the church. The differences between capital and labor will never be removed without the church's influence," wrote Matthews. "The next step is for the church . . . to go forth with a determination to destroy the agencies of evil."[30]

The Church Is My Force, the City My Field

The Social Gospel critique of prevailing ethical standards in the American business community also influenced Matthews's thinking. "The money-getting spirit dominates the life of nearly every man," lamented the Seattle pastor. "Men are measured by the dollar standard, and society is largely controlled by financial interests."[31] Following the open attack of the Social Gospel proponent Washington Gladden on John D. Rockefeller, Matthews called Rockefeller "the greatest sinner on the American continent."[32] Matthews never seemed fearful of alienating the more wealthy members of his congregation. In one sermon entitled "The Inconsistencies of Capital in the Light of the Golden Rule," he condemned the capitalistic ethos. "Capital is governed exclusively by the right of conquest. It rules with an iron hand. Everything must yield to its power or be crushed by it. Capital will never be met by kindness and goodwill until it learns the lessons of the golden rule."[33]

Matthews frequently urged his First Presbyterian congregation to address the needs of the poor. In a sermon called "The Practical Church," Matthews expressed his vision for the role the church should play in being an effective force for social and spiritual improvement. "The rich and poor we have with us always. . . . The interests are common, and the bond of union between them should be perfect. The rich should assist and make comfortable the poor." He further suggested:

> The Protestant church is the friend and sympathizer of the oppressed, the needy and the friendless. The trouble is, men do not appeal to the church, use the church, and appreciate the church as they should. However, they are rapidly learning that the church has a remedy for their every condition. . . . The church is preaching a practical gospel, a gospel that meets the everyday condition of men. The church is using its influence for the enforcement of law, the betterment of society and the elevation of the submerged class.[34]

Matthews often spoke about the need for the church to provide basic social services to the less fortunate. For example, he preached, "Employment must be provided for the unemployed; church farms opened, soup houses and cheap lodgings erected, in order that the tramp and homeless may be provided with physical comforts and Christianity at the same time."[35] In another sermon he urged construction of asylums for the blind and "workshops for the deaf, dumb and blind. In such shops they could be taught useful occupations by which

The Church Is My Force, the City My Field

they could be self supporting. . . . We should have a circulating library for the deaf, dumb and blind. We should also build homes for the aged and infirm."[36]

Matthews seemed ahead of his time regarding several issues concerning the aged. He objected to the common practice of firing older employees in favor of younger ones. He argued that a system of pensions should be paid out of the common treasury of the state and that the general public should support the pensions through taxation, and he even suggested that employers be required to reserve some positions in their companies for older men.[37]

The Seattle cleric emphasized health care and recreational needs out of a belief that this was part of God's grand design. Before the end of his first year in Seattle, Matthews suggested that the city needed an emergency hospital that could serve the poor. From the beginning, he advocated free care for those unable to pay. Even more remarkably, he suggested that the hospital be built in conjunction with the University of Washington in order to provide the university with a great medical school. This idea required considerable imagination in 1902, but Matthews remained undaunted. "It would, in a short time, cause to be added to the University, a medical school," the preacher offered. "Said medical school would bring to the city scores of students[;] . . . it would occupy, without rival, the broad field of the Puget Sound coast and Alaska. Its equipment should be so scientifically attractive and advantageous that the entire field would knock at its door for admission."[38] Matthews's dream of an outstanding medical school did take shape, but not until after his death and the end of World War II.

Throughout Matthews's ministry, he pushed his church and the city to improve health care at all levels. In addition to calling for an emergency hospital and free health care for the poor, he organized members of First Presbyterian into one of the first groups to address effectively the problem of tuberculosis in Seattle. The church established the city's first antituberculosis tents, which were the genesis for the Firland Sanitarium. "Rev. M. A. Matthews is entitled to much credit," stated the secretary of the King County Anti-Tuberculosis League, "for the position he took a year ago in the movement to combat the disease."[39] Matthews also served on the board of directors for the Society for the Prevention and Relief of Tuberculosis.[40]

The commitment of Matthews and his church members to health care and the relief of suffering was exemplified by their involvement with the King County Red Cross and the local humane society. From

1906 to 1914 and later, from 1926 until his death in 1940, Matthews served as president of the King County Red Cross.[41] He received citywide recognition in 1908 for directing the relief drive following an Italian earthquake. Using the power of his pulpit along with the local press and workers from his church, Matthews organized an appeal that sent $13,000 to Italy in January 1909.[42] As president of the local humane society, he actively promoted efforts to protect animals. "The man who does not love a horse is fatally diseased," he preached. "His heart is not in the right place. . . . Therefore, I appeal to all who own horses, mules, dogs, cows and other animals, to give their assistance in purchasing an ambulance to be used by the King County Humane Society."[43]

In September 1902, Matthews drew additional attention by proposing construction of a huge civic auditorium. Arguing that Seattle lacked the proper convention facilities to host great national events, he suggested a brick hall that would seat 4,000 and cost approximately $25,000. He further suggested specific individuals from the business community who ought to serve as the board of directors, as well as a possible time and place for the first meeting. Though his idea was never realized, it was indicative of the organizational tendencies in his thinking as well as the scope of his vision.[44] On other occasions he suggested that city engineers build a great sea wall in order to facilitate commerce in Seattle's harbor; thoroughfares should be constructed throughout the city; streetcar lines rapidly expanded. Matthews loved to dream and plan for the future of the city.[45]

Matthews did more than simply propose new facilities for the city. For example, he believed that the church should be responsive to the needs of Asian immigrants. Seattle and Tacoma had manifested extreme anti-Asian prejudice; in the 1880s, Tacoma experienced a series of anti-Chinese riots, and Seattle had deported Chinese in the same decade. Matthews's church became very active in the Seattle Asian community. The first baptism of a Chinese baby in Seattle was performed at First Presbyterian.[46] Beginning in 1903, Matthews's congregation sponsored a night school for Chinese immigrants. Run mostly by the women of the church, the school had the dual purposes of assisting recent arrivals in finding jobs and converting them to Christianity. During the first year, approximately thirty Chinese attended the school. By the second year, a conversation class was organized in which all speaking was done in English, with violators being fined a penny. On average, there appeared to be approximately sixty to sixty-

The Church Is My Force, the City My Field

five people in attendance during the winter. The school ran six nights a week, ten months a year. English language was taught four nights, the Bible the other two. Beginning in 1915, girls were allowed to attend. By the end of the decade, "graduates" from the school could be found as far afield as railroad camps in Montana.[47]

First Presbyterian also developed an extensive ministry in Seattle's Japanese community. Matthews secured the services of the Reverend Orio Inouye, who worked tirelessly at a Japanese mission built in 1906 at the corner of Seventh Avenue and Jackson Street, in the heart of Seattle's International District. Dormitory space, eating facilities, and reading rooms were provided in the mission, which held religious services every morning and evening. By April 1907, First Presbyterian's activities included publishing *The Mikado*, an English paper for the Japanese community, to which Inouye and Matthews contributed sermons and articles. By 1923, Inouye was succeeded by the Reverend K. Emura, and the Revered Soo Pui Kow served as pastor of the Chinese Presbyterian church that also was sponsored by the First Presbyterian congregation.[48]

The church supported several missionaries for many years in Sitka, Alaska, as well as a missionary at the Chinese mission home in San Francisco. First Presbyterian equipped and staffed a hospital in Fatehgarh, India, and several members of the church served in overseas missions in Africa, Siam, Korea, West Africa, West India, and China.[49]

Matthews, to be sure, considered evangelizing to be his most important work in the Asian community both at home and abroad.[50] Yet he also became very outspoken against West Coast racism and anti-Asian prejudice. He openly attacked the advocates of legislation that would restrict immigration in 1906 as "narrow, bigoted, full of race hatred and . . . asinine in spirit."[51] His views were so well known that he later was asked to contribute an article to *The Annals of the American Academy of Political and Social Science* on the issue of discrimination against the Japanese. Entitled "Racial Prejudice Un-American," the essay called for the United States to honor its treaty commitments to the Japanese people. Matthews argued that the percentage of Japanese on the West Coast, let alone in the country, was not sufficient to warrant concern. "Racial and national prejudice and suspicion are un-American," he wrote. "Why let un-American prejudice cause you to deny fundamental facts and laws? America must be impartial if she is to be truly American."[52]

In 1913 Matthews appealed for more support for the Japanese Presbyterian Mission and specifically for Inouye's ministry. He also hoped to construct a better building. In 1914, he sent letters to groups and individuals throughout the country soliciting money to erect a building that would include a dormitory, classroom, gymnasium, auditorium, and church facilities for the Chinese and Japanese. But Matthews was repeatedly turned down because, according to one possible donor, "the anti-alien sentiment created through un-American sources on the Pacific Coast [was] too great to make it possible to successfully launch and carry forward a campaign for the raising of such an amount of money."[53]

If Matthews expressed comparatively liberal attitudes toward Asian Americans, he found it more difficult to openly defend African Americans. Undoubtedly reflecting not only his Southern upbringing but also society's prevailing racist attitudes toward African Americans, he manifested a consistent paternalism.[54]

In the case of working women, Matthews and his church took a proactive role in trying to meet a number of critical needs. Though he preferred that women not work, his church organized child care. First Presbyterian received acclaim from all quarters for its day nursery and kindergarten.[55] Organized shortly after Matthews arrived, the day nursery, open from 7:00 A.M. to 6:00 P.M., was one of the first of its kind in the city. Children were fed a noon meal at a cost of 10 cents per day. "There are hundreds of parents, especially mothers with heavy burdens, who are compelled to have someone to care for their children while they go out and make an honest living," wrote Matthews. "The church maintains this Kindergarten and Nursery for the benefit of such mothers."[56] By 1911, Matthews was on the Seattle Day Nursery Board, as several churches attempted to band together and find day care for working mothers.[57]

First Presbyterian and its pastor also played an important role in the establishment of a juvenile court system. Matthews advocated this innovation largely because he was familiar with the work of the Denver reform judge Ben Lindsey, who had been born in Jackson, Tennessee. Matthews's congregation, led by the politically active Austin Griffiths, pushed for state legislation leading to the creation of the juvenile court in 1905.[58]

Matthews had always taken an interest in prison ministry; in Seattle he continued this effort and frequently made his way to city and

The Church Is My Force, the City My Field

Matthews cut a dashing figure during his early days in Seattle.
(Photography Collection, University of Washington Libraries;
Seattle Times photograph)

Under Matthews's direction, First Presbyterian became the largest church in the denomination. (Photography Collection, University of Washington Libraries)

(Above) Matthews believed that he could create
a righteous community in Seattle. (From *Men
Behind the Seattle Spirit,* ed. H. A. Chadwick, 1906.)

(Right) His outspoken views made Matthews news-
worthy; his stature made him a cartoonist's delight.
(Mark Matthews Papers, University
of Washington Libraries)

Matthews's battles and occasional truces with Hiram Gill
made good newspaper copy. (University of Washington Libraries)

FROM THEIR STANDPOINT

THAT TERRIBLE BOMB!

Matthews was often criticized for his views on woman's suffrage.
(University of Washington Libraries)

At times, Matthews appeared anything but progressive.
(Courtesy Ross K. Rieder)

UP TO HIM TO DO OR DIE!

THAT ATTACK ON THE MEADOWS

Matthews attacked numerous forms of vice.
(Mark Matthews Papers, University of Washington Libraries)

Matthews's heavy workload did not keep him
from taking an interest in a wide range of activities.
(Photography Collection, University of Washington Libraries)

county jails. He appointed John Cubbage to conduct regular jail services for inmates, and often Matthews was given parole supervision over first-time offenders.[59]

Matthews's view of social Christianity in his early years in Seattle also included a vision of ecumenical cooperation. He clearly believed that urban righteousness depended on achieving harmony, at least on key issues, among the major religious organizations. He often spoke of the inefficiencies of denominational competition and frequently argued that, if Christianity was to succeed in transforming the urban environment, it must abandon its doctrinal squabbling.

> It is folly for Protestants to try to maintain several divisions of the same denomination. All divisions of the Presbyterian household should be united into one great American Presbyterian Church. The Congregationalists and Presbyterians might, with great profit to both, and our common cause, unite. You could see what the two denominations might accomplish united, by imagining the union of the First Presbyterian Church and the Plymouth Congregational Church. Look at the decrease of expense and the increase of efficiency. Glorious would be the results.[60]

In 1905, Matthews seized on the idea of an interdenominational urban revival that might galvanize the middle class and establish Seattle as a righteous city. To accomplish this, Matthews invited one of the premier Presbyterian evangelists, J. Wilbur Chapman, and his team of ministers to Seattle in the spring of 1905.

Historians of American religion traditionally have presented urban revivalists, from Dwight Moody and Billy Sunday to Billy Graham, as being concerned not so much with social concerns as with the issue of salvation. One historian of urban revival in the early twentieth century found a clear division between those who directed their attention to the problems of poverty, unemployment, and poor health and those who focused on salvation. "Revivalistic pastors could not see that such activities had much to do with the real business of Christianity," one historian said, "which was, in their view, to lead sinners to find atonement in the blood of Jesus."[61]

Indeed, Matthews's bringing to Seattle revivalists who were concerned solely with salvation and not with a broader social message would have been contradictory to his basic vision. So he undoubtedly chose his revivalists quite carefully; he selected a team that preached the mix of spiritual regeneration and social commitment that was so important to him.

Chapman and his group hoped to create a religious experience that would stimulate all of Seattle, but especially the middle class. The visiting evangelist also hoped to encourage middle-class commitment to social reform and to foster cooperation between management and the working class. He attempted to do this by appealing to a key value of the middle class—specialization. Chapman brought with him a converted gambler, a children's evangelist, a Methodist preacher, and, most interesting, the foremost spokesman of the Social Gospel in the Presbyterian church, Charles Stelzle. In general, historians of late-nineteenth- and early-twentieth-century urban revivals have not seen a connection to the Social Gospel. But Stelzle's relationship with Chapman suggests again the complex way that evangelical Christianity addressed social concerns.[62] "Our party is so made up that we can assign one man to every department of work," Chapman told the Seattle press. "One has to approach different characters of men and women in a way that meets their condition."[63]

The revival began on April 11 and extended through Easter Sunday, April 23. Over the week and a half, Seattle hosted downtown tent revivals, marches through the red-light district, numerous services in the downtown and suburban churches, and countless meetings led by the team of revivalists. While the tent revivals led by the reformed gambler Daniel Toy received a good deal of attention, the revival was aimed primarily at the middle class. There was a distinctly nondenominational tone. "There are two things I will not do," said Chapman, "and that is I won't allow anyone to tell me the days of revival are over, for they have just begun, and I will not preach a denominational sermon. I am first, last, and all the time a Christian."[64]

Organizers believed that, if members of the middle class were to support the revival, a large congregational experience must be carefully orchestrated. Chapman made sure that Seattleites did not see his team of revivalists as a wild-eyed group of frontier itinerant preachers but as respectable ministers infused with the power of the Holy Spirit. "We are not a sensational party of preachers as some people insist on calling us," Chapman told Seattle reporters upon his arrival. "At least we are not sensational in a ridiculous and outrageous way, although there are many that consider our way of telling the truth sensational."[65] In order to legitimize revival within the middle class, Chapman used

The Church Is My Force, the City My Field

the major downtown churches, selecting First Presbyterian as his central base of operation. Always well organized, the services in these sanctuaries included excellent musical performances and sermons by Chapman.

A facet of the revival in which Matthews directly participated was the downtown march through the red-light district. On the night of April 17, a crowd estimated at more than 15,000 took to the streets, hoping to gain converts. The Salvation Army furnished a marching band, and each of the nine districts into which Chapman had divided the city provided a contingent of marchers. Newspapers reported that the event was the most remarkable evangelistic demonstration in Seattle's history. As the evangelists marched up and down the streets of the district, ladies of the night and saloon patrons came out on the streets and gawked. "The procession was headed by the First Presbyterian contingent," said one reporter. "This part of the line was headed by Wagner's band and was led by Dr. Chapman, Dr. Matthews, Dr. Wharton and a number of other ministers."[66]

On the afternoon of the following day, the children's evangelist C. T. Schaeffer led a parade of young people. A hundred boys and girls marched in the formation of a cross; another 1,000 followed them through the business district. Periodically, Schaeffer yelled to the marchers, "How many of you can honestly say, 'I love Jesus,' put up your hands," to which all of the children responded enthusiastically. At the end of the march, Reverend H. W. Stough, one of Chapman's associates, told the children that God had "more interest in the boys and girls of Seattle than in any others,"[67] because they would be the future leaders of the church. Subsequently, he proceeded to tell them the story of the Crusades in the Middle Ages, when Christians marched off to recover the tomb of Christ from the Moslems.

Perhaps the most interesting phase of the revival, and one in which Matthews would have been keenly interested, was the work of Charles Stelzle. Stelzle had a national reputation for supporting unions and the laboring class. He preached a message of reconciliation between labor and management. He pushed the Presbyterian church as well as other denominations to support labor unions. Stelzle expressed great concern that blue-collar workers were turning away from Christianity and toward socialism because the church was not responding to their needs. Stelzle attacked socialism for being non-Christian, but he also attacked the clergy for being insensitive to the problems of the poor.

Personally, I will acknowledge that the average minister would be hopelessly lost if he were suddenly confronted with the problem of taking care of a convert of the slums. He doesn't know what goes on down there. He doesn't know the terrible life those people live. He doesn't understand their temptations and how they must be led carefully back into the right path.[68]

Stelzle believed that evangelism and social reform, if done in the right spirit, could be a powerful combination. "I have a conviction that the right kind of an evangelist," he wrote, "who has a message which is broad and deep and thoroughly evangelistic, but with a social spirit backed by knowledge of social conditions and principles, could win his way in every community in this country."[69]

On a number of occasions, Stelzle exhorted his middle-class listeners to apply a Christian ethic to the system of capitalism. "We should make the working man understand that the church does not uphold the present social system if it is wrong," he argued. "That we stand simply for the principles of Jesus Christ applied to society in all its ramifications. That we favor only so much of the present system as will stand the test of these principles."[70]

Stelzle was generally well received in Seattle, and he organized meetings between delegates from labor organizations and from the city's ministerial alliance. On only one occasion did he meet significant opposition, and that occurred when one business banned him from speaking after the owners heard that he was a member of the International Association of Machinists.[71] Stelzle met almost daily with labor unions and held several large rallies that stressed the responsibility of the church to the working man.[72] This issue was of great concern to Matthews too; three weeks before Stelzle arrived in the city, Matthews had preached a sermon entitled "The Church's Delegate to Labor Organizations." "The church is the only power, force, or organization able to solve all the problems of the different divisions of society," he argued. "The church should be officially represented, by an accredited commissioner, in ever[y] labor organization. . . . Capital and labor will never be united, except by the Grace of God regenerating the men composing the two factions."[73]

The revival was considered a moderate success, although the denominational divisions were not healed and the middle class was not set on evangelistic fire. What the incident does suggest, however, is the variety of methods that Matthews employed to bring social Christianity to Seattle. More specifically, his involvement with the revival reflected his commitment to the church as the institution through which social change could take place.

Clearly, Matthews saw the church functioning on a variety of levels; he attempted to make the institution attractive to the middle and upper-middle classes by appealing to the heart of middle-class ideology. But he saw the institution as a force that could help create the healthy environment needed for Seattle to become a righteous city. He continued to hope that the church would be the means by which social divisions were healed. A righteous city must be united in purpose and values. Whether the divisions existed between Protestant sects, rich and poor, or capital and labor, he saw the church functioning in a way that would heal these divisions.

By the time Matthews had finished his first decade of work in Seattle, he had established himself as a leader in the field of social Christianity. His experience with farmers' movements in the South, as well as his belief that Christianity was engaged in a battle against the forces of evil, helped provide him with both a political and theological worldview that justified social commitment. He harangued his congregation to become more involved with the social issues of the day. He argued that First Presbyterian should be a major influence in the public policy of Seattle, and this position led him to embrace the major tenets of the Progressive movement. Matthews never hesitated to engage in local, regional, and national politics in pursuit of his aims. His efforts to redeem Seattle drew him directly into these realms and in doing so presented him with some of his most serious challenges.

≈ CHAPTER 5 ≈

Progressive Impulses

The man who refuses to cast his ballot for good govern-
ment, clean men and a righteous administration every time
the opportunity is given, is an infamous traitor and de-
serves financial and political death at the hands of the citi-
zens of this city.

—Mark Matthews (1908)

From his first day in the pulpit, Mark Matthews never questioned his conviction that a minister should be involved in politics. The combination of his Cumberland Presbyterian background and his exposure to the Farmers' Alliance had made it relatively easy for him to feel justified in his attacks on everyone from William McKinley to local county officials. After his arrival in Seattle, Matthews, more often than ever, voiced his opinion that a preacher had every right to comment on public policy. "The clergyman is the expounder of the *truth* and the preacher of righteousness," he said. "Therefore, his voice should be heard on all questions involving the existence and perpetuity of the government."[1] In another sermon, he argued, "If the church is entrusted with the duty of giving to the world pure citizens and a perfect citizenship, then the church should turn its attention to the work of purifying cities and inducting into the offices of the city governments of this nation God-fearing, personally righteous, Christian men."[2]

As Matthews fashioned First Presbyterian into one of the leading Social Gospel churches in the country, he was not content to leave Seattle politics to someone else. He believed from the outset that Christian participation in the political process was vital to reforming the city. Simply to preach the gospel week after week did not occur to him. He loved to meet Seattle's leaders and talk politics in their offices or at the prestigious Rainier Club. He constantly sought political involvement in virtually every issue of his day. He believed that he deserved to be considered among the most influential of Seattle's political leaders.

> The building of a city cannot be left to men of mediocre brains or determination. In other words, a city cannot be built by parasites who simply live because they have commercial or clerical positions. It must be built by men who have broad views, whose perspectives are those of giants. Cities are built by dreamers, plus those who execute the dreams. . . . We are truly a city set upon a hill; we cannot be hid.[3]

By the beginning of the twentieth century, Matthews's interest in specific issues and strategies was influenced by the movement that historians identify as Progressivism. His vision of a righteous community drew much from the political rhetoric and ideology of the period. He provides an excellent example of the way in which Progressivism appealed to elements of the religious community and helped shape the interaction between the church and the political sphere.

Historians describe Progressivism as a series of political and economic reforms at the local, state, and national levels during the first two decades of the twentieth century. Consisting of various coalitions of reformers and organizations, Progressivism at the local and state levels often sought political reforms such as the initiative, referendum, recall, and direct primary. Governmental reforms such as the commission form of government, municipal ownership, and city-manager systems were popular in many cities as ways of ending perceived corruption and, according to some historians, restoring the middle class to political power. Progressive platforms at all levels of government included economic reforms such as the regulation of public utilities, consumer protection, and the control of corporate power through anti-trust legislation. Many Progressives also favored the prohibition of alcohol as well and argued for woman suffrage.

Historians are less united regarding the motivation and objectives for these reforms. Until the mid-twentieth century, most historians understood Progressivism to be part of a liberal framework in which the reforms were clear attempts to restore the democratic process, abolish special privilege, and enact a series of laws ensuring social justice. Scholars saw a direct connection between the spirit of Populism and the spirit of Progressivism.[4]

However, by the 1950s, Richard Hofstadter and other historians had begun to argue that democracy had little to do with Progressive reforms. Hofstadter argued that by the late nineteenth century clergymen, lawyers, professors, and members of the older Anglo-Saxon Protestant families found themselves increasingly outside positions of power, replaced by a plutocracy of businessmen and urban political machines controlled by ethnic Europeans. Hofstadter and others concluded that the middle class sought political reform as a way of eliminating the old ward system of politics. The middle class favored the new city council, commission, or city-manager forms of government because they could be manipulated to allow the "right sort" of people to regain power and recover lost status.[5]

Other historians have argued that Progressivism is best understood as the attempt by corporate America to control competition, establish consumer confidence, and dictate how businesses would be regulated. Still other scholars have focused on the importance of scientific management and the value of efficiency.[6] Political reforms have been interpreted as attempts to make the "expert" more powerful. The city-manager and commission forms of government have been seen by some historians as efforts to make city government conform to ideals of efficiency and rational planning. Another group of historians has focused on many of the Progressive reformers who attempted to pass legislation that would exercise a measure of social control over working-class and immigrant behaviors. Efforts to prohibit alcohol consumption, outlaw gambling, control prostitution, and regulate public amusements have all been identified with the Progressive movement.[7]

It is within this context that Matthews participated in the politics of his day in order to develop a set of strategies for redeeming Seattle's social environment. He embraced many of the initiatives of the Progressive period in a way that helps reveal the paradoxes and complexities of the movement. He spoke passionately about democratic ideals and yet at the same time vigorously fought for laws that regulated social behavior. He preached often about capitalist exploitation of the working class and yet clearly argued for business efficiency and organization. In the end, Matthews reflected the complicated relationship among religious, economic, and class motives for political reform.

Progressive Impulses

Examples of Matthews's Progressive embrace of scientific management and efficiency can be seen in many of his sermons and activities. He embodied a spirit of organization as he developed First Presbyterian into the largest congregation in the denomination. But he also accepted the Progressive belief that this spirit of organization and management should be extended to the Seattle political infrastructure. He believed that "economy, efficiency, system, and saving" would result from changing to a commission form of city government, such as those operating in Galveston, Texas, and Des Moines, Iowa.[8] According to him, the judicial system needed to be reformed in order to allow for more institutionalized expertise. He argued that the practice of electing judges seemed to lead to nothing but incompetence and graft. "Divorce the bench from politics. It is not a position to be sought by candidates, but one to be filled by character and brains, regardless of partisan, party affiliations," he wrote. "Appoint the most learned and profound lawyers as judges for a term not exceeding twenty years."[9] In a 1907 sermon, he took the argument one step further and argued that judges should be allowed to serve on the bench for life.[10]

Matthews may also have seen Progressivism as a way of restoring lost status and power to white Anglo-Saxon Protestants. Even though he vigorously opposed immigration restrictions against the Japanese, he occasionally spoke of the need to lengthen the naturalization process. "As a nation we should raise the standard of citizenship and increase the requirements for naturalization," he urged. "To admit one . . . after only five years of residence in this country is preposterous and criminal."[11] Elsewhere, he stated that the qualification for naturalization should be increased to twenty-one years. "Even those of the better classes admitted to this country," said Matthews, "should not be permitted to become citizens until they have lived here twenty-one years."[12] At times he could sound extremely xenophobic. In 1913 he wrote,

> There is no reason why we should become an asylum, hospital or a land of refuge for undesireables. . . . Christianization and Americanization should precede naturalization. We have followed the dictates of the infamous parasitic politicians and have enacted laws whereby the illiterates of Europe may come to this country and be naturalized within five years. They have no right to the ballot until they have been in this country at least as long as our own American sons have

to live before they are entitled to vote. Fifty-five percent of our immigration comes from Southern Italy. You could not make American citizens of them in twenty-five years of incessant labor.[13]

While reforming the naturalization process frequently drew Matthews's attention, his real interest lay with legislating moral behavior and social control. He believed that Progressivism could help achieve a righteous society, and historians have generally agreed that Progressive reformers throughout the country shared a capacity for moral outrage and indignation. "For Progressives of all stripes . . . ," wrote the historian Paul Boyer, "questions of social injustice, corporate wrongdoing, governmental corruption, and personal morality were inextricably linked."[14] Many Progressives opposed child labor and the exploitation of women because these things undermined the moral and spiritual development of their victims, not because the work was physically harmful. Progressives condemned graft and misgovernment at the local level not only because it wasted taxpayers' money but also because it destroyed the moral climate of the city. To read the muckrakers—the investigative journalists of the late nineteenth and early twentieth century—is to read accounts by individuals who often saw themselves as moral crusaders.[15]

Frederic Howe, who wrote *The British City: The Beginnings of Democracy* in 1907, is often seen as the typical Progressive reformer. His autobiography attests to the moral fervor that influenced his work.

> Physical escape from the embraces of evangelical religion did not mean moral escape. From that religion my reason was never emancipated. By it I was conformed to my generation and made to share its moral standards and ideals. . . . Early assumptions as to virtue and vice, goodness and evil remained in my mind long after I had tried to discard them. This is, I think, the most characteristic influence of my generation.[16]

For Matthews, the moral context for politics encouraged him to rely on Old Testament imagery. It was common for Social Gospel ministers, such as Walter Rauschenbusch and Washington Gladden, to utilize Old Testament examples of the ways in which politics and religion mix. Matthews often justified his political involvement in the Progressive movement by referring to Old Testament prophets, in particular Isaiah, whom Matthews called "the greatest political reformer the world

Progressive Impulses

has ever had." Matthews wrote that the Biblical prophet "denounced political corruption and encouraged civic righteousness. . . . With all the power [Isaiah] possessed, he denounced corrupt political leaders, teaching in every sentence of his denunciation that the sins of political leaders were the greatest of political sins."[17]

On another occasion, Matthews called Moses the "Father of Constitutional Republican Government."[18] The Seattle preacher liked to cite 1 Kings 20:40, in which the king of Israel said, "So shall thy judgment be; thyself has decided it." Using that text, Matthews warned his parishioners of the "responsibility of present-day citizenship. . . . We are not only the custodians of prisoners taken in the battle of civic righteousness, but are keepers, defenders and protectors of the women and children for whom the battles of civic righteousness ought to be fought."[19] This particular emphasis on the protection of women and children may have reflected the preacher's Southern perspective. The Southern code of honor, under which Matthews was raised, required all gentlemen to serve as guardians for women and children.

Matthews's zeal for urban reform was born in that Southern climate. His religious background, his political experience in Georgia, and his general belief in a view of progress tied to the Christianization of the world contributed to his assertion that urban reform and civic righteousness were appropriate goals for his ministry. His experiences led him to see the general urban moral awakening of the 1890s and the first decade of the twentieth century as something in which he ought to participate. Progressives across the country believed that moral reform had to accompany structural reform in order to effect any meaningful change in the social and political ethos of America's burgeoning cities. The challenge to Matthews and other reformers was to organize and direct these moral energies against the evil forces that propagated vice in the form of corrupt government, gambling, prostitution, and alcohol.[20]

In sermon after sermon, Matthews attempted to rally support and infuse a moral energy into his congregation that would be translated into Progressive reforms at the ballot box. "The man who refuses to cast his ballot for good government, clean men and a righteous administration every time the opportunity is given, is an infamous traitor and deserves financial and political death at the hands of the citizens of this city," he said.[21] Matthews implored his congregation to understand their crucial role in bringing about a righteous society.

In fact it is the duty of Christian men who are citizens of God's Internal Kingdom to go out as citizens of this world and correct every evil, remove every curse, lift every burden and assuage every sorrow. You cannot correct the evils in society simply by saving individuals. Society must be corrected by the activity of the lives of those in whose hearts the kingdom of God has been established. It cannot be corrected otherwise. By the power of individual Christians the wicked are to be opposed and their wicked plans are to be defeated. One good man in society or politics who will act consistently with the laws of God's kingdom can change any condition.[22]

Matthews never ceased to see political action as part of a cosmic battle between the forces of good and evil. He understood his responsibility to be identifying evil and rallying his forces to combat it. "There [was] no time for whining, pining, complaining or shirking" when it came to one's political responsibility.[23] On one occasion, he urged his parishioners to believe that "it is the business of the Christian to be active in society, in business, in the domestic world and in the political sphere. . . . We are in no danger from bad citizens, but we are in serious danger from the bad citizenship of good citizens."[24]

Many Progressive reformers began with efforts to throw corrupt politicians out of office, as Matthews had advocated as early as his Georgia days. But even if they were successful, the problem remained of how to achieve moral righteousness once the middle class or "better" elements had regained power. Consequently, Progressives adopted two distinct but complementary strategies for moral control and civic uplift that appealed to Matthews. One strategy emphasized legislation against specific behavior such as gambling, prostitution, and alcoholic consumption. The second approach, though less direct, gained in popularity among Progressives and focused on transforming the city's physical environment in order to improve the moral disposition of its residents, particularly its children.[25]

The first strategy, the more coercive form of social control, focused on prohibition. There are some historians who argue that prohibition was the quintessential Progressive reform because of its moral emphasis. The historian James Timberlake concluded:

If the Progressive Movement was nourished in a belief in the moral law, so was prohibition, which sought to remove from commerce an article that was believed to despoil man's reason and undermine the foundation of religion and representative government. If progressive America's growing devotion to efficiency also reflected an optimistic belief in the desirability of material progress, the attack on alcoholic beverages as an enemy of efficiency mirrored the same faith. . . . If progressivism desired to curb the power of an industrial and financial plutocracy, prohibition aimed to remove the corrupting influence of one branch of that plutocracy—the liquor industry. . . . And, finally, if progressivism sought to improve the status of the lower classes by direct legislation, prohibition sought to uplift them by the same means.[26]

Progressives and other urban reformers attacked the saloon and brothel with the conviction that their elimination was necessary for the moral uplift of American society. According to one historian, as long as those two institutions stood, "the dream of an urban moral awakening would be no more than that; if they could be subdued, the purified, morally homogeneous city might at last become a reality."[27]

Matthews embraced this view of moral and urban reform. As previously discussed, his style and emphasis must certainly have been modeled in part on the work of T. DeWitt Talmage from Brooklyn. Matthews may also have been influenced by an even more militant reformer, the Reverend Charles Parkhurst. Parkhurst became pastor of New York's Madison Square Presbyterian Church in 1880 and soon began openly attacking brothels, gambling, and saloons.[28] His efforts helped elect the reform mayor William Strong in 1894, and, for the next three years, moral statutes were enforced with unprecedented vigor. Matthews's scrapbooks contain articles about Parkhurst's work. But there were many models and examples to choose from as Matthews attempted to find ways of bringing Progressive reform to the Pacific Northwest.

Seattle, however, proved to be a particularly challenging city for the implementation of the Progressive legislation against vice that was sweeping the nation. The Alaskan gold rush in 1897 helped create a fertile environment for gambling halls, saloons, and houses of prostitution. The Seattle historian Richard Berner has observed:

The spectacle of uprooted people with money to spend, idling away their time as they passed through the city, the dramatic growth of a permanent population, these things and the city's reputation for loose law enforcement, proved irresistible lures to gamblers, salooners, thugs, pickpockets, thieves, pimps, and prostitutes. . . . Gambling was rampant in the saloons, cigar stores, at the Meadows racetrack, at amusement parks and in the various incorporated clubs where laws against boxing were easily evaded by subterfuge.[29]

Seattle's law enforcement remained largely disorganized and vulnerable to significant political corruption during the early twentieth century, with no precinct stations in operation. Middle-class business owners and residents continually fought for more police protection in addition to improved streetcar, electric, sewage, and water service.[30]

Reformers, including Matthews, achieved some success during the first decade of the twentieth century by convincing officials of the need for ordinances to close saloons on Sunday. However, very few of these regulations were seriously enforced. Despite his relative ineffectiveness, Matthews relentlessly pursued coercive legislation. From his earliest days, he had participated in various crusades against social problems such as alcohol abuse, gambling, and prostitution. Whether they concerned ending gambling at the racetrack or prohibiting messenger boys from entering saloons, his sermons constantly attacked various vices. "We have no one to blame for the existence of the saloon, the liquor traffic, the gambling halls, and all other appurtenances to the saloon but society," he preached in "Society's Crimes Due to a Diseased Nervous System" in 1907.[31] Three years later, he delivered a typical series of sermons in which he described a number of civic conspiracies. He preached first on the "Liquor Conspiracy," followed by the "Vice Conspiracy," and ended with "The Conspiracies of Crime and the Interests against the Government." Like many Progressive reformers, Matthews loved to regale his audiences with statistics and investigations, either personally conducted or pursued by a committee, that gave an "objective" flavor to his sermons. For example, in his sermon on the liquor conspiracy, he cited an article from the *Chicago Tribune* in which the writer estimated that during the previous ten years 53,556 murders had been committed by men under the influence of alcohol. Matthews went on to provide additional figures on the social costs incurred by some "30,000 alcoholic maniacs." He argued that the saloon was directly responsible for eighty percent of all poverty.[32] Matthews described the saloon as "the most fiendish, corrupt and

Progressive Impulses

hellsoaked institution that ever crawled out of the slime of the eternal pit.... It is the open sore of this land. It has broken more hearts, wrecked more homes, blighted more lives, and damned more souls, than perhaps, all other agencies."[33]

Seattle residents also associated Matthews with fervent attacks on brothels; frequently, he sent investigating committees from the church into the red-light district in order to uncover illegal operations. Among his sermon notes is a letter from a First Presbyterian vice committee that he had organized. The letter describes in detail the committee's tour of the lower end of town, comparing Seattle's Tenderloin district to that of Butte, Montana (referred to in the letter as "The Hell Hole of Iniquity") and San Francisco ("The Sodom of the Pacific Coast"). Describing hundreds of half-clad women propositioning men on streetcar lines, the committee reported to Matthews that "conditions are so bad in [the Tenderloin] that the filth and odors are enough to disgust even those who have fallen down in the underworld."[34] Whether Matthews went on any of these "investigative" trips is not entirely certain; it is clear that he expressed great interest in discovering as many specifics as he could regarding the various expressions of vice in Seattle. He is credited with coining the phrase "Skid Road" to better describe the Seattle Tenderloin district. Playing off the fact that Yesler Avenue, south of First Presbyterian, had served as the original path by which logs were skidded down to the sawmill at the bottom of hill, Matthews apparently seized on the image. He described the plight of individual souls unable to resist the temptations of the underworld as skidding to perdition, and the term stuck.[35] During 1908, Matthews publicly urged that liquor be prohibited at Luna Park, an amusement park on Alki Point in West Seattle.[36] Two years later, the *Post-Intelligencer* reported that Matthews had provided the police with a tip that resulted in a raid on the Spellmine Brewing Company for selling liquor without a license.[37]

By mid-decade, reformers like Matthews felt encouraged that Progressive legislation could in fact change the ethos of the city. Mayor William Moore, elected in 1906, achieved greater success than previous administrations in enforcing Sunday saloon closures. And in 1908, in the waning days of his administration, Moore closed down a significant number of gambling houses. However, Matthews and other Seattle clergy pushed for even greater enforcement and additional legislation to close Chinese gambling houses and lotteries as well as "blind pigs" in amusement parks that offered the chance to consume alcohol undetected.[38] Both mayoral candidates campaigned on a platform of enforcing Sunday closings, and when John Miller defeated Moore, reformers rejoiced that better days were ahead.

Nevertheless, the pastor at First Presbyterian seldom articulated a particularly optimistic view of human nature. Matthews often justified his coercive view of reform with a rather traditional view of original sin. "Human nature is not changed by environment, education or evolution," he preached. "The nature remains the same, regardless of circumstances; it has never been affected by any power except that of the Holy Ghost in regeneration."[39] In another sermon he said,

> Sin is an act or a condition, or it may be both. It is the violation of or the nonconformity to the law of God, or the will of God. . . . Therefore, the soul of Adam, being tainted by a biased will, and we, the descendants of Adam, have had transmitted to us the taint that rested upon his soul in consequence of his apostasy from God. . . . Consequently, each descendant is born with the loss of original righteousness, and with the inherent tendency to corruption.[40]

With this attitude, Matthews rarely hesitated to demand rigorous law enforcement throughout society.

Yet Matthews also adopted an environmental approach to civic problems. Like many other Progressive reformers, he insisted that changing the environment would result in moral improvement. Parks, schools, playgrounds, and health-related concerns, from proper medical treatment to garbage collection—all had caught the attention of both religious and secular reformers by the turn of the century. From bond issues to ordinances, Progressives were attempting to shape the city in ways that reflected traditional moral values and healthy living.

Many of Matthews's sermons offered an environmental explanation of criminal behavior: "There are many forces contributing to the life of the criminal and to the creation of the state of crime. There is much that can be said in explanation, if not in defense of the criminal. He is largely a creature of society. Society has either made him by direct creation, or by neglect, or by permitting him to germinate and grow without restraint." Matthews further argued that climatic conditions contributed to crime, although Seattle hardly provided a good example of harsh conditions. "The winter months are conducive to robberies, hold-ups, and crimes of a similar character. The summer months are conducive to suicides, murders, riots and other crimes growing out of heated blood and aroused passions incident to an excessive high temperature of heat."[41]

Frequently, Matthews preached about the need to develop a healthy environment by constructing parks and public facilities to break down the alienation endemic to a large city. "A favorable environment renders indispensable service in the development of character," he claimed.[42] Asked in 1903 about the most pressing needs of the city, he stressed the "poverty of public facilities" and the absence of suitable playgrounds. Matthews, like Progressive reformers throughout the country, was convinced that disorder would result if concerned citizens made no systematic effort to create a healthy urban atmosphere. "It is cheaper to establish schools, parks, amusement halls, art galleries, libraries, and places of refinement, culture and morality," he said, "than it is to support a standing army of hundreds of policemen, jails, penitentiaries, and asylums for inebriates."[43]

His concern for the urban environment and the underlying issue of social cohesion was evident in Matthews's proposed criminal justice system reforms, which were quite advanced for their time. "The first change should be the substitution of psychological and physiological treatment for penal punishment," he believed. "It is a false theory to think you can punish a criminal and reform him or benefit society."[44] He argued that the concept of a prison should be based on ideas gleaned from the field of health care. Principally, he believed that this meant the creation of a healthy environment for the prisoner or "patient." On one occasion, he suggested that the city purchase twenty to twenty-five acres close to the city and build cottages, erect workshops, and establish forges, shoe shops, and small manufacturing plants. "To this farm every vagrant, every petite criminal and worthless, indolent person in the community should be forced to go."[45]

Matthews shared the Progressive concern for the circumstances that influenced character formation in young children. Leaders of the movement optimistically believed that if one could just raise moral, healthy children, social problems would disappear. All through the country, reformers like Matthews argued that parks and playgrounds would help create a healthy environment. "Every patriotic father and son ought to vote for the Park-bonds and give to Seattle's children playgrounds and rose gardens. Vote for your children," preached Matthews in a sermon entitled "Roses for Seattle's Children."[46]

Matthews's concern for child welfare led him on at least one occasion to argue for rather extreme measures of state intervention to control those individuals suspected of being unfit parents. "All of the parents in society afflicted with constitutional diseases of the body and of the mind should be under constant inspection, investigation and treatment, and whenever a child is born to such parents it should be under constant examination and protection. The very first time the slightest symptom displays itself in the child, he should be sent to an institution for the correction of the evil indicated by the symptom."[47]

The problem of child labor also drew Matthews's attention, as it did many other Progressive and Social Gospel reformers. He supported legislation prohibiting such labor and exhorted the city and his parishioners to be vigilant against it. He frequently spoke of unscrupulous capitalists who exploited children simply to make a profit. "Society sacrifices children to the god of gold," he preached. "They are the victims of all kinds of patent medicines, foods and concoctions made only to enrich the manufacturers and enlarge the business of undertakers."[48]

The Seattle preacher often vented his rage against what he considered the robber barons of his day. He continued to employ rhetoric that he had honed in Georgia, speaking for the Farmers' Alliance—rhetoric that fit the Progressive movement's desire to control business monopolies and create a healthier capitalistic environment.

> In the field of business these ubiquitous parasites rob you by the power of the oily tongue, a hypnotic pen or a rose-covered threat. The eighth commandment prohibits oppression, and every form of injustice. . . . When wood yards combine to extort money from the common people; when coal mines enter into a league to rob the hearth stone of warmth and comfort; when meat packers and whole-sale merchants consolidate to wrench from the brawny hand of toil the last dollar—you have monumental graft and the most violent infraction of the eighth commandment.[49]

Progressives, like Matthews, condemned the monopolistic practices of corporate businessmen. "Rockefeller is nothing less than a robber, a criminal," said Matthews. "I am speaking of Rockefeller, of course, simply as the most conspicuous representative of a certain class of monopolists in this country."[50]

Antimonopolism was a major issue in Seattle politics during the early twentieth century. Progressive reformers argued that municipal ownership of utilities would be both more efficient and less corrupt.[51] Matthews supported the general concept of municipal ownership. "The method of grafting franchises," he said, "has caused the people to demand municipal ownership of public utilities."[52] On one occasion, he was so upset at the exorbitant cost of ambulances and funerals that he argued for city control. "The time has come for the city to own its cemeteries and protect the survivors who want to bury their beloved relatives in a decent and respectable manner. The time has come for the city to own its own ambulances."[53]

Early in his Seattle tenure, Matthews often sided with labor on civic issues. He opined that the growth of monopolies forced labor to demand ownership of the means of production. "If the government would exercise a more rigid, more thorough, and a more satisfactory control over the implements of production, of commerce, and public-service utilities," he argued, "the cry for government ownership would cease."[54] He believed that labor could then rely on the protection of the law and "keep the implements and tools of production and wealth free for the service and benefit of all alike."[55]

Progressive reformers throughout the nation believed that social harmony depended on assisting the victims of industrial capitalism. Matthews was no exception. During those first ten years in Seattle, he not only chastised big business, but he also supported labor's struggle for better working conditions. He had been an early advocate of the construction of a labor temple, which was finished in September 1905, five years before a similar labor temple was constructed in New York City under Charles Stelzle's leadership. When the building was completed, Matthews was asked by Seattle labor leaders to ride in the lead automobile in a parade and give the dedicatory speech.[56] Frequently, in those first few years in Seattle, the *Seattle Union Record*, a paper highly sympathetic to labor's interests, praised his leadership. For instance, the paper supported the pastor's efforts to force businesses to distribute paychecks early in the day so that they could be cashed in a bank and not in a saloon.[57]

Matthews always hoped that the middle class and working class would come to share the same worldview—the middle-class worldview. The principal task for civic and religious leaders like himself was to bring the two groups together. "When the common people own their own homes," he preached, "and have the privilege of owning small manufacturing establishments, prosperity and peace will abide in every hamlet and city."[58] In that same sermon, he felt compelled to remind each side of its fundamental dependence on the other. "Capital and labor are on the verge of a passive revolution," voiced Matthews. "They seem to have forgotten that they are indispensable to each other."[59] Much of the problem, he believed, could be solved if both sides would agree to sit down as rational human beings and listen to one another. For this purpose, he proposed the establishment of a general court of arbitration.[60]

Matthews also shared the Progressive concern about the environment and consumer health. Whether Matthews read *The Jungle* by Upton Sinclair, first published in 1906, is unclear, yet he surely was aware of its spirit when he preached the following:

> Suppose we were to severely test all the food-stuffs or ingredients for food, found in the markets; we would discover the cause of much of our suffering. Thousands of men have been driven almost to the verge of insanity by indigestion, caused by the chalk and alum in baking powders. Tens of thousands of children have suffered and died as the direct result of poisoned and adulterated candy. Chemically impure catsups, sauces and syrups have wrecked the happiness of more homes than war. . . . If there is a hydra-headed curse in this country, its name is breakfast food.[61]

Matthews became quite active on issues of consumer protection. For example in 1911, he was named with four others to the Seattle Milk Commission, which was responsible for establishing and enforcing health standards pertaining to the production and distribution of milk throughout the Seattle area.[62]

One issue advocated by many Progressives that Matthews did not accept was woman suffrage. His views undoubtedly stemmed, in part, from his upbringing in the South, where it was an ingrained belief that each sex should operate in its own sphere of responsibility. For Matthews that meant only men should participate in politics. But his arguments also seem to reflect an unusual amount of chauvinism, even for his day.

> No sir! This country will never adopt female suffrage. If the ballot were extended to the women the star of America's glory would go down immediately never to rise again. . . . The deluded women who cry for their "right" of the ballot do not seem to understand that the

Progressive Impulses

right to vote is not an inalienable right.... Universal suffrage is wrong in theory and would be a curse in practice. The advocates of female suffrage are, many of them, advocates of divorce, small families, few household responsibilities and no children, all of which is unwomanly and dangerous. No gallant, patriotic, chivalric man can afford to vote for or advocate female suffrage because when ever you put burdens upon women which will compel them to neglect their duties as mothers or absent themselves from their home obligations you will undermine the government, destroy the constitution and wreck the nation.[63]

Matthews eventually accepted woman suffrage after it was passed. However, he never relented on the issue of whether women should preach from the Presbyterian pulpit. Interestingly, he did support efforts to hire more female faculty at the University of Washington. He argued for a fair salary scale for faculty and criticized the fact that of the 137 members of the faculty, only 12 were female. Matthews asserted that at least a third of the faculty in a co-educational institution should be women.[64]

Apart from his generally conservative attitudes toward women, Matthews believed in the overall agenda of the Progressive movement. He believed that his church could be an effective force in favor of a number of initiatives associated with the political and social reforms of the period. In 1910, he stated, "The facts justify us, when looking at the world from a political standpoint, in saying that this church is, or ought to be, in politics. Perhaps there are seventeen or eighteen hundred voters connected with this church. Therefore, every political question confronting the people should be a question of thought, prayer and consideration by the men of this church."[65]

Matthews worked diligently to establish voters' bureaus within his church so that information on local issues and candidates could be distributed. He pushed hard for the direct primary and even drafted his own version of the legislation that would be submitted before the state—legislation that was passed in 1908. Two years earlier he had orchestrated a "Blue-Pencil Campaign," in which he asked each voting member of his congregation to give close examination to every candidate and vote against anyone who seemed to be the pawn of special interests.[66] In 1908, Matthews wrote an open letter to all the mayoral candidates and asked them to express their positions on such issues as the selection of police chief and the handling of vice. All of the candidates, with one exception, felt compelled to respond to Matthews's queries. The lone dissenter was Lewis Levy, who showed some indignation with Matthews's approach. "My Dear Doctor—Yours of the 13th received," Levy wrote, "to which I hasten to reply: If it was not for the fact that I know you personally to be an all-around good fellow, I would not deign to reply to what I consider your attempt to put yourself up as a dictator to an American citizen."[67] How many of the other candidates had similar feelings but were afraid to express them is uncertain. What is important is how comfortable Matthews felt involving himself in public policy; he very much hoped that he could shape policy.

Like most Progressives, Matthews combined civic boosterism with moral reform. For example, he welcomed the Alaska-Yukon-Pacific Exposition in 1909 as a chance to demonstrate the greatness of Seattle to the world. He harangued other civic leaders for not giving the fair their full support. "The spirit of selfishness which is today threatening the future of the city is represented by the Atwood, McGilvra, Kinnear letters antagonistic to the AYP Exposition, which have recently appeared in the columns of the *Post-Intelligencer*. . . . It is evident that a coterie of patriotic and progressive citizens have agreed to assassinate the Exposition and impede the progress of the city."[68] Once the exposition opened, Matthews expressed his opinions on everything from various exhibits to the amusement rides. With Judge Thomas Burke, Matthews agreed that the South Seas island people could be viewed by the public. But he vigorously objected, to no avail, that the fair's entertainment area, the Pay Streak, should be closed on Sundays.[69]

When Matthews arrived in Seattle, the city was already experiencing the zeal for civic reform associated with Progressivism. According to the historian Mansel Blackford, Seattle reform politics after the 1880s had focused on the restriction of gambling and prostitution. During the early twentieth century, municipal ownership emerged as a major issue of Seattle politics.[70] On the cutting edge of most social reform in Seattle, Matthews pushed and prodded members of his congregation to involve themselves in shaping public policy, simply because it was their religious duty. He constantly held out the carrot of a righteous society that would reflect middle-class as well as Christian values, and at the same time he brandished the stick of sin and damnation to those people who failed to act.

Matthews must surely have felt some optimism about the strides taken toward fulfilling his aim of building a righteous city. He must have congratulated himself on many occasions: not only had he built a remarkable church in terms of size and influence, but he had also seen many of his ideas come to fruition. He could help set public policy with his work on the Seattle Milk Commission as well as shape public opinion regarding upcoming elections. On the surface, all seemed to be going on schedule in those first ten years.

Yet he must have sensed that all was not well with his battle plan to achieve a position of leadership and make Seattle a holy city. To preach from the pulpit was important, but this was a holy war, and it required covert as well as overt action. Matthews became increasingly bold not only about seeking more power but also about using all kinds of power for the implementation of his vision of righteousness.

Progressivism became an important vehicle for Matthews's journey toward civic righteousness. The national movement had provided a series of issues, a set of strategies, and a broad consensus for reform that fit well with his understanding of his role as a pastor. Matthews is a superb example of the way in which Progressivism influenced a Protestant minister. The difficulty for him, and for many clergy in the country, was that not everyone was convinced that ministers should be at the helm. One person who definitely objected to Matthews's role in Seattle politics was Hiram Gill. The struggle between the two of them emerged as the city's most famous political contest during the first half of the twentieth century.

~ CHAPTER 6 ~

The Great Feud

Dr. Matthews announces now that he is again against me. I would rather him out in the open against me than pretending to be my friend and then working against me secretly.

—Hiram Gill (1911)

Mark Matthews had been engaged in politics since the days when he first pleaded with the residents of Dalton, Georgia, to throw the "good ol' boys" out of office. His interest in the political arena had separated him from many of his ministerial colleagues in Seattle, as it had in the South, although it was not uncommon for other clergy to express interest in politics for a variety of reasons. But perhaps most striking in Matthews's case was the intensity with which he pursued politics; no issue was too trivial for his interests. Whether it was in Calhoun, Dalton, Jackson, or Seattle, Matthews embraced politics as the necessary means for creating a righteous city. For much of his first ten years in Seattle, Matthews's influence on Seattle politics stemmed largely from either his pulpit oration or his work on specific legislative initiatives. Without question, his activity allowed him to become a major influence in the politics of early-twentieth-century Seattle.

However, by about 1910, another side of Matthews's political activism began to emerge, specifically, his relationship with one of Seattle's key politicians, Hiram Gill. In Gill, Matthews found a nemesis who could frustrate the preacher's vision of urban righteousness and who, at the same time, served as a scapegoat whom Matthews could blame for the problems of the city. Even before Seattle voters elected Gill mayor, this relationship played itself out in almost melodramatic fashion, with Matthews attacking Gill in his sermons, and Gill occasionally lashing back at Matthews in public meetings. But after a number of unsatisfactory encounters, Matthews began to resort to covert methods in order to defeat Gill. Matthews's frustration with Gill ultimately led to the preacher's subtle shift from reliance on moral suasion to a willingness to use undercover investigation and the courts to enforce his opinion and further his vision of urban righteousness.

Hiram Gill was one of those political figures who emerged so frequently from the backrooms of American political dens in the late nineteenth and early twentieth centuries. Rather diminutive and balding, he sported a pair of glasses that made him look somewhat timid. Caricatured by Seattle's cartoon editorialists, Gill hardly looked like a powerful leader of public opinion. But his appeal to Seattleites was exactly the opposite of Matthews's. Gill voiced no expectations for proper behavior or for the demeanor of the city in general; he simply sold himself as "one of the boys," who was hoping to promote Seattle's economic interests by letting the loggers, sailors, and miners have a little fun. In 1904, Gill was elected president of the city council. And by the end of the year, Mark Matthews set in motion events that would culminate in heated conflict between the two men.[1]

In January of 1904, Matthews contributed an article to the *Seattle Times* expressing his views on the city's religious outlook for the upcoming year. In the article, he came out swinging, with his usual rhetorical passion: "Our city cannot be built on coin, out of gold, or by the hands of lecherous, licentious, avaricious men," he wrote. "The year 1904 will find the moral forces of Seattle aligned with but one purpose, namely, to elevate the moral tone of the business circles."[2] However, the year seemed not to produce the anticipated results from Matthews's perspective. In December, in an address to a prayer group, the preacher focused on the city council more than the business community. What seemed to provoke the speech was the fact that the voters had defeated a bond issue for more parks. Matthews blamed the city council, claiming that the people of the city did not trust the council with proper appropriation of the money. Specifically, he charged that all but four members of the council suffered from "graftitis." Picked up in the newspapers, the term caused a great deal of public discussion. When the council next met, members decided to demand that Matthews explain more fully his charges.

The Great Feud

In less than three years, Matthews had gained such prominence that most of his pronouncements were taken rather seriously. The preacher agreed to provide specifics to the council on January 30, 1905.[3] During the three weeks prior to the meeting, speculation and tension mounted. Interested observers launched a petition drive to demand that the proceedings be moved from the council chambers to the Grand Opera House in order to accommodate the expected throng. Matthews, however, opposed the suggestion on the grounds that he did not want to turn the event into a circus. Nonetheless, the atmosphere on the evening of January 30 was highly charged as a huge crowd of people gathered outside the city council chambers several hours before the 8:00 P.M. meeting; approximately 300 were allowed inside. When Matthews arrived, the crowd greeted him with raucous cheering, while the council members were met with "hisses and sneers" and aggression that verged on pushing and shoving. More than once, the sergeant-at-arms had to take action to control the crowd. Once the proceedings began, the rules were suspended in order to allow Matthews to read an opening statement.[4]

Matthews accused council members of specific acts of graft, political favoritism, and coercion. He charged that the council had erred by not allowing the Snoqualmie Power Company to compete with the Seattle Electric Company for the city's contract. He alleged that the council had favored a dredging company by supplying city water free of charge, and he criticized the council for not demanding the payment of interest on funds the city had deposited with local banks. He charged that the election of Hiram Gill as president of the council smacked of chicanery; he asserted that certain individuals had been favored unfairly with the granting of liquor licenses and that there was graft in allowing construction companies to combine and set prices. In all, Matthews leveled nineteen charges against the council, and the crowd, already worked up in support, cheered each of his indictments. When the preacher finished, he stated that he would say nothing further unless a grand jury was called, and only then would he reveal his sources. He claimed that it had been agreed that no questions would be asked of him at this time. With that, he turned and walked through the crowd as the people unsuccessfully attempted to lift his six-foot-five-inch frame to their shoulders.[5]

By this time, the president of the council, Hiram Gill, had become enraged at Matthews's charges and committed what was, in retrospect, a tactical error. Losing control, the politician began yelling at Matthews

The Great Feud

to return and answer questions. When this failed to bring the preacher back, Gill launched into a personal attack. The *Seattle Times* and the *Post-Intelligencer* reports differed slightly, but the essence of Gill's attack on Matthews was clear. He wanted to destroy the Seattle minister's personal reputation.

> I want to say that I was here in this city striving to make an honest living when he was a gambler in Tennessee running a "nigger" crap game. He was run out of his state, and the people in the county in which he was raised would not let him stay there a minute if he went back there today. I know his reputation. When he came here he was entangled with a disreputable woman of the under world and went down there to see her regularly. He is still going, too in close hacks with the curtains drawn. Had it not been for . . . the desire to save the name and family of a young girl from disgrace he would have been in the penitentiary today.[6]

In light of these fireworks, the *Seattle Star* called the confrontation between Gill and Matthews "the most dramatic incident in the history of the city council."[7] Gill's personal attack on Matthews's character seemed to most citizens to have gone much too far. Matthews must have let his Southern friends know that he had been attacked; letters came in from Georgia and Tennessee defending him, and all the city newspapers chastised Gill for his hostile behavior. It is possible, however, that if Gill had remained calm, Matthews would have been much more vulnerable to criticism. When the points of his attack on the council were individually dealt with by more rational respondents, every one of Matthews's criticisms failed to hold up. The prosecuting attorney, Kenneth MacKintosh, saw no grounds for calling a grand jury to investigate council behavior, and the entire incident was seen as a symbol of the ongoing battle between the open- and closed-town advocates.[8] Hiram Gill served as an excellent representative of the realistic politicians and "good ol' boys" who knew how to use power. Matthews, of course, emerged as the great symbol of Protestant moralism and eternal vigilance against corruption.

Ironically, however, the incident seemed to affect Matthews at a deeper level. His confrontation with Gill seemed to alter his own view of the use of power and his perception of how change should be effected. In this initial fray, the preacher had relied almost entirely on his powerful rhetoric and his ability to sway public opinion. He had not solicited the help of powerful allies either within the city council or within Seattle business and social circles. He attacked his enemies from the pulpit but did not apply any behind-the-scenes pressure. However, upon reflection, he must have seen how fruitless this approach had been. Consequently, by the end of 1905, Matthews, at thirty-eight years old, seemed to change course slightly and to pursue his quest for a holy city in a different way.

By that time, Matthews had become increasingly sensitive to the political realities of power and, therefore, was more cautious about alienating possible allies. This political awareness helps account for a rather curious permutation in attitude concerning one of the most controversial political issues in Seattle's Progressive period—municipal ownership of transportation systems. Matthews's Populist tendencies, basic distrust of big business, attraction to strong municipal government, and desire to eliminate opportunities for graft and corruption would lead one to expect that the Southern preacher would have favored municipal ownership of public transportation. Indeed, as previously noted, Matthews supported the general concept of municipal ownership on many occasions.

Consequently, one should not be surprised to find Mark Matthews among the civic leaders calling for a meeting in 1905 to discuss strategies for organizing the municipal ownership of streetcar lines. Along with the reformers George Cotterill, William Wood, Austin Griffiths, J. Allen Smith, T. S. Lippy, and other Seattle Progressives, Matthews expressed irritation at the city council's refusal to grant a competing streetcar franchise to the Seattle Electric Company.[9] The meeting resulted in the formation of the Municipal Ownership League.

The drive for municipal ownership gained momentum in late 1905, when the Municipal Ownership Party was created, and in January 1906, when William Moore ran for mayor as the party's candidate.[10] The Republicans nominated the city comptroller, John Riplinger, who, while favoring the general concept of municipal ownership, believed that the city was incapable of financing its own public transportation system. Matthews, when forced to choose, sided with the Republicans and Riplinger, largely because Riplinger advocated a tougher position on vice.[11]

Matthews may also have chosen to support Riplinger because of the Presbyterian minister's close relationship with two powerful figures who opposed municipal ownership, John McGraw and Judge

Thomas Burke. McGraw, a member of Matthews's church, was a former governor of the state and still active in Seattle politics. Burke had been highly prominent in Seattle affairs during the 1880s and 1890s and was particularly well known for his relationship to James J. Hill, the railroad baron. By 1906, McGraw and Burke were leading the Seattle Economic League, which stimulated discussion concerning political issues that affected commercial affairs. Matthews was a minor officer in the league; more important, he viewed Burke and McGraw as people he could not afford to alienate. In the fall of 1906 the Seattle Economic League opposed a citywide bond issue to fund a street railway system. Assisted by the *Seattle Times*, the economic league worked feverishly to convince Seattle voters that other cities had failed miserably at similar ventures. The appeals succeeded and the measure went down to defeat.[12] Whether Matthews was convinced to oppose municipal ownership solely on the merits of McGraw's and Burke's argument is difficult to say; it is certainly plausible, however, that Matthews was assuming a more pragmatic view toward political power. His two friends were influential figures, and Matthews certainly found their support useful. It is possible that he simply calculated the future benefits of their friendship in a way that made him abandon his earlier support of municipal ownership.

Despite Matthews's support for Riplinger, William Moore won in a very close election. However, Matthews must have felt good that voters passed a Sunday-closing law against saloons. The prospect of extending closing laws to other forms of entertainment seemed bright in 1906, and Matthews and the Seattle Ministerial Federation continued to apply pressure for such action.[13]

Over the next several years, the issue of vice control continued to dominate city politics. Matthews and various other ministers and social reformers continued to keep enforcement of closing laws and the general vision of a righteous community before voters and city officials. In 1908, Seattle voters elected John Miller to the mayor's office, and he promised to continue to enforce the Sunday-closing law. Miller, however, came under fire from a variety of quarters for his failure to rid the city of prostitution. Miller argued that such a cleanup would take time and that, in fact, there would still be a need for a restricted district somewhere in the city. From the fall of 1908 through the spring of 1909, Miller made repeated efforts to clean up the restricted district, only to have prostitutes move to other parts of the city. The net result was that vice continued to be an issue in city politics, and Matthews continued to preach sermons reflecting his own position concerning the way in which it should be regulated.[14]

As for Matthews, for a short time in 1908 he attracted the attention of the local press by apparently reconciling with his old enemy, Hiram Gill. Matthews's motives were undoubtedly complex and most certainly included a genuine longing to heal wounds. However, he also seemed to believe that Gill might be brought around to his side, given the fact that so much of the city's middle class expressed interest in the control of vice. The apparent accord between the two former foes caught many Seattle residents off-balance. Greeted with the headline "Gill Smokes Peace Pipe with Matthews," Seattle readers were reminded of the considerable distance that had to be closed. "For the benefit of the recent arrivals in the city," the story's reporter stated, "it may be said that once upon a time, Hi Gill and Dr. Matthews engaged in the most bitter, bloodless personal war of words that was ever pulled off in the city limits with or without the Marquis of Queensbury rules."[15] A meeting between the two men took place only after much effort. Gill had expressed considerable skepticism concerning whether the two would ever get together. The president of the city council swore that he would "see the doctor paddling a canoe upon the peaceful bosom of the Swanee River before he would call at 'The Manse' or anywhere else."[16] But Matthews persisted, and Gill came to hear the preacher explain his plans for the city and to say how very much he needed Gill's support. Whether Gill saw himself in Matthews's corner is very questionable, but Matthews must have appreciated the newspaper reporter's observation that "with Gill and Matthews hooked up together, there isn't another team in the city that can even get out upon the track."[17] The leader of the First Presbyterian Church must have felt quite confident that most of the roadblocks had been removed from his path to a position of greater influence in the city.

The reconciliation of Matthews and Gill lasted only a short time, however, because when Gill chose to run for mayor in 1910, he argued that Seattle must return to a policy of providing a restricted district for prostitution. To Matthews, this was clearly unacceptable. Challenging Gill for the Republican nomination was A. V. Bouillon, and the preacher soon publicly committed to Bouillon by asserting that a Gill administration would lead directly to "the gospel of corrupt politicians and infamous political bodies."[18] Matthews claimed that First Presbyterian

Church would cast its votes for Bouillon, and the Reverend George Cairns of the Temple Baptist Church reportedly urged his congregation to do the same.[19]

Election tactics, as usual, were questionable: Gill vigorously denied that he was responsible for "colonizing" the once-empty hotels and lodging houses of the First Ward with hundreds of men at fifteen cents per night and then transporting them for voter registration. However, grand jury detectives identified approximately 700 men who would be arrested if they tried to vote on February 8. On the Sunday before the election, Matthews delivered a vitriolic attack on Gill and any Christian who supported him: "The infamous cowards, slothful sluggards and stupid Christians who have refused to register and who are now taking no part in politics, are the greatest enemies to good government and the most formidable impediments in the way of the establishment of righteousness we have in the community."[20] Despite Matthews's efforts and the hint of scandal, Gill soundly defeated Bouillon in the primary and Moore in the general election.[21]

Yet the election results did not end the public debate over vice. Matthews, along with other clergy and social reformers, kept a sharp eye on Gill's activities. And almost immediately, the mayor raised concerns by appointing as his police chief Charles Wappenstein, a man who openly argued that vice could not be effectively regulated.

Wappenstein came to Seattle after working for the Pinkerton Detective Agency and serving as a police chief in the Midwest. Looking like a typical Keystone Cop with his large mustache, Wappenstein dated from Seattle's gold rush era. But from his early days on the force, rumors circulated regarding his tolerance of scam artists, kickbacks, and protection rackets.[22] A biographical description of Wappenstein in a local publication about Seattle police and fire personnel raised the hackles of Matthews and other middle-class Seattle residents: "Chief Wappenstein has the widest acquaintance with crooks of any peace officer in the West. He has also a very wide circle of friends and acquaintances among the business and professional men of Seattle."[23] One of those friends was Colonel Alden Blethen, publisher of the *Seattle Times*, who defended Wappenstein against any and all charges.

As the Seattle historians Sharon Boswell and Lorraine McConaghy assert in their biography of Blethen, "Wappy was back and so was the Tenderloin. The saloons and dance halls, gambling dens and hurdy-gurdy joints all swept away the dust and unboarded their windows as the 'lords of vice' once more opened for business."[24] In fact, Wappenstein relaxed the boundaries of the restricted district and attracted many new arrivals from outside the city, who, according to Boswell and McConaghy, "engaged in every form of debauchery imaginable."[25]

Gill's troubles began when he left town for a few days in September 1910, and acting mayor Max Wardall, outraged by the developments in the city, decided to exercise his power and remove Wappenstein for alleged improprieties. Gill quickly returned and reinstated Wappenstein, much to the general disgruntlement of the city. Beginning in October, the Public Welfare League started to circulate petitions for the newly approved recall election. Charging that Gill was "a menace to the business enterprises and moral welfare of said city," the Public Welfare League by December had gained the required signatures to force an election in February of 1911.[26] Matthews's role in the recall has been variously described but, in general, local historians have credited him with organizing the Protestant clergy and mobilizing his own congregation of voters to undermine his old enemy.[27] The picture is one of Matthews, the puritanical preacher, using his pulpit to motivate his congregation to work against the corrupt politician. He is seen as both facilitating the fight against corruption and, at the same time, riding the crest of a wave of moral reform sweeping the city as part of the Progressive period. These would appear to be the same methods he used during the first confrontation with Gill before the city council in 1905. But closer examination reveals that, indeed, Matthews's tactics had changed, and perception of his role in the recall must be revised to some degree.

The recall movement did, in fact, involve a great many of the city's clergymen. In early October, the *Post-Intelligencer* noted how many Methodists and Baptists were behind the petition drive.[28] Dr. Adna Wright Leonard was so outspoken in his attacks on Gill and Wappenstein that he was reportedly threatened with bodily harm.[29] But Matthews was uncharacteristically reticent during these months of October, November, and December. He did speak out concerning the necessity for a morally righteous city and on one occasion suggested that if he were mayor he would exercise very tight control over his police chief. But in general, his sermons varied little in substance and tone from what he normally preached on any given Sunday. It would be impossible to deduce from his sermons that a recall was in process.[30]

The Great Feud

Matthews's uncharacteristic silence became so noticeable that the editor of the *Post-Intelligencer*, Erastus Brainerd, who had been very outspoken in his own criticism of Gill, wrote Matthews in late January 1911 and asked why the preacher had not been more involved in the campaign.[31] The letter seems to have caught Matthews by surprise. In an extremely defensive reply, he claimed that he had in fact opposed Gill from the very beginning but had not received adequate coverage from the newspapers. He further claimed that his sermons were filled with indictments of the present administration.[32] Whether Matthews's memory was failing or he purposely exaggerated is difficult to say, but the newspapers had not covered him because he had said very little. He indicated to Brainerd that he would write an article explaining his precise position and would ask Brainerd to print it.

On January 24, the day of his reply to Brainerd, Matthews feverishly penned a letter to Gill asking him to resign. In the letter, Matthews again expressed his concern for the state of Gill's soul, and he reminded the mayor that he had offered his help in the past. Gill refused to resign and perhaps did not even respond directly to the preacher's letter.[33] Matthews subsequently submitted an article that was featured on the front page of the *Post-Intelligencer* on January 27, 1911, just eleven days prior to the February 7 election. In very direct terms, Matthews condemned the Gill administration and urged voters to elect George Dilling. "Every ballot cast will be either for or against righteousness, civic purity, and law enforcement," he wrote. "There isn't the slightest doubt in the minds of the general public of the fact of police graft, chicanery, double crossing and the infraction of the law at the investigation of the authorities."[34]

Matthews's position was at last clear, but one wonders whether he would have said anything if Brainerd had not prodded him. Certainly, Gill's response to Matthews's attacks indicated that the preacher had indeed been quite successful in maintaining a low profile. "Dr. Matthews announces now that he is again against me," said Gill on January 28. "I would rather him out in the open against me than pretending to be my friend and then working against me secretly."[35] The *Seattle Times*, published by Colonel Alden Blethen, was a strong supporter of Gill, and it too indicated that Matthews's position was only recently known. "Rev. M. A. Matthews finally has come out for Dilling," said the *Times*. "Mr. Dilling seems to be having more than his share of hard luck. The 'hoodoos' are flocking to Dilling."[36]

The Great Feud

Why Matthews waited so long to speak out is not entirely clear, but the evidence suggests that the Southern preacher was in the middle of a very complex game of power in which the stakes included his ultimate influence over the mayor's office. Since his reconciliation with Gill in 1908, Matthews had hoped to convince the politician to do things the preacher's way. After Gill's election, Matthews openly supported the mayor, but shortly thereafter, Matthews must have realized that Gill would not conform nearly enough to Matthews's desires. In his letter to Gill in January 1911, Matthews recalled their meeting the previous July and their discussion of illegal operations in the restricted district. At that time, according to Matthews's recollection, the minister demanded that Wappenstein be removed, but Gill refused, leaving Matthews to stew about his next move during an extensive trip back east.[37] Whether Matthews attempted to pressure Gill on other occasions is not known, but by September, the actions of Max Wardall and the Public Welfare League were making Gill's position more tenuous. Matthews may have agonized about whether to join in and openly declare himself against Gill or find another way of exercising influence.

In fact, Matthews did opt for an alternative way of pressuring Gill, and this approach had the advantage of allowing him to wait and see how successful the recall, a virtually untested form of democracy, would be. To strengthen his overall political position, he decided to take more covert action. Borrowing money on his insurance policies, the preacher hired one of the most famous detective agencies of the day, the William Burns Agency. Matthews wanted specific evidence of Wappenstein's activities, because the preacher did not want to be caught unprepared if it became necessary to oppose the mayor publicly, as it had been in 1905.

In mid-November 1910, Burns operatives began supplying Matthews with daily reports on various people.[38] The Seattle minister pored over the reports, hoping to find evidence that would be damaging to Gill and Wappenstein. Matthews made certain that his role was kept entirely secret, although Brainerd's accusation that Matthews had not done his share for the recall almost stirred him to reveal his efforts. "I hope what I am doing will be successful and if it is," he replied to Brainerd, "you will find that I have done more in the last four months than all the Welfare Leagues in this city have done to rid this city of the infernal corruption."[39] The preacher must have realized that secrecy had its continued advantages. If the investigation proved unsuccessful, he would not have to be associated with its failure. Matthews might

The Great Feud

also have believed that certain information could be used to make Gill more pliable even if the recall failed.

Matthews must have faced the election day anxiously: he had invested money and emotional energy in his effort to influence the future of Seattle politics. And as the results came in, he must have felt great personal satisfaction in Gill's defeat. Women in Seattle had just gained the right to vote the previous November, and they went to the polls with banners that read "Dilling for Decency"; this was enough to counteract a reported 500 "ladies of the night" who had been brought by limousines to vote for Gill. The election produced an obvious irony in the fact that Matthews, who had fought so vigorously against woman suffrage, now obviously reaped the benefits of women being able to participate in the electoral process.[40]

But the success of the recall did force Matthews to make a decision regarding the Burns investigation of Gill and Wappenstein. Although there is no direct evidence of any extended discussion between Burns and Matthews, the two probably rationalized that criminals should be prosecuted and Wappenstein brought to justice.[41] Consequently, one week after the election, Burns went to the prosecuting attorney, John Murphy, with the evidence collected. After reviewing it, Murphy said he believed that he should seek an indictment of Wappenstein before a grand jury.[42] At the time, Burns boldly stated to the press that the conviction of Wappenstein would be a "cinch." While holding Gill blameless, the famous detective confidently claimed, "We've got the goods on Wappy."[43] On February 25, the grand jury indicted the former police chief on the charge of accepting a $2,500 bribe for the protection of illegal gambling establishments and houses of prostitution.[44]

From the day of the indictment, rumors circulated regarding who might be responsible for bringing Burns to Seattle. A number of prominent businessmen were mentioned as possibilities, but Matthews's secret was extremely well kept.[45] In April, newspapers reported that Matthews had been seen meeting with the Burns detective, the prosecuting attorney, and the foreman of the grand jury, but still reporters doubted that the pastor of First Presbyterian possessed the financial resources necessary to fund such an operation.[46] Finally, on May 7, 1911, the *Post-Intelligencer* printed Matthews's version of how and why he had brought Burns to the Pacific Northwest. "Many people have been charged erroneously with instituting and backing this campaign and investigation," Matthews said, almost appearing to be trying to save others from being blamed for the campaign.[47] In fact, a number of

The Great Feud

Seattle papers criticized what they perceived to be Matthews's smug self-righteousness.[48] Additional indictments were handed down on May 24, 1911, and the most startling one was against the publisher of the *Seattle Times*, Colonel Alden Blethen, for efforts to protect gambling.[49] However, most attention focused on the trial of Wappenstein, set to begin May 26. Matthews continued to fund the surveillance of Wappenstein right through the trial. The clandestine flavor of this affair appears in the report given to Matthews on May 25. It appears here in the form in which Matthews received it.

C. W. Wappenstein came from his home and went to W. A. Morris office at 8:50 o'clock this A. M. left Morris office at 9:15 A. M. in company with Morris and went to the Court House and gave his additional $20,000 bail. The bail was put up by D. Ham and wife, who own a Dairy Farm and Eugene France a lumberman. He left the Court room at 10:00 A. M. and went to the Italian American Club in company with D. Ham and E. France. He left the club at 12:30 P. M. and went in the Saloon by the side of the Canadian Bank of Commerce, came out of Saloon and went in the Bank at 12:50 P. M. He left the bank at 1 P. M. and went to the Court room where his attorney filed about one hundred affidavits signed by citizens of Seattle, asking for a change of Venue on the grounds that the Newspapers had published so much about Wappenstein that a fair trial was impossible. The attorney for State filed an equal number of affidavits that he could get a fair trial in this county. The motion for a change of Venue was denied. C. W. Wappenstein then filed an affidavit asking to be tried by some other Judge that he couldn't get a fair and impartial trial before Judge Mains on account of Mains being of the same Church and a personal friend of Dr. Matthews. This was denied. Wappenstein left the Court room at 4:25 P. M. and went in a Saloon at 115 James St. He left the Saloon at 4:35 P. M. in company with France and went to the Club at 7 P. M. and went in a Saloon by the side of Canadian Bank of commerce and returned at once to the Club. I didn't see him any more but remained in the vicinity until about 9:30.[50]

From the outset, Wappenstein's attorney protested the influence of Matthews and his church members; not only was the presiding judge, John Main, a member of Matthews's flock, but so too was the foreman of the grand jury, C. W. Corliss. Jury selection was dominated by the defense stipulation that no member of First Presbyterian be chosen.[51]

The Great Feud

By May 30, the jury was sworn in and the prosecution began to present its case. The heart of its argument rested on the testimony of two individuals associated with the vice syndicate—Gideon Tupper and Clarence Gerald. Both gamblers and proprietors of houses of prostitution, Tupper and Gerald testified that they had bribed Wappenstein for the protection of their establishments. The defense attorneys were seeking primarily to establish that Wappenstein's acquisition of $1,000 was the result of his brother-in-law's gift and not a bribe. But more persuasively, the defense argued that Tupper and Gerald were turning against Wappenstein only to make themselves immune from prosecution. The argument raised enough doubt in the minds of the jury that the vote was seven to five for acquittal, and thus the trial ended in a hung jury.[52]

Matthews's specific reaction is not known, but one can safely assume that he was not pleased with the verdict. Whether he personally put pressure on John Murphy to retry the case is uncertain, though he was undoubtedly involved in discussion about doing so. Nonetheless, Murphy did proceed with a retrial that began on June 26, 1911. The defense secured a new judge, J. T. Ronald, who was not a member of First Presbyterian. The cases for and against were essentially the same, as the defense continued to emphasize the motives behind Gerald's and Tupper's testimony, but the final jury instructions from Ronald were noticeably more pointed than Main's had been:

> Truth is truth, no matter how polluted the sources from which it comes. If it is true such a polluted source does not make it false; but if you believe any evidence to be the truth, then you should accept it no matter what methods or means were resorted to procure it, no matter what motives prompted it.[53]

With that, the jury returned a guilty verdict, and Charles Wappenstein was sentenced to three to ten years at the state penitentiary in Walla Walla.

How much direct influence Matthews had with Murphy, Main, or Ronald is unclear. Whether he attempted to persuade them of Wappenstein's guilt is perhaps not the important point. What is crucial is to see this incident in juxtaposition with Matthews's early years, when he attempted to mold Seattle only from his pulpit. By 1910, he believed that he needed various forms of political power to effect change. He worked behind the scenes, analyzed the flow of events, and calculated the risks of public involvement. If Gill and Wappenstein did not fear Matthews's power, they certainly respected the influence of this preacher who was willing to hire private detectives and who had cultivated powerful friends, including C. W. Corliss, John Murphy, and John Main. This was not some wild-eyed cleric but a sophisticated power in his own right who was committed to his vision of a righteous city and who was able to do more than just persuade from the pulpit.

There were many in Seattle who supported Matthews's efforts, including the editor of the *Post-Intelligencer*, Erastus Brainerd, who said in 1910, "The best single individual influence at present exerted in Seattle, is probably that of Mark A. Matthews."[54] Even two years earlier, Bobby Boyce, writing for the *Argus*, depicted rather colorfully Matthews's political influence: "I have seen him jump into politics and ma[k]e Teddy's big stick look like a splinter in a small boy's thumb. I have seen him win over a belligerent chief of police, snap his fingers under the nose of a prosecuting attorney and get away with the goods."[55]

In many ways the events surrounding the Gill-Wappenstein affair must have encouraged Matthews to think about other ways in which he could extend his power and influence. The combination of moral suasion, political organization, and even covert activity seemed to result in the desired outcome. Few other ministers across the country could claim as much influence on the political and social issues of a city the size of Seattle. Yet as Matthews entered the second decade of the twentieth century, the dynamics that allowed him to exercise such influence seemed to be subtly changing. From demographics to middle-class culture, Seattle's context continued to be in flux.

Compared to other cities, Seattle in 1900 was remarkably homogeneous, due largely to its geographic location. Blue-collar jobs, such as logging, fishing, and mining, tended to be outside the downtown region. By 1910, city residents had developed a much greater sense of class awareness, if not class consciousness, than had been the case ten to fifteen years earlier. The upper-class and professional people were separating into nicely secluded neighborhoods, usually with views of Lake Washington or, in the case of the Highlands and Queen Anne Hill, Puget Sound. The skilled working class gravitated toward the Wallingford, Fremont, and Ballard neighborhoods. In terms of political issues, these class distinctions arose over the issue of prohibition, which was generally supported by the middle and upper-middle classes

The Great Feud

and opposed by the working class. Class differences arose in regard to city government, with the upper and middle classes pushing for abolition of the ward system and the working class trying to retain it.[56] Matthews had hoped to temper the influence of the rich, unite the business and skilled working classes, and get the unskilled to accept the values of the middle class. This game plan was increasingly obsolete in a sociological environment with increasing class consciousness, distrust, and fear. At the very least, among the upper and upper-middle classes, the movement to private neighborhoods had what the Seattle historian Roger Sale describes as a somewhat anesthetizing effect. "The ideal of a withdrawn private life makes for comfort, and when best achieved makes for hope, but it can yield indifference to everything outside, and this indifference can cost the community dearly in the way of cohesion, or in a common sense of problems and solutions. To retire is to abdicate."[57] This sense of indifference was exactly what threatened Matthews's status. His vision rested on his ability to convince the middle-class leadership that it needed to do more than simply retire or fight for narrow self-interest.

Matthews's continued influence also depended, in part, on the continued commitment on the part of the middle class to view issues of public policy from primarily moral grounds, thereby allowing ministers like Matthews the authority to speak. In general, there is a variety of evidence to indicate that the middle class perceived many political issues from a moral perspective—prohibition being the most notable. The issue of whether Seattle was to be an open or closed town dominated politics during the first two decades of the twentieth century and in large part was perceived as a moral dilemma. But, as the middle class attempted to deal with the problems of a complex urban environment, emphasis gradually shifted away from seeing these problems from a strictly moral perspective and moved toward an approach that required specialized training. Efficiency and expertise gained acceptance as ideals. Matthews objected neither to these values nor to the idea that the trained expert should be given public authority. What he did not see, however, was that this professionalization ultimately would undermine his authority as a spokesman on public policy. When issues were seen less in moral terms and more as problems of logistics, engineering, or innovation, the minister was relegated simply to the spiritual dimension of life. The institution that fostered this change in middle-class thinking was the state university, and in Seattle, of course, this was the University of Washington.

Until the 1870s, higher education in the United States was dominated by small denominational colleges whose express purpose was the development of moral standards and mental discipline. Operating with a limited curriculum that emphasized classical languages and philosophy, these colleges had small faculties composed primarily of ministers. The professional schools of law, medicine, and ministry did not require a college education for admission. Matthews himself is an excellent example: he was essentially self-taught and was able to pass the Tennessee bar exam and ultimately to practice law in Washington State. However, in the late nineteenth century, due to a number of factors but especially the impact of the forces of industrialization and urbanization, the university began to change its orientation. Scholars began forming professions that claimed expert knowledge of discrete subjects; they also established processes of certification that gave them the right to say who was and who was not a member of their field. Scholars in the social sciences established associations and journals for the purpose of enhancing their professional standing and providing a vehicle for the communication of specialized knowledge. And, perhaps most important in regard to the impact on Matthews's life, scholars saw the university's purpose as the shaping of public policy.[58]

This development at the University of Washington can be clearly seen in the efforts of two university presidents, Thomas Kane and Henry Suzzallo. What can be traced with some precision is the growth of the university under these two presidents and the shift toward specialization and expertise. Thomas Kane was inaugurated in 1902, the same year Matthews arrived in Seattle. At that time, the university had only 650 students and a faculty of 33. By 1914, Kane had worked to increase the enrollment to 2,381, of whom 1,529 were Seattle residents. At the very least, it could be said that more upper-middle- and middle-class students were attending the institution. They were being taught by a faculty that had grown to 194 in 1914 and included J. Allen Smith, a major scholar in political science. Smith wrote numerous articles on Seattle city politics and was active in the Seattle Municipal League.[59]

Smith's success in his profession is not as important as his message—that the middle class could have power if it would educate itself. He said that the trained specialist and not the minister could solve the problems of the inner city, that the trained specialist could end corruption, and that the trained specialist could provide the secrets to sustained prosperity. The university was committed to one notion: leaders must be professionally educated. If and when this notion gained acceptance, the general moralist, and more specifically the minister, would not be as effective as the specialist in public policy.

But Matthews did not easily relinquish power to the university-trained expert. He vigorously defended his role in attempting to shape Seattle's public affairs. His sermons from the pulpit of First Presbyterian continued to thrust him into a number of public events and arenas, but increasingly he understood that this holy war required covert as well as overt action. Matthews's feud with Hiram Gill revealed the larger cultural struggles at work in most American cities during the early twentieth century. The outcome could hardly have seemed certain to the combatants by the time of the First World War. Matthews's belief in the righteousness of his cause willingly encouraged him to employ strategies and tactics that proved objectionable to many parties. Nevertheless, he successfully achieved a level of power and influence that allowed him to remain a central figure in Seattle political and social life for the next three decades.

❧ CHAPTER 7 ❧

"Shall Matthews Run the City?"

The pastors of this city represent more people than all the papers combined, and have not only a human but a divine right to lead the people in all questions of morality, righteousness, virtue and truth.

—Mark Matthews (1914)

Ntional interest in the endeavors of Mark Matthews reached a new peak when, on December 28, 1912, *Collier's Magazine* published a story by Peter Clarke MacFarlane entitled "The Black-Maned Lion of Seattle."[1] MacFarlane traced Matthews's ministerial career and regaled readers with stories of the preacher's encounters with Hiram Gill and Charles Wappenstein. "The man is a born trouble maker, a congenital disturber of the peace," MacFarlane wrote of Matthews. "He troubles his town, he troubles his church, he troubles himself. He can never let well enough alone. He is the best hated, most feared man in Seattle. But also he is the best loved."[2] Matthews's reputation for sensational preaching was enhanced by MacFarlane's colorful depiction of the tall pastor's rhetorical abilities. "It is doubtful if in the American pulpit there is a man more skillful in the arts of public denunciation than Mark Matthews," noted the *Collier's* writer. "Few men can paint black blacker than he. He is a master of smashing similes that stick and scald and burn."[3]

MacFarlane's article epitomized the attention Matthews received throughout the second decade of the twentieth century. During these years, the preacher established himself as a significant force in national Presbyterian circles; he further expanded his role within Seattle politics and developed an important relationship with Woodrow Wilson.

Matthews's success with Gill and Wappenstein encouraged him to attempt to exercise more influence over politicians, police chiefs, and even presidents. This chapter examines his efforts to utilize all of his power in pursuit of his version of a righteous society.

Matthews's battles with Gill and Wappenstein left the preacher with one additional enemy—the publisher of the *Seattle Times*, Colonel Alden Blethen. Blethen deeply resented the fact that in the early months of 1911, Burns detectives, at Matthews's request, had attempted to find incriminating evidence against the head of the *Times*. Burns operatives believed that they could prove that Blethen owned an interest in the Morrison Hotel and the Arcade Dance Hall, where illegal gambling was believed to exist. This information helped the prosecuting attorney John Murphy win an indictment from the grand jury against Blethen for allegedly libeling a city councilman, for conspiring to protect illegal gambling, prostitution, and liquor sales, and for helping to maintain what was described as a "public nuisance," the Arcade Dance Hall. The *Post-Intelligencer* delighted in the dilemma of its chief competitor and printed on its front page a telegram from Blethen to Wappenstein implying the possibilities of a protection racket.[4]

Blethen lashed out at Matthews and his other enemies. "It is because *The Times* would not join this gang of marauders, headed by Dr. Matthews, an elder of whose church is foreman of this grand jury, that Matthews' friends have been determined to get an indictment," he explained to reporters. Blethen also attacked the *P-I* and its editor, Brainerd, for being political and unfair and consequently filed a $100,000 libel suit against the *P-I* for Brainerd's editorial. In the midst of this public hoopla, Matthews had the Burns operatives continue their investigation of Blethen.[5]

The Burns detectives pressed a Tenderloin businessman by the name of Charles Berryman in hopes that he would provide more evidence of Blethen's involvement, but the effort came up empty. Detectives worked closely with the editor of the *P-I* to find additional information but came away with nothing.

Ultimately, the indictment was dismissed for lack of evidence, but Blethen placed the blame for this public spectacle squarely on Matthews's shoulders. On May 28, 1911, the *Times* launched a full-scale attack on Matthews's alleged control of Seattle city politics. Blethen devoted two entire pages to Matthews's career as "Boss" of Seattle. The publisher admitted that he himself had played a role by providing Matthews with space to reprint his sermons. "He was always good

copy.... His sensational pulpit utterances—at first—made good headlines," said Blethen, but he added that he had soon found that the publicity was out of control. The editor traced the highlights of Matthews's
political activity and leveled a stinging indictment of his own:

> From an academic standpoint this new amalgamation of church and
> state—even circumscribed as it is by the boundaries of one city—is
> extremely interesting. Matthews' church—in the broader sense—is
> feeling the wrath of its own members. Business has suffered so se-
> verely from church interference that hundreds of formerly good
> church-going men have been compelled to feel that the new attitude
> of their church means nothing but demoralization and destruction.
> The entire membership of other denominations in Seattle resent
> fiercely the attempt of the Presbyterians to assume political dictator-
> ship. And the end? It is inevitable. Caesar waxed great but he had his
> Brutus. Matthews has reached the very pinnacle of his political power
> and his ministerial fame. His Brutus will come quickly—in the guise
> of Matthews' own overweening political ambition—an ambition sure
> to lay him stark and cold and with all the stab wounds of popular
> disfavor. So far like Caesar. But unlike Caesar—Matthews will be
> forgotten.[6]

Though Blethen's comparison of Matthews with an eastern city
boss, in that same editorial, may have been overstated out of his personal animosity for the preacher, it is indicative of the perception that
many others shared concerning the cleric's role in the city. However,
Blethen's prediction of the preacher's fall missed the mark, for
Matthews had only just entrenched himself in a position from which
he would influence Seattle city politics for many years to come.

Many people believed that Matthews dictated the tone and direction of the administration of George Dilling, the mayor who defeated
Gill in the recall election of 1910. Perceived by some observers as overzealous in the enforcement of restrictions against vice, but seen by most
as the puppet of Matthews, Dilling became the subject himself of a
recall movement. "Dr. M. A. Matthews, the tall Sycamore of the Sier-
ras, is the sole and only issue," the *Argus* reported. "As the Gill recall
was aimed at Wappenstein, so is the Dilling recall aimed at the tall one
with the effervescent nerve. And the war-cry will be, 'Shall Matthews
Run the City?'"[7]

"Shall Matthews Run the City?"

Dilling survived the recall, but more than a few people still harbored doubts about just how separate Matthews's office was from the mayor's. The election of 1912 seemed to blur further any distinction. In February of that year, Matthews plunged into the campaign by once again publicly denouncing Gill, who was attempting a political comeback.

As chairman of the Seattle Ministerial Federation committee on civic righteousness, Matthews claimed that the hotel and liquor interests, as well as seventy percent of the police, favored Gill out of the belief that his reelection would signal the return of protection rackets.[8] Though Matthews's ultimate influence on the election is impossible to gauge, many people saw Gill's defeat, and the election of the longtime reformer George Cotterill, as the product of the preacher's work. "But for Dr. Matthews, George Cotterill would have been defeated," observed one reporter. "Just how clever he is only those who are connected with him know. But he gets away with the stuff."[9]

Just what "stuff" Matthews got away with during the Dilling and Cotterill administrations is impossible to document. It is clear that he pushed hard for the regulation of vice, and when Cotterill's police chief, Claude Bannick, formed the "Purity Squad" in an effort to step up enforcement, Matthews lent his verbal support. When the Purity Squad was opposed by Matthews's friend, parishioner, and city councilman Austin Griffiths for being too zealous, Matthews worked diligently to prevent any restrictive legislation against the police.[10] Mostly the pastor's influence surfaced in the form of advice regarding political appointments or city policy. The Seattle press tended to reinforce the idea that Matthews wielded the most important voice within several administrations, although according to the *Town-Crier*, it was to the detriment of the city:

> Certain it is that Dr. Matthews has never hesitated to use church and congregation to inspire in seekers of office, great and petty, an extraordinary desire for his personal favor and fear of his personal wrath. He has forced himself into every political argument that has taken place since he came to the city. He has demanded of every candidate for every office specific answers to lists of arbitrary questions prepared by himself—not by the officers of his church or the people of his congregation, but by Matthews the man. He has done all in his power to thwart the wishes of those who have resented his arrogant interference, and he has never turned a hand to help those whose answers—had the ques-

"Shall Matthews Run the City?"

tions been put in good faith—should have been most satisfactory. In politics he has always been an unfair inter-meddler, desiring only to create a profound impression of his personal power.[11]

The second ten years of Matthews's tenure in the Pacific Northwest found the preacher resorting to a variety of methods to build and wield his personal power. From his pulpit, he criticized and cajoled Seattleites into accepting his ideas and conforming with a prescribed behavior. The campaign of 1912 revealed that he had attempted to galvanize the Seattle Ministerial Federation, which comprised a significant number of Christian ministers in the city, to further his political and social agenda. For years this organization had actively supported interdenominational cooperation. But, beginning in the second decade of the twentieth century, it began to espouse more specific political positions.

In 1912, Matthews convinced the federation to put its weight behind a specific list of candidates, much as First Presbyterian traditionally had done. Controversy surfaced almost immediately, however, when the list of candidates for the fall election failed to include the name of Judge John Main, who had presided over Charles Wappenstein's first trial, which ended in a hung jury. Main's absence created a public stir; many pundits thought that Matthews purposely excluded Main because of the preacher's displeasure with the first Wappenstein verdict. The great protest forced Matthews to respond before the federation; he indicated that an error had been made and that, indeed, Main's name should have been included.[12] The *Post-Intelligencer* attacked the federation for bungling the affair, and a number of people were unconvinced by Matthews's explanation of the omission and believed he was purposely sending up a trial balloon. "Dr. Matthews seeks to close the incident, after bungling, crude and transparent efforts to cover up the broad evidences of his personal malice and uncharitableness," said the *Town-Crier*. "Dr. Matthews intended to 'get' Judge Main. . . . Dr. Matthews does nothing except for a purpose. He knew, if no one else did, just what was in the ministerial report."[13] The *Town-Crier* was probably right.

As indicated previously, Matthews frequently felt the need to assert the cultural authority of the clergy, and of course, by implication, of himself. On more than one occasion Matthews's thoughts must have turned to Calvin's Geneva and seventeenth-century New England, where the ministers' status as leaders was widely accepted and their

"Shall Matthews Run the City?"

will directly reflected through political candidates. Perhaps with his Puritan forefathers in mind, he told Seattle voters just who he believed should run the city. "Who gave a few men who may own a press the right to dictate the policy of the city?" Matthews asked. "The pastors of this city represent more people than all the papers combined, and have not only a human but a divine right to lead the people in all questions of morality, righteousness, virtue and truth."[14] To foster the power of the preachers, Matthews, in 1912, called for the development of the King County Evangelical Ministers' Congress. "The province . . . shall be to discuss, legislate and handle all moral, civic righteousness, educational and literary work belonging to, evolving from or in any way vitally connected with ministers."[15]

Although Matthews did not abandon collective action when the congress failed to materialize, he felt more comfortable and more effective operating alone. He involved himself in almost any issue of his choosing. For example, he felt responsible for reviewing the possible pardon of Charles Wappenstein. Pressure for Wappenstein's release had been generated by members of the Seattle press shortly after the former police chief's incarceration in the Walla Walla penitentiary. However, Governor Ernest Lister felt obliged to solicit Matthews's approval before he would consider Wappenstein's release. Indeed, it was the pastor who set the conditions for Wappenstein's pardon: he recommended that for one year the former police chief be allowed to live anywhere but in the city of Seattle. Lister agreed with Matthews's stipulation, and Wappenstein chose to live on a family farm near Lake Sammamish, about ten miles east of Seattle.[16]

A much riskier form of political involvement arose for Matthews in 1912, when Seattle experienced several serious outbursts of violence involving one of the most radical labor groups in the country, the Industrial Workers of the World, better known as the Wobblies. The first serious incident took place during a May Day parade in 1912. Seattle's ardent patriots, led by Colonel Blethen, expressed outrage that Mayor Cotterill tolerated soapbox orators who denounced the American flag. Blethen argued that the mayor had threatened the safety of all citizens by allowing the Wobblies to speak.[17] Matthews, much to his credit, quickly came to Cotterill's defense and attempted to make distinctions among radical groups. "The I.W.W.'s are not Socialists, and the Socialists are not I.W.W.'s, though there are members of both classes in both organizations," Matthews told his congregation. "The flag incident was not for the purpose of punishing I.W.W.'s. The stars and stripes were used for dirty political ends to bring disturbance and odium upon the present administration."[18]

The following summer witnessed an even larger controversy over the mayor's handling of a violent incident during Potlatch, Seattle's annual summer festival. Josephus Daniels, secretary of the navy, had arrived in Seattle with a few thousand sailors as part of the ceremonies for the opening of the Panama Canal. During their visit, near the waterfront, a brief scuffle occurred between a woman socialist, three sailors, and a Seattle resident. The next day, Alden Blethen, in his *Seattle Times*, portrayed the incident as an event in which "a gang of red flag worshippers and anarchists were brutally beating two blue-jackets and three soldiers who had dared protest against the insults heaped upon the American flag."[19] Blethen's description apparently helped spur a crowd, the following evening, into sacking the I.W.W. office, looting socialist headquarters, and overturning various printing presses. Mayor Cotterill condemned the action and appealed to Seattle's citizens to act responsibly. He called up reserve firemen to help monitor the city and ordered the chief of police to prevent any copies of the *Seattle Times* from being delivered, since he blamed Blethen for inciting the riot. Again, Matthews rushed to Cotterill's defense and tried to convince people that the Wobblies' right to free speech had to be protected. "We cannot do away with free speech, for if we do, we will shortly find ourselves in the position of asking that it be reestablished," Matthews argued, although he ignored Cotterill's shutting down of the *Seattle Times*. "The law's provision is a prison term for anyone who vilifies the flag or makes seditious utterance. This seems to have been lost sight of in the agitation against the I.W.W. as a body."[20] But Matthews seemed to want it both ways. While quick to defend Cotterill, he urged his congregation in a sermon entitled "Free Speech and Its Possibilities" to be vigilant against libel, sedition, and blasphemy:

> Therefore, it is ridiculous, and more than asinine for you to wage your war against free speech. If you are really patriotic, honest, loyal, righteous and true, take down stenographically the utterances of men who may be anarchistic, seditious, blasphemous and depraved. Get the names and addresses of two witnesses who may be standing by you at the time the man makes the blasphemous or seditious statements. Apply for a warrant and bring the felon into court, convict him, make him suffer the penalty for his crime, and, if he is an unnaturalized citizen, deport him.[21]

"Shall Matthews Run the City?"

In spite of Matthews's somewhat ambivalent response to the incident, Cotterill was determined to go after Blethen. The mayor went to the *Post-Intelligencer* to explain what had happened. Cotterill related that in May 1911, while he had been in the publisher's office, Blethen had reached into his desk and retrieved two clearly doctored photographs of Mark Matthews and the prosecuting attorney John Murphy. "With singular boldness he forced upon my attention two disgraceful photographs," said Cotterill, "bearing the heads of the two gentlemen upon human figures in indescribably loathsome relations."[22] The mayor charged that Blethen lacked a basic sense of decency and was willing to go to most any length to distort the truth if it served his purposes. The mayor's charges against the publisher brought further criticism from other newspapers of Blethen's methods. Pressed for an explanation of the 1911 incident, Blethen recalled that the Matthews-funded Burns investigation had led to his own earlier indictment for owning an establishment where illegal gambling was believed to take place. Even though the indictment had been dropped, Blethen charged that Matthews and Burns had planned to use doctored photographs if the case came to trial; in response, Blethen had his own doctored photographs made to prove how easy the process was. But because the charges were dismissed, Blethen never displayed the photographs publicly, though he did show them privately to people like Cotterill. Blethen's explanation received little sympathy from the public, and the newsman was forced to weather continued criticism.[23]

Matthews refused to become involved in the charges and counter-charges; he maintained an aloof posture in the face of a very emotional situation. But in a larger sense, the publicity associated with the Potlatch and photograph incidents continued to demonstrate how seriously Matthews was regarded as a public figure.

Perhaps less serious, but no less indicative of Matthews's wide-ranging influence, was his willingness to speak out in the controversy surrounding Mount Rainier. Periodically, Tacoma residents expressed a desire to change the mountain's name to "Tahoma," thus fostering a running battle between journalists of Seattle and Tacoma over the merits of each name. On one occasion in late 1915, Matthews publicly stated that, though he believed there might be some justification for the name change, Tacoma residents could do nothing about it. Once again, the local press felt that they must respond to Matthews's opinions. Seattle newspapers agreed with Matthews, while one Tacoma weekly devoted an entire issue to "The Shame of One Seattle Pulpit," in which the editorialist lambasted Matthews. "There he stood, the pastor of the First Presbyterian Church, resisting the onward and upward movement," wrote the editor of *What's Doing*. But the editor also confirmed Matthews's standing in the Seattle community. "I am convinced that this one man could have brought the quarrel to an end. Such, I believe is his influence over there in Seattle."[24] Matthews was undoubtedly the last Seattle pastor to be consulted on such an entirely secular affair as the name of a mountain. The incident attests to the highly visible position that he had attained during his second ten years in the city.

This visibility and influence encouraged Matthews to continue to articulate his vision of an empire in the Pacific Northwest and of moral righteousness for his city. He urged his congregation to increase its power and establish its domain in unparalleled ways. "You have been a power in the purification of your city, and in the construction of this Western empire," Matthews told his people. But he added that they must think in ever-larger terms and suggested that their backs were to the Rockies and their feet were in the Pacific, with their arms stretched along the Pacific coast, bidding the Orient to come.[25]

Many of the specifics of that vision during Matthews's second ten years remained consistent with the objectives that he had expressed during the first ten years. He continued to urge Seattle residents to authorize money for public improvements, although he spoke less frequently. "Our cities need perfect sanitation . . . ; [they] need public baths, comfort stations, playgrounds, recreation parks and outdoor amusements," Matthews said in 1912. He called for restrictions on tenement housing and the construction of more public auditoriums.[26] As a member of Seattle's Municipal League, Matthews remained politically active in the movement for political reform. Specifically, he pressured voters and civic leaders to enact the commission form of government.

In 1914, Seattle voters approved a plan for freeholders to formulate a new city charter and, in an advisory vote, favored a commission form of government. However, the charter submitted by the freeholders centered on the city-manager system and not the commission form. As a result, Matthews opened his own campaign through the newspapers in an attempt to defeat the proposed reform in the July election. He criticized the city-manager concept and opposed the charter's reduction of mayoral power.

His opposition to the city-manager system is interesting, given his generally favorable attitude toward Progressive legislation. Several key leaders opposed the proposal, including the former mayor John Miller,

"Shall Matthews Run the City?"

George Cotterill, and, perhaps most notably, J. D. Ross, head of Seattle City Light and a parishioner of Matthews's.[27] Perhaps Matthews also feared that he might not have as much personal influence over a city manager as he had had over Seattle's mayors. At the very least, he expressed his concern that the mayor would simply be a figurehead. "In other words, he is to be an ornamental dummy, with the exception of the duty of presiding over the council and appointing the chief of police," Matthews argued. "The manager is to be the real czar, the real head, and the real director of the city."[28] In late March 1914, Matthews debated one of the freeholders, Josiah Collins, in a series of articles in the *Post-Intelligencer*.[29] The voters agreed with Matthews, J. D. Ross, and George Cotterill, as well as with organized labor, which opposed the concept, and defeated the charter.[30]

Matthews's civic vision continued to focus on vice control. Specifically, Matthews during this period stepped up his lifelong fight for the prohibition of alcohol. As early as 1905, First Presbyterian had employed one of the most vigorous prohibitionists in the region, E. B. Sutton, to speak on the street corners of Seattle.[31] Matthews continued his personal campaign against alcohol and frequently proposed the coffeehouse as a substitute for the tavern. Approximately eighty years ahead of its time, the idea of the coffeehouse appealed to Matthews as a possible alternative for the saloon-goer.

> The coffee house substitute for the saloon is not intended as a hoboes' resort nor a pauperizing institution. It is a legitimate, respectable place for any man who desires to enter, read the papers, study the magazines, inform himself on current literature and write a letter home to his aged mother, who anxiously watches the footsteps of the coming and going postman for some tidings of her lost boy.[32]

Even though Matthews consciously phrased the idea to attract middle-class support, it failed to do so. However, in November 1914, Seattle residents had an opportunity, along with the rest of the state, to go dry, and Matthews actively campaigned for the measure. The interest in the issue was so intense that, according to the historian Norman Clark, 94.6 percent of eligible voters participated in the election, a state record that still stands. And in this election, prohibitionists scored a resounding victory.[33]

On January 1, 1916, the state went dry, and Seattle was soon advertised by the Anti-Saloon League as the largest dry city in the world outside of Russia.[34] Ironically, the mayor responsible for enforcing the dry law was Hiram Gill. Gill, running on a platform of repentance, had been given a second chance in 1914 by Seattle voters, and he had added considerable credibility to his claim of reform by appointing a prohibitionist, Austin Griffiths, as police chief. Matthews, not easily convinced of the depth of Gill's reform, had counseled Griffiths not to take the job. Nevertheless, Griffiths accepted and returned, along with Gill, to the task of enforcing prohibition.[35]

Gill tackled his assignment with great vigor. Often appearing in shirt-sleeves with an ax in hand, Gill helped the Dry Squad demolish drugstores that were illegally selling alcohol. Cheered on by most of the radical reformers, Gill, however, could not allay Matthews's fears that the mayor remained among the unconverted. In late January 1916, Matthews unexpectedly criticized the police for being overzealous in their raids on private homes and private clubs, such as the Rainier Club, of which Matthews was a member. Whether the preacher was receiving pressure from his wealthier friends is difficult to say, but he claimed that the wet forces were behind the raids in an attempt to make the law look bad.[36]

Generally, however, Matthews seemed satisfied with the effect of the law and its enforcement, as were many of Seattle's civic leaders. Norman Clark pointed out the number of former opponents who switched positions after they saw the social benefits that could be derived from its enforcement.[37] Support for the law continued to gather momentum throughout the summer of 1916 and culminated in a mass meeting called by the ministers' federation on August 13. Thirty-five hundred people came to hear Governor Ernest Lister, Mayor Gill, James Duncan of the Seattle Central Labor Council, and Mark Matthews urge compliance with the law and support for its enforcement. "Law is supreme," stated Matthews in the form of a public resolution. "The people must respect and obey the law."[38]

However, Matthews's prestige and power suffered a minor setback during 1917, when he became publicly involved with two trials concerning alleged police protection. The first trial took place in March 1917 and rocked the town, because the defendants were Mayor Hiram Gill, Police Chief Charles Beckingham (who had replaced Griffiths), and King County Sheriff Robert Hodge. All three had been implicated in a protection racket by Logan Billingsley, a Seattle bootlegger. Billingsley, after his arrest, confessed that he had paid Gill money for protection; as a result of his admission, the grand jury quickly returned

"Shall Matthews Run the City?"

the indictments.[39]

The prosecution relied primarily on the testimony of Billingsley until it shocked the city by calling Mark Matthews to the stand. The preacher previously had been subpoenaed by the defense, but now he was asked to corroborate Billingsley's testimony. In typically dramatic fashion, Matthews recited a series of events extending back to July 1916, when he had first met Logan Billingsley in his church. At that time, the bootlegger had pleaded with the preacher not to blame the Billingsley brothers for the shooting deaths of two policemen in a gun battle outside a warehouse. While acceding to Billingsley's request, Matthews had then attempted to convince the bootlegger to go straight and help clean up the illegal operations. Consequently, in August Matthews received $1,000 from Billingsley and Clarence Gerald, another bootlegger, for the purpose of cleaning up the city. Matthews explained that he had used the money to facilitate the Dry Squad's work and to hire the Burns Detective Agency again for further investigation. By September, the pastor explained to the jury, he believed that Billingsley had not reformed. He confronted the bootlegger with the rumor that he had paid Gill $7,500 for protection. According to Matthews, Billingsley neither confirmed nor denied the rumor, and so the Seattle minister went to Gill. The mayor flatly denied that money had changed hands but did admit, according to Matthews, that he had met with Billingsley on one occasion. Though not as convincing as the prosecution had hoped, Matthews's testimony seemed, in the eyes of many, to implicate Gill.[40]

At the time of his testimony, Matthews believed that some type of compromise had been reached at the end of August 1916 between Billingsley and Gill. Though he had no direct evidence, the preacher believed that this compromise explained why Billingsley went back into the bootlegging business. However, further testimony revealed that Billingsley had attempted to frame Gill by purposely lying to Matthews about the protection scheme. Amid charges and counter-charges of perjury, the trial degenerated into a circus, with the end result that all three defendants were acquitted. Matthews appeared to be an innocent pawn, but the incident did little to increase his prestige in the Seattle community.[41]

Matthews, however, was playing hardball by 1916; he decided to finance a phony gambling operation in order to try and uncover police corruption. Burns detectives kept him regularly informed of clandestine operations. "We have received the word from gamblers, people who are running gambling houses, bootleggers and even policemen that there will be nothing doing until after the Grand Jury has adjourned," Matthews was told. "We propose to open a gambling house for which we have prepared; we will pay protection money for which we have prepared; we will pay protection money . . . then insist upon paying the money to someone higher up so that we will know absolutely that we are getting the protection for which we are paying . . . until if possible we are able to pay directly to the Chief or to the Mayor's Secretary."[42]

Using evidence provided by Matthews, prosecutors brought charges in June 1917 against a prominent Seattle police officer, Mike Powers, for taking a bribe for the protection of a gambling operation. Ultimately, the jury acquitted Powers, and Matthews received considerable criticism when reporters disclosed that he had been responsible for setting up the operation. "Dr. Matthews is going entirely too far," said the *Argus*. "Is it the province of a minister of the gospel to operate a resort where young men may be tempted to gamble away possibly their pilferings from their employers, in order that a public official may be tempted to be a crook?"[43] Occasional criticism aside, Matthews continued to be perceived by most Seattle residents as extraordinarily influential.

Mark Matthews's relationship with Woodrow Wilson, during this period, enhanced this perception even more. The Seattle preacher's attempts to lobby presidents had begun a few years earlier, with William Howard Taft. Never intimidated by the office or the occupant, Matthews always spoke his mind. "I am frank to say that the first twelve or fourteen months of your administration did not impress me favorably with your work as an executive, and that was because I was not familiar with the impediments that were persistently thrown in your way," Matthews wrote Taft in 1910. "That opinion has been entirely dissipated and I believe you are doing conscientious, faithful, constructive, and permanent work." In the same letter, Matthews elaborated on his rather interesting views regarding Theodore Roosevelt and the prospects for the Progressive Party.

The attitude of your predecessor in the last few months is extremely unfortunate, undignified and dangerous. In fact, his utterances in the last few months make him the most dangerous man in public life. I wish he would do the only thing left for him to do, namely step out of

"Shall Matthews Run the City?"

the party and ask his followers to assist him in making a new party. He would then be eliminated and the insane enthusiast who may be following would also be eliminated. It would be a great benefit to this country. In fact the time has come for a new alignment of the parties. The old-time, constitutional gold-standard Democrats and the old-time, constitutional Federal Republicans could come together and form a party that might be called the "Conservatives"; and, into the other party could be put the Socialists, the Radicals, the insanes, the Progressives and all political riff-raff of this country and call them the "Progressives." Then we could go before the people on the issue of sanity and insanity.[44]

Clearly Matthews hoped to win favor with Taft by appealing to the president's political leanings. Matthews would make a habit over the next few years of doing all that he could to draw as close as possible to the highest levels of political power in the land.

By 1912, Matthews had emerged as a national figure within the Presbyterian church. In that year, the Presbyterian General Assembly elected Matthews moderator, the church's highest elected position. His rise within the national church will be discussed in a subsequent chapter, but it is important to note here because it provided him with the opportunity to meet Woodrow Wilson, himself a Southern Presbyterian. Invited for the presidential inauguration in March 1913, Matthews quickly concluded that he might try to influence Wilson to direct some of the "pork barrel" Seattle's way.[45]

By the time Wilson reached the White House, Matthews must have felt confident that good times were ahead. And the Seattle pastor soon used his relationship with the president for political purposes. On more than one occasion, people ranging from the territorial governor of Alaska to generals in the United States Army channeled requests to Wilson through Matthews. For example, Seattle Mayor Ole Hanson asked the preacher to aid the Hanson-led delegation in its search for federal money for hydroelectric projects. "The last thing he said before boarding his train," Hanson's secretary wrote Matthews, "was that I plead his cause to you and to ask if you would so greatly assist him and Seattle as to wire someone in Washington, stating generally that Seattle needs the right to develop more power immediately for war industries."[46]

Matthews's standing with the Wilson administration led other local officials to use the preacher as a reference. On one occasion, William Short, president of the Washington Federation of Labor, and Robert Proctor, president of the Seattle Central Labor Council, wrote Wilson concerning mismanagement of the Alaskan railroad and asked him to check with Matthews. "We have been informed by members of congress within the last week that the republican national committee has in its possession [a] mass of documents showing criminal waste in expenditure for the Alaska railroad," Short and Proctor wrote Wilson. "We understand that the Rev. Mark A. Matthews can confirm above facts by material obtained by his own investigation."[47]

Indeed, during the years prior to America's entry into the First World War, Matthews seems to have been highly respected not only by the president but also by his cabinet members. Considered a loyal follower of Wilson, Matthews could expect to receive at least a hearing on nearly all of the issues he raised. "I want to call your attention to the enclosed telegram from Rev. Dr. Matthews of Seattle, who is one of the most eloquent and brilliant men in the United States," wrote Secretary of the Interior Franklin Lane to Attorney General A. Mitchell Palmer in 1919.[48]

The president frequently wrote personal notes to Matthews as well as responded to him through his secretary, Joseph Tumulty. "I want you to know how real a comfort it was to me to get your telegram of sympathy," Wilson wrote Matthews in 1914 on the occasion of his first wife's death. "It is very delightful to feel the warm touch of a friend's hand at such a time, and your message has served to give me strength and courage."[49] The president expressed to other cabinet members his high regard for the Seattle preacher. "I became interested in the case," Wilson wrote his first attorney general, T. W. Gregory, "because it was presented to me by the Reverend Doctor Matthews of Seattle, a man of high character and fine spirit."[50] On a few occasions, Wilson solicited Matthews's opinion on an issue. "I need not tell you that anything that comes from you has great weight with me, and my first impulse was to acquiesce at once to your suggestion," the president wrote Matthews in 1916.[51]

Matthews's ability to gain Wilson's ear was apparently the key factor in the appointment of William Parry, a Seattle businessman, to the first Federal Trade Commission in early 1915.[52] Earlier, Matthews had been involved in a bitter fight over the Seattle postmaster position and had succeeded in having his candidate appointed. However, his greatest plum for Seattle came in 1916, when, after eighteen months of

"Shall Matthews Run the City?"

struggle, the city was named the western immigration port of entry. Up until that time, immigrants could come through Vancouver, British Columbia, and enter the United States at any of a number of points. But Matthews argued persuasively for Seattle's interest to Secretary of Labor W. B. Wilson and recommended the following:

First, to order immediately that all orientals coming to the United States shall enter the United States at some Pacific coast water port of entry, there to be received, passed, entered, or rejected. This can be done without notice to the Canadian transportation companies. Canada has such a rule and she does not permit any oriental to enter her borders unless said oriental enters by a Canadian water port of entry. Why not the United States be just as fair to herself and to her citizens and their interests[;] Second, in the interest of economy and better enforcement of the immigration laws, abolish the Vancouver office and consolidate it with the Seattle office[;] Third, put all immigration situations west of the Rocky mountains in the Seattle office[;] Fourth, urge Congress to build an adequate immigration building in Seattle.[53]

By August 23, 1916, Matthews's proposal had received approval, and Seattle was named the immigration point of entry.[54] In the same year, Matthews urged Wilson to appoint Judge J. T. Ronald, the judge who had presided over the second Wappenstein trial, to replace Charles Evans Hughes on the United States Supreme Court, but obviously in this case Matthews failed to make a compelling case to the president.[55]

But Matthews's tendency to dominate relationships and to try and influence people in power led him occasionally to overstep the fine line between trusted confidant and annoying meddler. His problems with the Wilson administration tended to increase after America's entry into the First World War. For example, shortly after having Vice President Thomas Marshall dine at his home, the preacher wrote Marshall and told him to direct other cabinet members to heed Matthews's advice concerning the enforcement of war-time regulations.[56] "Please say to Mr. Baker Secretary of War and to Mr. Daniels Secretary of the Navy that I am trying to help them," Matthews wrote Marshall. "Ask them to listen to me because I would not make a suggestion to be unbeneficial. They may be bombarded with telegrams to lift the bans and to let the crooks loose and go free. Ask them to please let me be heard. In other words tell them to please let me help them by listening to what I say."[57] It is difficult to imagine Marshall being quick to respond to such a directive.

Matthews pushed exceedingly hard for a person in whom he believed, and this led him to misconstrue into promises statements by Wilson's cabinet. On more than one occasion, people with whom he corresponded denied that they had said what Matthews claimed. "You have greatly exaggerated my promise as to Mr. Ballaine," Franklin Lane wrote Matthews. "I am not 'in covenant with you to make Mr. Daniels put him into the Alaskan coal field.' I expressly told you so."[58]

By 1918, Matthews had lost some of his influence with the Wilson administration. Although still respected as a loyal supporter, the Seattle pastor increasingly began to irritate key advisors to the president. For example during World War I Matthews had become a strong supporter of General H. A. Greene of Camp Lewis, located just south of Tacoma. When Greene was dismissed, Matthews's heated response led Wilson to question the preacher's judgment. "The Reverend Doctor Matthews, who sends the enclosed telegram," Wilson wrote his secretary of war, Newton Baker, "is a very excitable and not a very wise person, but he is a live wire in all matters of patriotic action, and I know his heart is thoroughly with us."[59]

By 1920, Matthews had realized that the favors of Washington, D.C., were slow in coming to Washington State. "The fact that you have made no appointments in the state of Washington in the last few years is hurting us very much," Matthews curtly wrote Wilson.[60] The preacher's frustration reached its highest level in October 1920, when his intense lobbying effort to place a Seattle resident on the shipping board failed. "In refusing our reasonable request to appoint Captain J. S. Gibson on the Shipping Board," Matthews wrote Wilson, "you have without cause violently wounded justice, judgment and true friendship."[61]

The frustration expressed by Matthews in his letter to Wilson was indicative of much more than disappointment over the rejection of a recommendation. Undoubtedly, the Seattle preacher was venting anger that had been building for a number of years over the general course of political events. Matthews's world in 1920 was distinctly different from the one in which he lived prior to the First World War, and he could not have been very pleased with the changes. Events had diminished his optimistic faith in progress, altered his theological emphasis, and made him politically more conservative. It is necessary now to look more closely at the impact of the First World War on Mark Matthews.

　　　　　　　　　"Shall Matthews Run the City?"

CHAPTER 8

The Great War and the General Strike

*Please do not discuss peace any more. The infamous forces
against which we are contending must be crushed. We do
not want peace until they are crushed. We do not want
them to break. We want to strike them down. Prophecy is
clear on this question.*
       —Mark Matthews to Woodrow Wilson (1918)

W hen the United States entered the First
World War, the titanic struggle between the Allies and the Central Powers had degenerated into hideous trench warfare sending thousands
upon thousands of young men to their deaths. America's entry promised the possibility of an end to this horrible conflict. But while the
battlefield impact of America's 1917 entrance was uncertain, there was
no question that the declaration of war drastically changed the way
that most Americans understood the meaning and purpose of the conflict. Certainly, the debates over preparedness had failed to unite the
country, and Woodrow Wilson had won reelection primarily because
he had kept Americans out of war. But by January 1917, when Germany resumed unrestricted submarine warfare against the United
States, it became apparent that America could avoid the conflict no
longer.

Church leaders all over the country faced the task of interpreting
the meaning of the war through their respective faiths. For the most
part, Protestant and Catholic leaders as well as the Federal Council of
Churches had supported Wilson's policy of neutrality. But war itself
presented a host of difficulties, not the least of which were the moral

conflicts associated with combat. Just weeks before asking Congress for the declaration of war, Woodrow Wilson expressed his fears to a journalist that war might mean "that we should lose our heads along with the rest and stop weighing right and wrong" and that "the spirit of ruthless brutality will enter into the very fibre of our national life, infecting Congress, the courts, the policeman on the beat, the man in the street."[1]

According to the historian John Piper, three Protestant positions emerged during the first summer after America's entry into the war. A number of clergy and parishioners chose pacifism, which objected to all participation in war and understood war as evil. Many, however, including Mark Matthews, took a much more militant position. Matthews and others believed that victory in the world war could bring righteousness; the First World War was interpreted as a holy crusade. And still others took a middle position that focused on wartime ministries and sought not to condemn either war or the enemy.[2]

The First World War helped exacerbate anxieties that had been building among many people throughout the country for several years prior to the outbreak of the war itself. Some Seattleites, like the Reverend Sydney Strong, a Congregationalist, and his activist daughter Anna Louise Strong, came to believe that capitalism was seriously flawed, as did the labor leader Hulet Wells and the lawyer George Vanderveer. They and others argued that the American system needed serious reform in order to progress and prosper. But Matthews responded differently. After the Gill and Wappenstein affair, Matthews became obsessively concerned with legal authority and his own power. Specifically, Matthews moved in a much more conservative direction in the years prior to and immediately after World War I. He simply refused to tolerate most groups and individuals that would not accept his view of Christianity, his view of Seattle, his view of economics, and his view of America. He wanted to rid his community of anyone who did not share his opinions.

In regard to Matthews's relationship to the middle class, two developments took shape during these years. First, the Seattle preacher felt compelled to abandon the notion that labor could adopt middle-class values. In turn, spokespersons for the middle class demanded that religious leaders denounce radicalism and support capitalism. Second, Matthews believed that the world war made patriotism essential. Nationalism and, more specifically, Americanism became the holy creed that the middle class required. Matthews embraced more drastic measures in his fight for righteousness; his holy war against Germans, his blistering attack against Christian "liberals," and his battle against alien thinkers—all reflected a growing intolerance and, more important, the sense that he no longer believed consensus could be achieved. He abandoned the notion that just the right sermon or just the right pressure, properly applied, could bring the lost sheep into the fold. Consequently, he shifted his energies from supporting constructive legislation associated with Progressivism to advocating more exclusivist legislation aimed at destroying what he believed were demonic forces. The First World War fostered these tendencies, and the radical labor movement in the Pacific Northwest deepened his suspicions of anyone who sought too much change.

Matthews's concern for American foreign policy can be traced back to the Spanish-American War and his blistering attacks on McKinley's policies. Once Wilson became president, Matthews took a renewed interest in the affairs of the world. He publicly supported the president's controversial Mexican policy and argued that the United States should take disarmament seriously. "The disarmament of the world is the work and duty of the Christian Church. . . . Peace is blighted by the preparation for war," he told his congregation in 1913. He deplored the fact that the world had spent $60 million for navies and only $24 million for missions during the previous year. "There was never a more damnable sentence uttered than the sentence, 'In time of peace prepare for war.'"[3]

Once the war in Europe began in August 1914, Matthews quickly fell in line and supported every aspect of Wilson's foreign policy. He strongly endorsed American neutrality from the outset of the war, and, as president of the Seattle Ministerial Federation in 1915, Matthews presented a resolution calling for nonalignment:

Resolved, by the citizens of Seattle of every creed and nationality in mass meeting assembled:
1) That we deplore the existing conflict as an offense against civilization and a crime against mankind.
2) That we rejoice in the strongly expressed position of this country's neutrality.[4]

As late as May 1915, in Billings, Montana, Matthews told an audience that preparation for war brought war. "In time of war prepare for peace. We have prepared for war so assiduously that we have brought on wars. There are always plenty of people subject to being stirred up and there is always more than enough to do the stirring. This is a time for calm cool judgment, not a time to become excited."[5] His belief that Wilson was exercising cool judgment was exceedingly strong given that the secretary of state William Jennings Bryan—whom Matthews knew very well and with whom the Seattle preacher had much in common—resigned in protest of Wilson's policies in 1915. Matthews, though, never wavered in his support of the president.[6]

As public criticism of Wilson increased, Matthews dug in his heels and supported the president with greater resolve. In 1916, the Seattle preacher organized the Washington branch of the League to Enforce Peace. William Howard Taft, national president of the league, had written Matthews asking him to organize key Seattle leaders. Matthews convinced Professor Edmond S. Meany of the University of Washington, the Reverend Dr. Herbert Gowen, and General Hiram Chittenden to join him. Matthews was elected president of the local chapter, which had as its stated purpose supporting the actions of nations "against any state which breaks the peace before resorting to arbitration or conciliation."[7]

Once Wilson asked Congress to declare war on Germany in April 1917, Matthews quickly extended his support to the president. On April 5, the minister sent a public telegram to Wilson, offering to help in any capacity, as a "chaplain, in bureau office, in the trenches, on top of a ship or in a stoke-hole."[8]

Without hesitation, Matthews accepted Wilson's rationale for the war. Matthews literally viewed the war as a holy crusade in defense of Americanism and an extension of the democratic experiment. In his sermons and newspaper interviews, the Seattle preacher urged total devotion to the war effort and advocated merciless treatment for any who opposed it.

> Americans must believe . . . that we are going to establish universal liberty and representative government throughout the world [and] that we do not want peace until it comes as the result of absolute righteousness after the accomplishment of our purposes. We would not accept peace if it were offered to us by the Kaiser and his allies. . . . We are not fighting for peace. We are fighting for righteousness. . . . We will not submit to any qualifying word before the word, 'American.' The people of this country must be Americans, whole-hearted,

The Great War and the General Strike

and they must be absolutely loyal. We should take into consideration the danger to this country through Vladivostok. Thousands of our enemies may pour into this country in the guise of Russians. . . . They may plant themselves as German spies and agents of the German government.[9]

Prior to 1917, Matthews emphasized Christianity's commitment to peace; he now stressed its relationship to righteousness and the necessity of fighting for it. "Christianity does not invite war, does not seek war, does not want war," he argued. "Christianity does not teach Christians to be cowards; it does not teach them to run."[10] Clearly for Matthews, righteousness was cloaked in American patriotism.

By May 1917, Matthews had organized all the men of his church who had been exempted from the military into what he called the Home Guard. Its primary purpose seemed to be satisfying the patriotic urges of men like himself by having regular meetings and offering encouragement to members to be ever-vigilant for traitors.[11]

The war reinforced Matthews's belief that vice needed to be carefully controlled in order to protect soldiers stationed at Seattle's Fort Lawton and Tacoma's Camp Lewis. On numerous occasions, he wrote Wilson in an effort to have the zones prohibiting prostitution and alcohol enlarged. Overall, he approved of General H. A. Greene's emphasis on controlling vice among military personnel, and Matthews expressed great concern when General Greene was demoted and sent to the Philippines. Matthews pleaded with the president to have Greene reinstated, because he believed that the general was the only one capable of enforcing the restrictions. "The foreign elements—the I.W.W. forces, the vice syndicate fiends, the pro-German element, and the German spies in this section—are rejoicing at the removal and demotion of General Greene," Matthews wrote Wilson in 1918.[12]

In 1918, Matthews delivered a speech in San Francisco before the Associated Advertising Clubs of the World. He praised Wilson for his decision to commit America to the conflict and stressed the moral differences between the two sides. "Germany is fighting to make the world safe for Demonocracy—America is fighting to make the world safe for Democracy," Matthews charged. At length he condemned America's enemies at home and asserted that the only fair treatment for them was "eternal imprisonment or ignominious death."[13] He was so pleased with his rhetoric that he persuaded Washington's United States senator, Wesley Jones, to read the speech into the Congressional Record.[14]

The Great War and the General Strike   143

Although many clergy throughout the country took a more temperate view of the war than did Matthews, it is clear that others were at least as stridently pro-war as the Seattle preacher. One historian has described in detail the vehemence with which many prominent clergy, including Billy Sunday, Newell Dwight Hillis, Charles Eaton, and Lyman Abbott, attacked Germany and exhorted their audiences to view the conflict as a holy cause. "I tell you it is Bill against Woodrow, Germany against America, Hell against Heaven," preached Billy Sunday. "Either you are loyal or you are not, you are either a patriot or a black-hearted traitor. . . . All this talk about not fighting the German people is a lot of bunk. They say that we are fighting for an ideal. Well, if we are we will have to knock down the German people to get it over."[15] Dr. Hillis, pastor of Plymouth Congregational Church of Brooklyn, argued that 10 million German soldiers ought to be sterilized.[16]

Matthews's tendency to believe in conspiracy theories made him susceptible to the highly charged atmosphere that existed throughout the country. He became convinced that civilian courts were corrupt and incapable of dealing with the problem of sedition. "These combined seditious, treacherous and infamous forces are poisoning the avenues of justice, and it is most difficult to get convictions in Federal and State courts," Matthews wrote Wilson and several other cabinet members. "They have poisoned jury panels and in many instances have their friends on the juries."[17]

By January 1918, Matthews and many other Seattle residents had come to believe that internal security and patriotic loyalty were in an extremely fragile state in the city. In the same spirit in which he had previously written Wilson, Matthews attempted to convince the United States Attorney General, Thomas Gregory, of the seriousness of the situation. The Seattle pastor believed that Bolshevik activity was occurring within the city and that traitorous activity needed to be stopped. Matthews asserted that the "Kerensky overthrow . . . [had been] largely planned, schemed and executed in the city of Seattle." He believed that the city was in danger of falling into the hands of "the pro-German forces, the I.W.W. fiends and the vice syndicate agents of this country." He sought amendments to the Espionage Act so that military authorities might "arrest these fiends, court martial and shoot them." For good measure, he requested that Gregory name him provost marshal general in the Pacific Northwest so that he might have authority to "shoot all violators of the law."[18] Matthews and other Seattle leaders pushed the Wilson administration to construct an internment camp that might hold as many as 5,000 suspected traitors.[19]

Receiving little direct encouragement from the White House, the Seattle pastor took matters into his own hands and requested that Senator Jones sponsor amendments to the Espionage Act and the Army and Navy Act. Matthews desired legislation that would legitimize military courts in areas where civilian courts had previously maintained sole jurisdiction. "Courts martial shall have concurrent jurisdiction with civil courts," according to Matthews's proposed amendments. Jones did indeed offer the amendments, but Wilson did not support them and they failed.[20]

Nevertheless, Matthews continued to press for rigid controls on anyone who opposed the American effort, and he constantly propagandized against the Germans. Perhaps his most acclaimed speech on the war came in New York in August 1918. Widely covered in New York newspapers, the address created quite a stir as it lambasted the German people and suggested possible terms for peace. "Staid old members of the conservative Fifth Avenue Presbyterian Church stared in amazement yesterday as applause and cheers greeted the most heated pulpit attack on the kaiser and Germany that had been made in this city since the beginning of the war," said one reporter.[21] Using all of his rhetorical skill, Matthews offered a unique solution for the kaiser and insisted that no negotiated peace be accepted:

> Germany shall be crushed and made to submit to terms of peace dictated to her by America and her Allies. It is right to destroy a mad dog; you would not negotiate with him, would you? . . . Germany shall live on herself, within herself and to herself. She shall remain in isolation, in sackcloth and ashes for a hundred years. The Kaiser shall be exiled to some lonely isle, there to spend the rest of his life, and be permitted to read only literature which tells of the success, triumph, peace and prosperity of America and her Allies.[22]

Matthews argued that "any merchant or any person, a citizen of this government or of any Allied government, who buys an article in Germany for the next one hundred years" should be court-martialed and shot.[23]

It is interesting to note that anti-German sentiment throughout the country was so strong by 1918 that the *New York Times* thought that Matthews's solution might be too lenient. "Can it be that Dr. Matthews, fierce hater of Germany as he is, shares the reverence for a crown that still lingers in so many minds and would have the post-bellum shootings stop just short of the Great Offender?"[24]

Since March 1918, Matthews had pleaded with Wilson not to accept anything less than unconditional surrender. For the preacher, the war had begun to assume apocalyptic dimensions; in a battle for righteousness, he believed that only total victory was acceptable. In a revealing letter to Wilson, Matthews indicated how deeply he believed in the American cause.

> Please do not discuss peace any more. The infamous forces against which we are contending must be crushed. We do not want peace until they are crushed. We do not want them to break. We want to strike them down. Prophecy is clear on this question. Had I the right to make a suggestion, I should like to have you say to the world, 'There shall be no more peace considerations, suggestions or parleys so far as the United States is concerned. We will continue in the warfare for righteousness and liberty until the world is free.' I believe that sentence would save thousands of lives and would put terror into the infamous foe. He cannot be influenced unless we reach him through fear. . . . I would be perfectly willing to live in a dungeon on bread and water for the rest of my life if I could have the privilege of shooting the Kaiser.[25]

As late as October 1918, Matthews sent Wilson a telegram urging him to resist the temptation to settle with the Kaiser. "Please answer in most emphatic terms that we will never negotiate with Germany. These incarnate fiends are unworthy of consideration," Matthews wrote Wilson. "Their armies must be destroyed. We must gain an absolute victory and then dictate terms of peace governing their future lives. Fight on. Fight on. We are with you. God bless you and give our arms success."[26]

When the armistice came on November 11, Matthews undoubtedly experienced an emotional letdown. After he heard the news of the armistice, he apparently did not send the president a letter of congratulations. He next communicated with Wilson on November 14 and made no mention of the peace.[27]

The great emotional peaks and valleys associated with the war had drained Matthews. He had found it necessary to interpret the war in a theological context, and he defended the president from every attacker. But perhaps most of all, he felt justified as a patriot and as a Christian in using every method at his disposal to protect his vision of American society from a variety of enemies. Matthews had always been comfortable using the rhetoric of mortal combat to describe the struggle between what he believed were the forces of good and the forces of evil. The First World War seemed to confirm for him the images of conflict that had seemed so real for most of his life. Like many Americans, after the fighting stopped Matthews viewed the war ambivalently; as the armistice took hold, he must certainly have rejoiced at the end of the monumental carnage. However, he and other Americans wrung their hands in the face of Bolshevism's success in Russia. Matthews worried that the war had unleashed political and social forces that would be extremely difficult to control. Working men across the country were restless, and soon thousands of soldiers would be returning home and looking for work.

Matthews had plenty of company among the middle class in the Pacific Northwest who feared radical labor. Certainly the unrest associated with the Industrial Workers of the World made more than a few people nervous about possible violence. The I.W.W. had been organized in Chicago in 1905, and leaders proclaimed that their goal was to unite all workers into one class-conscious union. Before long, the Wobblies utilized strikes, propaganda, and sabotage to meet their goals. They first came to the Pacific Northwest in 1907, to Portland; subsequently, in Spokane in 1909, they fought for free speech. By 1916 they had emerged as a fairly sophisticated labor organization and one that most middle-class Americans greatly feared. In that year in Everett, Washington, a protest against a ban on street speaking erupted into violence at the local docks and a number of people were killed.[28] Matthews appears not to have commented on the event, but certainly his sympathies must have been with the local citizens who attempted to stop the I.W.W. from recruiting any more workers to their cause. Only few years before, during the Potlatch episode with Alden Blethen, publisher of the *Seattle Times*, Matthews had defended the right of the I.W.W. to speak freely. But now, Matthews and many others had changed their minds.

Throughout 1917, Matthews spoke bitterly about the I.W.W. as "America's most damnable enemy." He excoriated the Wobblies for acts of sabotage associated with their labor activity and became increasingly worried that their fanaticism would disrupt the war effort.[29] He and many others expressed deep concern that the logging industry had been shut down repeatedly by the I.W.W. during the first year of the war. At times, a hint of desperation could be found in Matthews's voice as he asked Wilson for help. "Would you authorize the lumbermen and vest them with authority to handle the I.W.W. agitators?" Matthews asked Wilson in 1917. "Or would you appoint someone and vest in him authority to handle the whole situation?"[30] Two weeks later, he wrote Wilson again and complained of the I.W.W. tactics of putting spikes in logs in order to ruin the saws at mills or nailing copper tacks in fruit trees. He recommended that Wilson accede to the demand for an eight-hour day, which Matthews believed was legitimate. Ultimately, however, Matthews argued that force should be used against the Wobblies. "If I were Provost Marshall of the State of Washington," he told Wilson, "I would court martial these infamous traitors and shoot them at the rise of the morning sun."[31]

Matthews loved to write Wilson and talk in belligerent terms about all of those who opposed Wilson's efforts.

> I am deeply interested—yea on fire with the problems confronting this country, and, her grave danger now and after the war. Of course you know the reason the wolves are criticising Baker, Creel, Burleson and others, is they are trying to reach you by criticising your secretaries and your workers. When the war is over, three years from today, the wolves from the infernal world will turn loose as they have never done before in this country.
>
> Now my suggestion is this: let those of us who are your friends and who would die for you and yours, go throughout the country and expose the infamy of the criticisms and of the critics. Now is the time to fight both in America and in Europe. We are going to win the war in both places. Give us the power; turn us loose; let us fight, fight, fight until we win.[32]

Wilson responded by encouraging Matthews in his general outlook regarding anyone whom he deemed to be an opponent of the government or the war in general. "Your letter of April twenty-seventh warms the cockles of my heart," Wilson wrote Matthews. "I feel just as you do. Whether it is the best thing to do to let loose on the wolves is a question in my mind, and I should not like to give advice about it, but you may be sure that I would forgive any friend of mine for anything they might do in that way."[33]

Perhaps because of Wilson's general encouragement, Matthews felt free to continue to express his concerns regarding un-American activities and foreign influence. He criticized the Pope and urged Wilson not to visit the Vatican in the year after the war ended. He conveyed his feelings to Vice President Thomas Marshall:

> If the President undertakes to visit the Vatican and pay homage to the Pope, it will mean the absolute defeat of the Democratic party in the next election. . . . The Pope has been pro-German from the beginning. . . . If the President visits that damnable "Dago," it will do more harm and produce more disaster in the Democratic party than any act that he could commit. For God's sake wire him and tell him to stay away from the infernal pro-German "Dago."[34]

Matthews's anxieties were not confined to Catholics, Wobblies, or Southern Europeans; in 1919, his latent anti-Semitism emerged in a particularly vicious context. In that year, Matthews had been introduced to the document entitled *Protocols of the Meetings of Zionist Men of Wisdom*. The tract claimed that the Bolshevik government in Russia was controlled and financed by Jews. Quickly convinced by the document, Matthews sent Wilson a copy and an accompanying note: "Jews are aiding, financing and assisting the soviets, radicals, I.W.W.'s, Leftwing Socialists, Communists and every other description of anarchist to attack this government whenever and wherever they can." The preacher praised the *Protocols,* and urged Wilson to read them carefully. "They will show you that there is in the mind and heart of the Jews mentioned and others to be mentioned the purpose to form a conspiracy to attack our form of Government and ultimately to assist in establishing a Government of their own."[35] Matthews's views reflected the feelings of many conservative and fundamentalist Protestants during the period. There seemed to be something about the *Protocols* that correlated to the prophecies of the Antichrist that were so popular during the First World War.[36] However, it is likely that Matthews found his attraction to the *Protocols* something of an embarrassment later in life when he vigorously criticized anti-Semitic activity in Germany during the 1930s.

Clearly, Matthews reflected the anticommunist paranoia of the period known as the Red Scare. Attorney General A. Mitchell Palmer organized the efforts to deport radical aliens. J. Edgar Hoover headed the Justice Department's General Intelligence Division, and he led the gathering of information on thousands of persons suspected of radical activity. Police raids in dozens of cities resulted in the arrest of more than 6,000 suspects with hundreds being deported. One historian contends that the First World War converted "thousands of otherwise reasonable and sane Americans into super-patriots and self styled spy-chasers."[37] Matthews's emotional commitment to the war had been so intense that he needed a further outlet after the shooting stopped.

Like many Americans who did not actually fight in the trenches, Matthews had become convinced that the best way to help the war effort was to root out all seditious activity. The Espionage Act of 1917 and the Sedition Act of 1918 had helped to create an intolerant attitude toward any act of nonconformity. "The home front, unable personally to lay hands on the hated Huns, had made scapegoats of the 'draft-dodger,' the 'slacker,' and anyone else who did not conform," according to the historian Robert Murray.[38]

Shocked by the Bolshevik revolution in November 1917, many Americans viewed the Bolshevik government's separate peace with Germany as a betrayal. Alarm gave way to fear as Bolshevism spread through Europe. American communists openly supported the Russian revolution, and American radicals rejoiced at the developments overseas. The combination of an intolerant attitude toward anything "un-American" at home, with the rise of Bolshevism abroad, helped lead directly to the Red Scare.

An important event that contributed not only to Mark Matthews's fear of communism, but to the nation's fears as well, was the Seattle General Strike of 1919, in which the preacher played a fairly significant role. The demands of the First World War had triggered an explosion of shipbuilding activity in Seattle and other coastal cities around the country. Before 1914, only one Seattle firm—the Seattle Dry Dock and Construction Company—was constructing steel-hulled vessels in the city. However, by 1918, five firms had gone into the steel-hull business, and the Emergency Fleet Corporation, the U.S. government agency responsible for orchestrating the wartime expansion, encouraged other firms in the city to build wooden-hulled ships. During 1918 alone, Seattle shipyards contributed ninety-six ships to the war effort, and it was estimated that during the course of the entire war, Seattle produced approximately one quarter of all the ships constructed. However, the labor dynamics were extremely complex. The U.S. government had an interest in controlling wages in order to prevent a mass exodus of workers from one part of the country to another. Employers, on the one hand, generally approved of wage controls because that generally meant a more stable labor supply; on the other hand, some employers occasionally hoped to gain an advantage in the labor market and attempted to raise rates in order to attract more and better skilled workers. Within the labor community itself, tensions arose between the American Federation of Labor and the Industrial Workers of the World over leadership and overall objectives.[39]

In August 1917, the Emergency Fleet Corporation established the Shipbuilding Labor Adjustment Board—known more commonly as the Macy Board after its chairman, V. Everit Macy. The board was to take responsibility for all bargaining over wages, hours, and working conditions for the duration of the war. According to the historian Robert Friedheim, the board's decisions were not well received. A good measure of distrust developed between labor groups on the West Coast and the board, which ultimately contributed to the situation that led to the later general strike. For the remainder of the war, the Macy Board moved toward standardization of wages in the shipbuilding industry; whatever compromises ensued proved generally unacceptable to the leadership of the metal-trades union in Seattle.[40]

Throughout the summer of 1917, tensions mounted and strikes threatened as the Macy Board attempted to settle on an appropriate wage scale. In something of a compromise, a slightly higher rate for Seattle shipyard workers was approved, but for a number of reasons, this proved generally unsatisfactory to the metal-trades unions. Conditions in the shipyards had been deteriorating even before the end of the war. Concern about wage control and the transition to a peacetime economy began to culminate in the fall of 1918. Matthews found himself integrally involved, and only three days after the armistice in Europe, he sent a telegram to Woodrow Wilson asking him to use his powers to prevent a reduction in wages. In fact, Matthews predicted a major strike if a reduction in wages occurred.

> Practically all the unions on the Pacific Coast engaged in shipbuilding have decided to appeal from the Macey Board and are sending a delegation of seven members to Washington to present their case before a board of appeal. Some of the shipyards in Seattle have been and are paying some of their men higher wages than the Macey Board provides. The Emergency Fleet Corporation or Shipping Board or the Macey Board may order shipyards to reduce all wages to the Macey scale which if done will result in a strike involving every shipbuild-

ing industry on the Pacific Coast. As I am convinced that most serious trouble will ensue if wages are reduced in the shipbuilding industry. At the present time I take liberty of urging you to issue orders that will prevent any interference in or reduction of present wage scale in Seattle shipyards for the present at least until the fullest consideration can be given the entire subject. Situation here is serious. Please act on this suggestion. Am appealing in the interest of a cause dear to us both. Please give me a favorable wire.[41]

Four days later, Matthews again wired Wilson and repeated his plea to intervene. "The situation is most serious. Everything is involved. . . . ," Matthews wrote. "Would you please wire reply at once in order that I might influence the meeting which convenes at noon tomorrow Tuesday. Please help at once and save the day."[42] Wilson responded courteously to Matthews, but indicated that he did not believe that he should intervene. "The process of appeal is plain and I shall count on the sober second thought of all concerned," wrote the president.[43] Matthews made one additional effort to convince the president to intervene in the wage dispute, but failed to change Wilson's mind. Most likely, Matthews's principal concern centered on the potential radicalization of the labor movement. He likely assumed that if wages were reduced the rank and file would probably bolt from the American Federation of Labor and accept the more radical I.W.W. Matthews had come to despise the I.W.W. and wanted to do anything in his power to prevent the labor movement from gravitating to the left.

Whether Wilson could have done anything to stem the tide of events in Seattle is difficult to say, but in any event, negotiations deteriorated. On January 21, 1919, 35,000 shipyard workers struck for higher wages and shorter hours. The Emergency Fleet Corporation, which contracted with the shipbuilders during the war, refused to negotiate with the strikers. As a result, the Seattle Central Labor Council, led by the fairly radical James A. Duncan, who also happened to be a dry Presbyterian, began promoting the idea of a general strike in support of the already-striking shipbuilders.[44]

In response, the permanent labor committee of the Seattle Ministerial Federation attempted to pressure the Emergency Fleet Corporation to compromise on the issue of wages. In addition, on January 31, civic leaders met and appointed an Industrial Relations Committee consisting of Matthews, Judge George Donworth, and James Spangler, president of Seattle First National Bank. Many Seattleites were aware of the congenial relationship between Matthews and Duncan. As Matthews put it, "We agree to disagree." Spangler had also earned the respect of the labor community for his work on Woodrow Wilson's investigatory committee of the timber strikes of 1917, at which time he had been critical of the employers.[45]

Matthews arranged a series of meetings between the committee and James Taylor, president of the Metal Trades Council. The preacher suggested that a committee of labor and management be established to contact government officials and international officers of various shipyard unions. However, by the first week in February, events had gone too far for meaningful negotiation.[46] On February 3, Seattle newspapers reported that a general strike would occur in three days. People jammed department and grocery stores to stock up. Hardware stores reported that they had more requests for guns than they could fill. A *Seattle Union-Record* editorial tried to allay the building hysteria, as the strike committee claimed that it would take care of the basic necessities for people.[47]

On February 6, an estimated 60,000 workers went out on strike, and the city came to a virtual halt. Schools closed, streetcars stopped running, and businesses failed to open. The strike committee did allow garbage trucks, milk wagons, and laundry trucks to continue to operate. At all times the city had coal, food, water, heat, and light. Mayor Ole Hanson requested federal troops from Camp Lewis to maintain order, but there was little need, as no violence broke out. However, the prevailing sentiment throughout the city during the strike was fear. Stimulated by the famous editorial by Anna Louise Strong in the *Seattle Union-Record*, Seattle residents conceived the worst possible scenarios. "We are undertaking the most tremendous move ever made by Labor in this country," Strong wrote. "We are starting on a road that leads—no one knows where!"[48] Matthews and others concluded, however, that Seattle might easily be on the road to revolution. "It is not a strike. It is a revolution," said the preacher. "It is a direct attack on the American government, and is an effort to crucify the American Federation of Labor."[49] A great sigh of relief could be felt not just in Seattle but throughout the country when, on February 10, most strikers decided to go back to work. There were few who disagreed with the observation made by the *Seattle Star*: "Full Steam ahead. . . . Today this Bolshevik-sired nightmare is at an end."[50]

The Seattle General Strike once again reflected Matthews's elevated standing within the city. The public exposure Matthews received for his negotiating efforts reaffirmed his image as a force for righteousness and stability. Seattleites believed the pastor to be one of the only people powerful enough to combat the forces of radical labor. Ten days after the strike, the *Argus*, not one of Matthews's traditional supporters, acknowledged his influence.

> Dr. Matthews is, even those who do not like him will concede, a wonderful man. . . . He is credited with having control of one of the greatest political machines in the West, and perhaps without that machine the city could not have been cleaned up. That machine, too, is responsible for much that happened here during the strike, although he neither asks nor wants credit for it.[51]

If the strike did not bear out the worst fears of many of Seattle's middle-class residents, neither did it signal a rapid decline in the fear of communism. One week after the strike ended, Matthews, along with Judge Thomas Burke and the businessmen J. D. Lowman, J. W. Spangler, and O. D. Colvin, formed the American National Committee. Based in Seattle, the committee established an office in New York for the purpose of investigating and bringing to justice anyone who opposed the American government. "It would be wise to bring to justice the guilty who commit the overt acts, who conspire against the government," Matthews wrote in the statement of purpose. "It would be equally wise to deport every alien in America. . . . It is necessary to meet the propaganda of the anarchists by a campaign of counteracting propaganda."[52] Though the group seems to have produced few results and apparently did not meet beyond the first year, the Seattle preacher's involvement does suggest the degree of fear that existed after the war, as well as his credibility with the business community.

Matthews's public visibility and prestige continued to grow throughout 1919. Most notably, the pastor convinced Woodrow Wilson to include Seattle on his trip around the country—made in an effort to sell the Treaty of Versailles. The Seattle preacher sat at the head table for dinner with President Wilson, Seattle's mayor, and Washington's governor. The following day, September 14, Matthews felt even more excitement when Wilson attended services at First Presbyterian. An estimated 4,000 people crammed into the church to worship with the president. Matthews selected some of the great gospel hymns, including "I Love to Tell the Story," and a quartet anthem, "My Faith Looks Up to Thee." Speaking on the topic "Precious Moments with Jesus," Matthews emphasized the virtues of service and sacrifice, and suggested that the world had not yet "tried Christianity."[53] Matthews seemed to want to serve in a pastoral role for Wilson; he therefore chose not to preach a political sermon. After the benediction was said, the packed congregation stood as the presidential party, including the president, Mrs. Wilson, and several Secret Service men, exited the church. For Mark Matthews and the many members of the First Presbyterian Church, this must have been a very proud moment.[54]

From 1912 to 1919, Matthews's activity in Seattle's civic life proved Colonel Blethen's prophesy about the preacher's impending demise to be at best premature. Saluted by the city for his role in the strike and listened to by the president of the United States, Matthews surely must have felt gratified and reinforced in his public positions. But clearly, he had not escaped the impact of the war nor the rapid social changes that took place during the period. Seattle momentarily reached out for a symbol of stability and a sign of "normalcy," and Matthews filled the bill. But few Seattle residents could deny that the city and the country had changed; the resolution of the strike had not solved the inherent conflict of interests, and the end of the war did not initiate the hoped-for triumph of righteousness no matter how much Wilson and Matthews fought for the League of Nations. The failure to establish a righteous community certainly troubled Matthews. In 1919, he once again reflected on what he believed the city of Seattle needed to achieve its future destiny. As he had on many previous occasions, Matthews exhorted city leaders and Seattle citizens in general to beautify the city with boulevards and parks; he emphasized the need for school construction, hotel facilities, hospitals, and more streetcar lines. He called for a reduction in taxes and predictably called for a commitment to civic righteousness. But there was one thread that seemed different from many of his earlier efforts to shape a civic vision; in 1919 Matthews stressed the theme of emancipation. Revealing the strain of the last three years, he spoke about the need to "emancipate this city from the tyranny of attempted class prejudice and restrictions." He asserted that the city was divided between those who loved the city and those who were enemies of the city. He hoped that business and labor could work together for a common end.[55] Still considered a significant figure in Seattle city politics, Matthews ended a tumultuous decade with a renewed commitment to the future. However, his response to the future was to become more conservative and more committed to defining the fundamental truths for his life and others.

The Great War and the General Strike 155

$\mathit{CHAPTER\ 9}$

Fundamentalism and Modernism

The fight for the great fundamentals has just begun and
no Unitarian can remain hereafter in a Presbyterian pul-
pit. He must go or be exposed.
                                    —Mark Matthews (1915)

For most of Mark Matthews's early ministry, he had struggled against people like Hiram Gill and Alden Blethen. He believed that monopolies, corruption, and greed posed the greatest obstacles to achieving the righteous community he so much desired. His preaching focused less on formal theology and more on the social and political problems faced by his parishioners. Yet Matthews gradually became drawn into one of the great conflicts in American religious history—the battle between fundamentalists and modernists. The controversy split Protestantism to its core. Nearly every denomination felt the effect of such division, but Presbyterians experienced a particularly painful conflict in which Mark Matthews emerged as a key figure on a number of fronts.

At the beginning of his ministry, Matthews could be described as evangelical, and he certainly believed in the efficacy of religious revival. He also participated in numerous interdenominational and ecumenical activities. On various occasions he argued for the unification of Presbyterian factions, and, at least theologically, he expressed a good deal of toleration for other Protestant denominations early in his career. Nevertheless, Matthews gradually became known as one of the Presbyterian church's most powerful conservatives, and at times he was labeled one of its most extreme conservatives. At a key point, however, the Seattle preacher assumed a mediating position between moderates and conservatives and played an important role in helping the Presbyterian church avoid a major schism. This chapter examines Mark Matthews's role within the national Presbyterian church and demonstrates how complex the fundamentalist controversy was during the second and third decades of the twentieth century.

The emergence of fundamentalism in the twentieth-century American religious landscape reflects a complex set of social, ideological, and theological issues. For much of the twentieth century, historians tended to see fundamentalism as an ultra-conservative religious expression that was focused primarily on preserving a dying way of life. Characterized by many as simply narrow-minded and ignorant, fundamentalists were dismissed as anachronistic reactionaries to the modern world. However, more recently, historians have argued that fundamentalism reflected complex doctrinal issues and social forces. The historians Ernest Sandeen, George Marsden, and Joel Carpenter have all contributed greatly to a more nuanced understanding of this movement within American Protestantism.[1] Rooted deeply in many of the theological, intellectual, and social movements of the nineteenth century, fundamentalism emerged more self-consciously in the second decade of the twentieth century. The movement captured the attention of the national media in the Scopes Monkey Trial of 1925, when Clarence Darrow was pitted against William Jennings Bryan over the teaching of evolution. But the movement was far more complicated than a simple battle over what interpretation of the origin of human species should be taught in the public schools. The core beliefs regarding Christianity were believed to be at stake; the role of religion in public policy was debated, as well as many of the traditional Victorian beliefs surrounding the family, gender roles, and maxims regarding moral behavior. Political, social, and economic battles were inseparable from the disagreements over the nature of Biblical truth and scientific fact. Christians all over the country engaged in bitter argument over these issues, and the very fabric of many denominations was significantly torn during the last three decades of Matthews's life.

Most adherents to fundamentalism believed that evangelism was the church's overwhelming priority; they maintained that converts were marked by a fresh infusion of the Holy Spirit in order to live a holy and effective Christian life. Fundamentalists believed in the imminent, premillennial second coming of Christ and the divine inspiration and absolute authority of the Bible, whose very words were free from errors. Belief in the virgin birth, the reality of miracles, the bodily resurrection of Christ, and the atonement of Christ for humanity's sins were understood to be fundamental beliefs for Matthews and many other conservative Protestants. Increasingly, these beliefs became a litmus test for religious orthodoxy.

However, as was the case with many other facets of his life, Matthews does not fit easily into the typical definition of a fundamentalist. George Marsden has pointed out that the term *fundamentalism* has been used in a number of ways, and as a result, Matthews can be categorized as a member in some senses but not others. For example, when the term *fundamentalism* is used to refer to a conservative religionist, Matthews should certainly be included. In the sense that *fundamentalism* refers to persons who hold to what they believe are traditional "fundamental" doctrines, Matthews should be included. But in the sense that *fundamentalism* is used to describe the distinct coalition of those who called themselves "Fundamentalists," Matthews should not be included. And for Marsden, this last is the most accurate use of the term.[2]

In other ways Matthews does not easily fit the strict definition of a fundamentalist. His social and political thought was often at odds with the free-enterprise liberalism so characteristic of fundamentalist economic and social thought. He was hardly ambivalent toward social reform in the way that most fundamentalists were. And perhaps most important, for all that Matthews hated about liberal theology, he held steadfast in his commitment to keep the Presbyterian church intact, whereas many fundamentalists believed that the preservation of truth called for separation from the denomination. As was the case with Populism, Progressivism, and the Social Gospel, Matthews's thinking and ministry was directly influenced by fundamentalism. And as was also the case with those other movements, he sometimes marched to the beat of a different drummer and charted a different trajectory for his life than did most of his colleagues.

Mark Matthews's journey in the context of fundamentalism is not an easy one to explain. Many of his early sermons in Jackson and Seattle chastised his fellow clergy for their narrow-mindedness and short-sightedness. He believed that no denomination had a monopoly on righteousness. Like many clergy of his day, Matthews was especially concerned with social, health, and economic problems. He embraced social Christianity in an effort to apply his interpretation of the Gospel. He confidently believed, as did many Protestants, that religious solutions could be found for social ills and that righteous communities

Fundamentalism and Modernism

would be a testimony to God's triumph over sin. Yet by the early twentieth century, as so many historians have found, the confidence expressed by Matthews and other Protestant leaders began to wane. Certainly, as we have seen, Matthews felt increasingly frustrated about his efforts to bring about a righteous society by simply preaching from the pulpit or initiating new legislation.

For most of Matthews's ministry, he had believed that the source of his frustration could be found in the guise of corrupt politicians or greedy capitalists. Yet by the first decade of the twentieth century, theological and intellectual problems began to weigh more heavily on him. Religion itself had come under increasing attack. Major problems arose for religious thinkers. The philosophical critiques from the eighteenth-century Enlightenment and the work of Charles Darwin from the nineteenth century presented certain theological difficulties regarding the accuracy of scriptural accounts of the creation and the miracles attributed to Jesus. The increasing reliance among intellectual circles on empiricism and rationalism raised enormous problems for theologians who attempted to justify the legitimacy of a faith experience. Increasingly, European theologians attempted to accommodate theology to these developments within philosophy. The German theologian Friedrich Schleiermacher influenced significant numbers of religious thinkers by linking theology to the intellectual life of the culture. Schleiermacher argued that religion and culture are inseparably connected and that theology must therefore be constructed on this integrated foundation. Higher Biblical criticism stressed naturalistic historical explanations for the development of cultural attitudes and values among Biblical people. This combination of reformulated theology and challenging intellectual developments tended to undermine the belief that Scripture could be understood as a testimony to transcendent truth for all peoples and for all time.[3]

The collective force of modern philosophy, new science, and new theology began to take its toll on orthodox assumptions by the beginning of the twentieth century. As one historian has argued, "The progressive abandonment of supernaturalism and the relativization and equalization of all religious belief systems" marked the advent of the modernist impulse.[4] This modernist expression often was referred to as a "New Theology" or "New Christianity." The historian William Hutchison wrote, "The dominating theme of the New Theology, God's presence in the world and in human culture, could not be articulated, to be sure, without negative commentary upon earlier ways of thinking."[5]

For the average clergyman and his parishioners, this was not a problem until the end of the nineteenth century. Certainly, Matthews did not spend a lot of time pondering these issues. But gradually, he and many of his fellow clergy grew more alarmed at the challenges facing orthodox Protestantism. By 1908, Matthews was referring specifically to Schleiermacher and to modernism.

> Then there came a wave of Altruism, not based on the love of God, but on vague ideas of development. . . . It is pictured in poetry and romance; Schleiermacher and Ritschl are the chief profits [sic] of this cult. That is the answer of modernism, which embraces all phases of Higher Criticism, Evolution, Pantheism, Unitarianism, and all diluted forms of Christianity which are akin to Buddhism, Confucianism, etc., such as theosophy and Christian Science.[6]

On another occasion, he compared the modernists to dogs, for "they attack the Bible, they deny Christ, they ridicule your faith, they repudiate the vicarious atonement, [and] they hoot at the physical resurrection."[7]

Anxiety continued to increase among many Protestant ministers over the issues associated with evolution, higher Biblical criticism, far eastern religions, and the massive social changes that were occurring in American society in the early twentieth century. The reaction to these phenomena manifested itself on a variety of fronts. For instance, in 1910 a group of Bible teachers, evangelists, and pastors edited a series of twelve small booklets called *The Fundamentals*. Though generally restrained in tone, particularly when compared with the fundamentalist tracts that emerged in the 1920s, *The Fundamentals* vigorously defended Scripture against the attacks of higher criticism. By 1915, the twelve booklets, written by a variety of conservative scholars, pastors, and lay leaders, contained some ninety articles and supported orthodox views of sin and salvation and the existence of the Trinity. *The Fundamentals* authors repeatedly attacked modern religious beliefs, from Mormonism, Russellism, and Eddyism to Modern Spiritualism and Romanism.[8] Articles clearly articulated concerns about modernism as an intellectual compromise and the abandonment of basic orthodoxy. Matthews read the tracts with interest, and shortly after their publication his sermons began to focus more directly on the themes and issues discussed in *The Fundamentals*, and he more frequently referred to himself as someone who supported "the fundamentals" of the Christian faith.[9]

Fundamentalism and Modernism

Matthews's shift toward greater theological conservatism probably stemmed at least in part from his training in Old School Presbyterianism, which was the root of his theology. Back in Calhoun when Reverend Hillhouse tutored Matthews in the specifics of Charles Hodge's systematic theology, the emphasis had been on the primacy of Scripture. Old School Presbyterians, as we have seen, understood that Scripture was a collection of factual information. There was little, if any, Scripture that should be interpreted allegorically. According to the historian George Marsden,

> Old School Presbyterians had preserved a distinctive view of the truth. They tended to view truth in its purest form as precisely stated propositions. This applied not only to the [Westminster] *Confession*, but also to the infallible Scriptures that the *Confession* summarized. In either case truth was a stable entity, not historically relative, best expressed in written language that, at least potentially, would convey one message in all times and places.[10]

Common-sense realism also underscored the notion that "basic truths are much the same for all persons in all times and places."[11] This view of truth tended to place a great burden on the accuracy of the written word. These tendencies, embodied in common-sense realism and Old School Presbyterianism, according to Marsden, Ernest Sandeen, and other historians, lent themselves to fundamentalism by the second decade of the twentieth century.[12] Modernists tended to reject the inerrancy of Scripture and accept the notion that religion was relative to time, place, and culture. Religious pluralism and higher Biblical criticism provided the foundation for the modernist response to religious orthodoxy in the nineteenth century. Matthews understood this and cast his lot with conservative Christians. He believed that a righteous community could not be constructed without a rigorously maintained orthodoxy.

By 1910, the Presbyterian General Assembly, the national body of delegates, had decided that it must delineate more clearly the "essential" doctrines by which it stood. In part, this desire for specified orthodoxy grew out of concerns regarding several graduates of Union Theological Seminary in New York who manifested a number of liberal tendencies. The subsequent five-point declaration by the General Assembly provided Matthews and other conservatives for the next two decades with a virtual creed by which they could measure any clergy within the church. In summarized form, these five points consisted of the following: 1) The Holy Spirit so inspired the writers of Scripture "as to keep them from error"; 2) "Our Lord Jesus Christ was born of the Virgin Mary"; 3) Christ offered up himself as "a sacrifice to satisfy divine justice"; 4) "He arose from the dead, with the same body in which he suffered"; 5) Christ "showed his power and love by working mighty miracles."[13]

The division between modernists and fundamentalists, and more generally between conservatives and moderates, began to widen at precisely the time during which Matthews emerged as a national figure in the Presbyterian church. The Seattle pastor attracted national attention when he made an unsuccessful bid for moderator of the Presbyterian church in 1911. Disappointed with the defeat, Matthews nonetheless did not give up. He convinced the Seattle and Spokane presbyteries to offer his name for moderator once again in 1912.[14] At that year's General Assembly in Louisville, Kentucky, Matthews emerged as the favorite and came away with a first-ballot victory.[15]

For the rest of the convention, Matthews received high marks for his parliamentary procedure as well as for his oratorical ability. "Dr. Matthews' first morning in the chair demonstrated his singularly fine capacity as a presiding officer," noted one observer. "Every matter at issue was stated by the moderator in terms unmistakably lucid and definite."[16] Speaking on a number of occasions, Matthews also shared the platform with William Jennings Bryan and Charles Stelzle, the noted advocate of the Social Gospel, before a crowd of 10,000.[17]

As moderator, Matthews traveled throughout the country and preached about the need for revitalized evangelistic efforts.[18] He also continued to hammer away at the ills of American society. "Covetousness is America's sin and it will be America's ruin if Americans do not repent," he told a crowd in Toledo, Ohio. "It is the blight of the church today. We are in the midst of the greatest crisis the church has yet had, because the spirit of materialism has settled upon the church."[19]

Matthews continued to make good newspaper copy, and, much to his delight, reporters asked his opinions on everything from the weather to presidential politics. "Taft should be nominated for the Supreme Court and Roosevelt ought to be at a plow," Matthews remarked in Buffalo.[20] In Philadelphia, Matthews's views received extensive coverage. "A mighty effort of 4,500,000 church members to add 500,000 names to the rolls in a year, led by a progressive minister from the far west, who believes America is ready to give up money grabbing and 'return to her throne of sanity,'" reported a Philadelphia newspaper, "is the program outlined by the Presbyterian general assembly."[21]

However, Matthews's suggestions did not always meet with universal approval, particularly when he advised specific cities about what they should do. "His words are the crackling of thorns under a pot, and vain as the babble of fools," one Omaha reporter wrote.[22] Buffalo residents took umbrage at being compared unfavorably with Seattle. "Buffalo may not be as clean morally as it could be made, but there having been no cry from any source to submit the city to a chloride of lime purification," one Buffalo newspaper noted, "just why we should be compared with the immoral Seattle of a few years since, does not appear."[23]

Nevertheless, Matthews greatly enjoyed his travels as moderator and looked forward to the 1913 General Assembly, which would be held in Atlanta, Georgia. He perceived it as something of a homecoming, and on his way there he made stops in Chattanooga, Tennessee, and Dalton and Calhoun, Georgia—the last his birthplace, where his longtime Southern friends treated him like a conquering hero.[24]

On the surface, the General Assembly of 1913 looked like a means of uniting Presbyterians. For the first time in the twentieth century, the Presbyterian Church U.S.A., the Presbyterian Church U.S., and the Cumberland Presbyterian Church held their conventions at the same time in the same city.[25] Matthews supported the unification movement. "There is no logical reason why members of the same family should be separated and it is certainly true that members of the same family are unchristian if they are antagonistic to one another," he said.[26] However, at a deeper level, the 1913 assembly revealed the growing concern among the more conservative members that liberal theology and higher Biblical criticism threatened orthodoxy. As a national leader, Matthews increasingly advocated fundamentalist theological positions.

When Matthews delivered his moderator's address to the assembly, he placed special emphasis on evangelism and fundamentalism. "The business of the church is to evangelize the world," he preached. "That is the church's mission and Christ commissioned and equipped her to do such superhuman work." The Seattle pastor pressed the members of his audience to commit themselves to fundamental truths and asked rhetorically, "Have we been preaching the plain, simple gospel and His vicarious atonement?" He further suggested that candidates for the Presbyterian ministry should be made to swear their conviction that only those with a personal belief that "Christ was God" could be saved.[27] Support for the speech poured in from all parts of the country, but there was also strong criticism. Liberal spokesmen condemned Matthews for being much too rigid. "That is a shocking doctrine, that no man can be regenerated who does not know by a living, personal consciousness that Christ was God," said one observer. "That condemns Isaiah and John Milton, and Edward Everett Hall."[28]

Conservative concern for the direction of the Presbyterian church led assembly members to form a special investigating committee to examine the affairs of Union Seminary in New York City and to name Mark Matthews as chair. Conservatives believed that Union no longer taught Presbyterian doctrine and had fallen victim to liberal theology. The specific task of the committee was "to make a thorough investigation of all the legal, ecclesiastical and doctrinal questions involved."[29]

Within the next month, Matthews initiated correspondence with the president of Union Seminary, the Reverend Francis Brown, and asked for the original charter and list of contributors and their gifts. Although Brown provided the charter and constitution, he refused to name the contributors. On October 13, 1913, Matthews wrote a detailed letter requesting that all records be sent to him and stating that, if possible, the seminary should open itself completely to the investigating committee. He also asked Brown to answer ten questions relating to the seminary's acceptance or rejection of the Westminster Confession of Faith, which was considered the statement of orthodoxy within the Presbyterian church. "Did not the constitution and original organizers, incorporators and charter require the directors, the faculty and all concerned," asked Matthews, "to subscribe to the doctrines taught in the Westminster Confession of Faith and the polity of the Presbyterian Church?"[30] Whether Matthews was trying to pressure the seminary into reaffirming the terms of its original charter or attempting to trap it into making self-incriminating statements is not entirely clear. Nonetheless, to him, Union's heresy was clear, and either it had to be rectified or Presbyterians should sever all ties. "Does the seminary intend to depart from its original purpose and constitution and teach the theological doctrines of Unitarianism, Judaism, Universalism, Congregationalism, Methodism, Catholicism . . . or Presbyterianism?" asked the Seattle preacher, in apparent disgust.[31]

Matthews sent the same letter to William Kingsley, president of the Union Seminary Board of Directors. Kingsley's reply was cordial, but he refused to answer any of the questions concerning doctrine and asserted that the General Assembly could not require him to. He fur-

Fundamentalism and Modernism

ther suggested that additional discussion would only injure the interests of the church.[32] Undaunted, Matthews pushed on with the investigation.

Between November 1913 and February 1914, Matthews must have had many uneasy moments over this quarrel with the seminary. As chairman of the investigating committee, he was expected to report to the General Assembly in May 1914, and as of the middle of February, he had been completely stymied. Several members of the committee wanted to resign. Facing complete failure, Matthews resorted to skillful diplomacy and kept the committee together, offering at the same time a more conciliatory approach to Union. He abandoned the combative stance and tendered an olive branch. "We, as a committee, wish to assure you that there was not any spirit of antagonism or criticism intended," Matthews wrote to Kingsley. "Let me personally assure you that the opposite spirit and motive prompted the all-inclusiveness and character of the inquiries." He requested that the lawyers from his committee be allowed to visit the seminary and examine its records. Brown and Kingsley agreed, although by then it was too late for Matthews to make a report to the 1914 General Assembly. The report was delayed for one year.[33]

By March 1915, Matthews knew that he would be going to the General Assembly with a report critical of Union Seminary. Perhaps as a way of building support for his case, he decided to initiate a nation-wide campaign by sending a letter entitled "Back to Fundamentals" to the major Presbyterian congregations in the country. Surely influenced by the many articles published over the previous five years as *The Fundamentals*, Matthews hoped to document the degree of support for fundamentalism. "In view of the deep unrest in the religious thought of the day," he wrote in the letter, "we believe that there should be a pronounced and persistent emphasis on the integrity and authority of the word of God, the deity of the Lord, Jesus Christ, and His vicarious atonement on the cross—the only way of salvation."[34]

Matthews received more than 200 responses offering support for his position; however, it is unclear how many letters he had sent out. Presbyterian journals were generally favorable. "For all it contains in explicit terms," wrote the *Continent*, "it could be heartily signed, we believe, by every minister and practically the whole body of lay members in the denomination."[35] "Praise God that [Matthews] has laid it upon the hearts of his children in Christ to sound the call to the Church of Christ," wrote one passionate reader of the *Sunday School Times*. "Will not the leaders of other denominations send out a similar message to their brethren?"[36] Some Presbyterians were more cautious: the *Presbyterian Banner* expressed concern, although it did respect the number of signatures penned to the statement. "Does a self-constituted 'Voluntary Committee' need to assert again what the whole Church has said in its organized capacity?" the journal asked. "Those who are so devoted to the 'fundamentals' of doctrine should not forget that the fundamentals of church government are equally a part of our official standards."[37]

As a result of the hoopla surrounding Matthews's "Back to Fundamentals," his committee report was eagerly anticipated by the General Assembly in Rochester, New York, and the Seattle preacher did not disappoint those who were expecting a pyrotechnic display. For two hours he addressed the General Assembly, reading the report and offering his editorial comments. Though the report concluded that no legal relationship existed between the church and Union Seminary, Matthews charged that the seminary had accepted money under false pretenses. Specifically, he argued that donors had been under the assumption that sound Presbyterian doctrine was being taught. He also accused the directors of Union of violating the trust they had been given. "It is teaching doctrines inconsistent with and subversive of the doctrines of the Westminster Confession of Faith, which the charter and purposes of the Seminary forbade," asserted Matthews. "The theological trust has been violated, the moral trust has been violated and the legal trust has been violated."[38]

The following day, President Brown responded to Matthews's charges, vigorously defending the integrity of his institution. He claimed that all donors understood the philosophy of the seminary, and he criticized Matthews's manner of attack. "It is difficult to determine where the category of fact ends and the category of opinion begins," Brown argued. "I can only say that it was a tissue of misrepresentations, not purposely made, but inspired, I am sure, of ignorance."[39]

As one would expect, Matthews's presentation received mixed reviews. Some considered it a courageous statement against the forces of liberalism, while others, including some members of his committee, believed that he had gone beyond the conclusions of the report.[40] Matthews viewed his address as one of the high points of his career. Relishing the national spotlight, he vigorously denounced Union Seminary as "an incubator of heretics." He believed that he had thrown down the gauntlet and was ready for the battle to begin. "The fight for

Fundamentalism and Modernism

the great fundamentals has just begun and no Unitarian can remain hereafter in a Presbyterian pulpit," he said. "He must go or be exposed."[41]

Matthews's role in the Union Seminary affair reflected an increased sense of self-righteousness and, more important, his growing identification with fundamentalism. He certainly believed that the declaration of five points by the 1910 General Assembly provided the basis for attacking both Union and modernists in general. In addition, Matthews's role as committee chairman typified the general pattern of leadership he would assume during his most influential years—whether in a political or a religious context. He used his power to build a fortress from which he could fight off all perceived enemies. In doing so, he contributed to the polarization of positions rather than to their unification.

Perhaps the most noticeable theological shift that Matthews made during this period was the change from a broad postmillennial view of Christ's return to a more premillennial understanding. Postmillennialists held that 1,000 years of peace and prosperity must precede Christ's second coming. Premillennialists argued that Christ could come at any moment and would certainly do so prior to the dawning of the millennium. Throughout much of the nineteenth century, both postmillennial and premillennial views could be found in most denominations. Gradually, however, in the late nineteenth century, premillennialism began to gain more adherents. A Church of Ireland expatriate, John Nelson Darby, linked premillennialism with dispensationalism. Darby argued not only for premillennialism but for a specific understanding of the unfolding of human history. He classified history into eras or dispensations, with each reflecting a dominant principle. Each dispensation ended with a major conflict, divine judgment on those in power, and the introduction of a new era. Although not all fundamentalists described themselves as Darbyites, Darby's ideas increasingly became some of the identifying beliefs of conservative fundamentalists.[42]

Matthews, early in his ministry and at least through 1910, reflected little premillennial influence. In 1909, for example, in a sermon entitled "Things to Be Accomplished before Christ's Second Coming," he listed several conditions, including the conversion of the Jews, that were required before Christ would come.

> Both the Old Testament and New Testament clearly reveal that the Gospel is to exercise an influence over all branches of the human family

Fundamentalism and Modernism

immeasurably more extensive and more thoroughly transforming than any it has ever realized. The end is to be gradually attained through the spiritual presence of Christ in the Providence of the Church.[43]

A few months later, Matthews preached, "His second coming is a part of the workings of God's moral government. I do not know when He will come. Whether He comes before or after the Millennium, it makes no difference, I know He is coming."[44]

As late as 1913, Matthews expressed views, in an interview with the *Los Angeles Tribune*, that had much more in common with postmillennial thinking than with premillennial and that did not reveal any dispensational influence. A reporter wrote, "One of his great beliefs is based on history—that the Church of the living God made its way from its birthplace through Europe to England, across the Atlantic to America, over this great hemisphere, and that the Pacific is to be the gateway for it to make its way back again, over Asia to its starting point, and plant the flag of triumphant Christianity, and then will be closed the last stage of the last great era."[45]

By 1915, the same year he wrote his letter on the "Fundamentals," Matthews was making frequent reference to Scofield Bible study leaflets in his sermons. The Scofield Reference Bible, first published in 1909, became a major tool for dispensational premillennialists. Enormously influential, the Scofield Bible combined paragraphing and cross-references with the theology of Darbyite dispensationalism.[46] C. I. Scofield's Reference Bible was based on the assumption that Christ's kingdom was totally supernatural in origin and therefore could not be realized in this age or in any natural development of human history. "For dispensationalists the prophecies concerning the kingdom referred wholly to the future," according to the historian George Marsden. "This present era, the 'church age,' therefore, could not be dignified as a time of the advance of God's kingdom."[47]

By 1916, Matthews had fully converted to dispensational premillennialism. In a number of sermons he spelled out the "signs of His coming." In "The Reign of the Righteous through the Millennium Period," he clearly reflected the new influence of dispensationalism:

This is the Church's dispensation. It is very distinct, however, from the millennium Kingdom, which is to follow the Church's dispensa-

Fundamentalism and Modernism

tion. The Church—the bride of Christ—is His companion in His humiliation manifesting His sufferings, and filling up the afflictions which are behind. The Kingdom is the manifestation of the glory of Christ which must follow the Church's dispensation.[48]

Sermon after sermon in 1916 emphasized these themes. Matthews became fascinated with prophesy. His language became much more eschatological, and though he did not go so far as to name a time and place for Christ's return, he clearly believed that events of the First World War corresponded to events prophesied in the Biblical books of Ezekiel, Daniel, and Revelation. "There are certain events which must transpire before the end of this age," he told his congregation in 1916. "In prophesy, these events are stated. We are rapidly passing through them."[49] On other occasions, he explicated the events surrounding the final battle of Armageddon. "The so-called great battle of Armageddon occurs just before Christ comes to the earth—just at the end of the period of the tribulation," said Matthews, "when Christ strikes his great final and effective blow and kills the armies of the earth that are arrayed against him."[50] In 1918, at the Philadelphia prophetic conference, the Seattle preacher delivered an address on the premillennial coming of Christ, and in the same year he published a collection of his sermons as a book entitled *The Second Coming of Christ*.[51]

As early as 1914, Matthews had become convinced that he could establish his own Bible institute for the purpose of educating people more specifically on the doctrines of scriptural infallibility, the Holy Trinity, virgin birth, Christ's atonement, justification by faith alone, and the premillennial return of Christ.[52] Bible institutes had become a key weapon in the battle against liberalism and modernism. Matthews hoped to build something that would compare favorably with the Moody Bible Institute in Chicago, the Northwestern Bible Training School in Minneapolis, the Bible Institute in Los Angeles, or the Philadelphia Bible Institute. For a few years, he succeeded in attracting students to his institute, and in 1917 he officially incorporated. However, Matthews simply could not raise the necessary capital to build a facility, and in the end he had to refer students elsewhere.[53]

Matthews's desire to build a Bible institute underscored his great concern over the ideological conflict within the Presbyterian church. In the early 1920s, the controversy over liberalism that had first appeared prior to the world war re-emerged in response to various ecumenical movements. Conservative Presbyterians considered the Inter-church World movement and the New Era movement to be tinged with liberalism.[54]

In April 1920, Matthews wrote an article for *The Presbyterian* in which he criticized the Interchurch World movement and argued that evangelical denominations should not "associate or affiliate with every cult or society that calls itself Christian." He proceeded to list nine fundamental principles that he believed defined an orthodox Presbyterian. He stressed the importance of an infallible Bible, virgin birth, and the existence of the Trinity.[55] By the time of the Presbyterian General Assembly in May 1920, Matthews and another former moderator, Dr. Maitland Alexander, were leading the opposition to continued Presbyterian participation in the ecumenical movement. After heated debate, the motion to withdraw was referred to the executive commission. The compromise motion attached specific conditions regarding budgeting and fiscal management for the interchurch organization but recommended that Presbyterians continue their support. A majority of the General Assembly approved this motion.[56]

Similarly, Matthews and other conservatives criticized the New Era movement. Designed in part as a way to modernize the machinery of the church and to instill evangelical fervor in the mission field, the New Era movement came under attack for not proclaiming the important doctrines of Christianity.[57] Matthews's attacks on these interdenominational organizations reflected the significant shift in his religious worldview.

In 1922, the fundamentalist-modernist controversy entered a new phase within the Presbyterian church. Conflict centered on the preaching of the Reverend Harry Emerson Fosdick. In 1918, Fosdick, a Baptist, began preaching as the associate pastor and preacher at First Church in New York City. The General Assembly had encouraged experiments in interdenominationalism, and Fosdick's tenure at First Church became one of the most visible expressions of ecumenical activity in the country. In May 1922, Fosdick preached a sermon entitled "Shall the Fundamentalists Win?" in which he argued the merits of liberal theology. He asserted that the doctrines concerning the virgin birth, Biblical inerrancy, and the physical return of Christ were not indispensable to belief in Christianity and therefore ought not to be the litmus test for Christians.[58]

Conservatives found Fosdick's sermon symptomatic of the worst of modernist tendencies. Many expressed outrage that a non-Presbyterian delivered such a sermon from a Presbyterian pulpit. The first formal response came from the presbytery of Philadelphia, a stronghold of conservative theology. In October 1922, the presbytery adopted an overture to the General Assembly indicating that in the pulpit at First Presbyterian in New York a sermon had been delivered that was "a public proclamation of the Word which appears to be in denial of the essential doctrines of the Presbyterian Church in the U.S.A."[59] Since Fosdick was a Baptist, and therefore not subject to Presbyterian jurisdiction, authors of the overture carefully referred to the pulpit and not the person. The Philadelphia presbytery asked the General Assembly to direct the New York presbytery "to take such action as will require the preaching and teaching in the First Presbyterian Church of New York City to conform to the system of doctrine taught in the Confession of Faith."[60] Opinion within the church regarding the overture was very divided. As the General Assembly in Indianapolis approached in the spring of 1923, forces on both sides began to rally.

Conservatives supported William Jennings Bryan, three-time candidate for president of the United States and now outspoken critic of Darwinian evolution, for the position of moderator. Mark Matthews delivered the seconding speech for Bryan. However, in a very close vote Bryan lost to Dr. Charles Wishart, a moderate.[61]

Then the General Assembly turned its attention to the Philadelphia overture and Fosdick, debating the issue for five hours. The original committee studying the matter recommended, by a vote of 22 to 1, to dismiss the Philadelphia overture since the New York presbytery had already started its own inquiry into Fosdick's preaching. Nevertheless, the minority report carried the day at the General Assembly, 439 to 359, meaning that the Philadelphia overture was binding. Bryan, Matthews, and other conservatives believed it would now be possible to curtail Fosdick and any other modernist preacher. As a result of the overture, the General Assembly directed the New York presbytery to

> take such action, either through its present Committee or by the appointment of a special commission, as will require the preaching and teaching in the First Presbyterian Church of New York to conform to the system of doctrines taught in the Confession of Faith; and that said Presbytery report its action in a full transcript of its records to the 136th General Assembly of 1924.[62]

Fundamentalism and Modernism

Following that action, the General Assembly reaffirmed its commitment to the five-point doctrinal deliverance of 1910.[63] Shortly thereafter, Matthews offered his congratulations to Bryan regarding the Philadelphia overture and downplayed his election defeat. "But it was much better for you not to be Moderator," he wrote Bryan. "You are in [a] position to lead the church, and if you arouse the laymen and show them what rationalism is costing them both in money and morals, you will be able to bring the church back to orthodoxy."[64]

Before the New York presbytery could complete its investigation or take action against Fosdick, two documents appeared that articulated very forcefully the conservative and liberal positions. In 1923, J. Gresham Machen published *Christianity and Liberalism*, which argued that the fundamental principles of Christianity were in total conflict with the assumptions of liberalism. Machen asserted that the only logical course was to purge Presbyterianism of such liberal beliefs.[65] "We shall be interested in showing that despite the liberal use of traditional phraseology modern liberalism not only is a different religion from Christianity but belongs in a totally different class of religions."[66]

With this publication, Machen emerged as one of the leading Presbyterian conservatives in the country, and he provided his supporters with a powerful printed weapon against liberalism. More moderate Presbyterians, however, rallied to a document published in January 1924, which came to be known as the Auburn Affirmation. When it first appeared, the document had been signed by 150 Presbyterian ministers. By May 1924, the number of signers had risen to 1,274. The Auburn Affirmation articulated a theological basis for toleration. The document also stated that the history of the Presbyterian church had been marked by tolerance of a diversity of opinion. Specifically, the authors declared that the five-point doctrinal mandates, approved by the General Assemblies in 1910 and 1923, were invalid.[67]

The Auburn Affirmation clarified the essential difference between the two positions. Machen and his supporters believed that two separate religions had emerged on the American landscape, and those two were incompatible. Signers of the affirmation believed the differences among most Presbyterians, and for that matter most Protestants, to be so insignificant as to be virtually irrelevant. The church historian Lefferts Loetscher divided Presbyterians of this period into three groups. The first group he labeled as extreme conservatives, many of whom supported Machen. Matthews appears at this point to best fit in this category. The second group, Loetscher described as the extreme party of toleration—essentially the signers of the Auburn Affirmation. And the third group consisted of those who would not sign the Auburn Affirmation but who generally wanted a spirit of toleration to prevail.[68]

Those groups all began to line up support for their respective positions at the 1924 General Assembly. The assembly began with a victory for the conservatives when Dr. Clarence Macartney became moderator by a close vote, 464 to 446.[69] Matthews was named chairman of the Committee on Church Policy. The assembly determined that the Permanent Judicial Commission should be charged with rendering a judgment on Fosdick's situation, since some members of the New York presbytery had filed a protest concerning the presbytery's handling of the affair. The General Assembly's judicial commission determined that, since Fosdick was a Baptist, he must either join on the assembly's terms or resign his preaching position; the New York minister chose the latter course. On the surface it appeared that the conservatives had won a major victory by having Fosdick removed. Yet more astute observers recognized that the judicial commission carefully avoided requiring all Presbyterian ministers to adhere to the five-point doctrine.[70]

The 1924 General Assembly was then given the task of either confirming or reviewing the findings of the commission; once again, this vote was seen as a major test for both liberals and conservatives. Matthews moved to review the findings of the judicial commission in hopes that the five-point doctrine would be required of all clergy. His motion, however, was rejected 504 to 311, indicating that extreme conservatives would have a difficult time achieving anything more than Fosdick's dismissal.[71] The five-point deliverance of 1910 would not be incorporated into the judicial and administrative policy of the Presbyterian Church U.S.A.[72]

In a second case before the 1924 assembly, the conservatives suffered another defeat on a resolution that would have required "all who represent the Church on the Boards, General Council, Theological Seminaries, and every other Agency of the Church" to reaffirm the five-point doctrinal statement of 1910.[73] The Permanent Judicial Commission ruled that it was unconstitutional for the General Assembly alone to construct new standards of belief.

Matthews openly criticized the results of the assembly and Fosdick's actions in a sermon to his congregation.

Therefore, you can see that the Commission did not render a judicial verdict in the strict sense of the law, but wrote an afternoon-aid-society-halting stammering essay on an interloping disturber of the peace of the Church, intending, of course, to express the determination of the Church, and, to say to the intruding, offensive quest that he should never come back to the First Presbyterian Church of New York City unless he would come in through the front door in the regular, standardized, orthodox, Confession of the Faith way of entering. If this unwelcome offending guest is a sincere Christian gentleman, he will never again try to preach in that pulpit unless he first joins the presbytery, after due trial and examination, and subscribes to all the doctrines and practices of our Church as taught in the Confession of Faith, including infant baptism, and the Holy Sacrament of the Lord's Supper.[74]

Between the General Assemblies of 1924 and 1925, Matthews corresponded with J. Gresham Machen on several occasions and expressed support for his position. In November, Matthews inquired, "How does the battle go? What do you think of the latest anarchistic acts of our rationalistic friends in New York?"[75]

By the spring of 1925, the men shared a concern for the direction of the upcoming General Assembly. Both men worried that the momentum had shifted away from the conservatives. Machen believed that the election of the next moderator would be crucial, and he very much feared that Charles Erdman would be elected. Erdman, although theologically conservative (he had been a major contributor to *The Fundamentals*), eschewed the intolerance of the extreme group. Two weeks before the convention, Machen wrote Matthews a detailed account of his dislike for Erdman. "One thing is clear to me—the election of Dr. Erdman would be a greater blow to evangelical religion than ever the election of an out-and-out Modernist."[76] Matthews wrote back, "I am deeply grieved over the awful situation. Do you know anybody who can influence Erdman? I have tried to get him to stay out of the mess. It is his only salvation."[77]

Despite Machen's efforts, Erdman emerged victorious in Columbus, Ohio. Machen wrote Matthews shortly thereafter.

The news from the General Assembly seems to indicate a rather sweeping Modernist victory. It is not only the election of Dr. Erdman that troubles me. . . . If our Church gets into the permanent control of the Modernists, I do not know what we as Christian men ought to do. There are many battles in a great war, and this war is not yet lost. It is

Fundamentalism and Modernism

evident, however, that the long policy of lying and deceit which has been pursued by the Modernists has been woefully successful. I think it is very doubtful whether the Presbyterian Church is going to remain Christian. But certainly we ought to contend earnestly for that, and ought at any rate to have faith in God as to the ultimate result, no matter what may become of our Church.[78]

Whether Matthews agreed completely with Machen at this point is not exactly clear. He certainly led Machen to believe that he agreed in spirit with the assessment of Erdman.

Almost immediately, at the 1925 General Assembly, Charles Erdman faced the perennial question of whether the ability to license clergy rested with the presbytery or with the General Assembly. The New York presbytery had made a formal request to the General Assembly "to determine by its Judicial Commission, the proper status of a Presbytery in its Constitutional powers in the matter of licensing of candidates."[79] At the 1925 assembly, the commission reviewed a case of the New York presbytery licensing a candidate who did not believe in the virgin birth. The commission ruled that, though licensing had originated in the presbytery, ultimately the General Assembly did have the right of review to determine whether the presbytery's standards were in line with the church's constitution. The judicial commission also cited the 1910 declaration that no candidate "who is in serious doubt concerning this doctrine should be licensed or ordained as a minister."[80] Conservatives rejoiced, but more moderate and liberal Presbyterians threatened to split from the denomination.

Under Erdman's leadership, a fifteen-man special commission was formed in order to examine the "present spiritual condition of our Church and the causes making for unrest."[81] Years later, Erdman credited Matthews with proposing the original idea for the commission. Appointed to the committee, Matthews was regarded as the most conservative of all its members.[82] Clearly the pressure would be on the Seattle pastor to make sure that conservative issues were faithfully represented. In many ways this would be the most significant moment in Matthews's life relative to his influence on the future direction of the Presbyterian church.

Erdman directed the commission to focus on the power of the presbytery and the General Assembly regarding the licensing of candidates for the ministry. He also believed that the commission needed to decide how binding the specific decisions on the part of the General Assembly were on the presbytery.[83]

Fundamentalism and Modernism

The commission heard testimony from a number of prominent spokespersons, including Machen and another leading conservative, Clarence Macartney, as well as from more liberal voices, such as Henry Sloane Coffin and William Adams Brown. These more liberal and moderate church leaders made it clear that the judicial decision of 1925, which required belief in the virgin birth, threatened to force the secession of the left wing of the Presbyterian church. Yet, if the commission changed the formula for subscription or seemed to abandon the Westminster Confession as the standard of belief, the right wing would inevitably leave. The commission never considered that the church should repudiate its historical positions. As the historian Lefferts Loetscher has argued:

> The practical problem, then, reduced itself to the question whether, without amending the constitution or the subscription formula, the constitution could be so interpreted as to remove the binding force from the 'five points' without repudiating them as doctrines of the Church. In other words, could it be shown that the Presbyterian Church's history and constitution, properly interpreted, pointed to a much broader toleration than extreme conservatives were willing to grant?[84]

The commission divided itself into five committees: Conference, Historical Background, Causes of Unrest and Possibilities of Relief, Literature, and Constitutional Procedure, the committee to which Mark Matthews was appointed with Nelson Loomis and Judge John H. DeWitt. In retrospect the committee on the Causes of Unrest and the committee on Constitutional Procedure were the most important. The causes committee attempted to deal with the conservative contention that the naturalistic liberal party within the church was essentially not Christian. As previously indicated, the conservative solution was to force the Presbyterian church to take a stand on the essential Christian beliefs—in other words, the five points—and in so doing, force the liberals out of the church. On the other hand, the liberals asserted that the church had always tolerated a diversity of opinion. In the end, led by the moderate churchman Robert Speer, the committee took a centrist approach that stressed tolerance, forbearance, and loyalty to the denomination.

Fundamentalism and Modernism

Matthews's committee on the constitution was responsible for evaluating the relationship between the General Assembly and the presbyteries, a key area of dispute. Minutes for the commission do not reveal the substance of discussion or debate.[85] But the committee offered a key recommendation by affirming the authority of the presbyteries and not the General Assembly in the decisions regarding the qualifications of the candidates for ministry. The committee report stated: "[I]t seems like trifling with sacred things to chance the fate of fundamental religious beliefs upon a mere vote of the General Assembly. An open and avowed change in the Constitution cannot be brought about without following a procedure which insures most careful consideration and action by the Presbyteries."[86] The committee further stated that in "every presbytery there must be ministers who represent both schools of thought—the strict constructionist and the liberal constructionist."[87] The historian Beau Weston concluded that the spirit of toleration was "most remarkable, from a committee of which Mark Matthews was a member."[88] In the end, Matthews signed off on reports from his own committee as well as the committee on causes of unrest, and these were subsequently included in the larger report of the commission.

Most observers regarded the report of the Special Commission to be the most important event of the 1926 General Assembly. In summary, the report argued that the Presbyterian Church in America had historically been far from homogeneous; Presbyterians had disagreed regarding many practices and beliefs. The report implied that it was those who tried to force the Presbyterian church into a much more narrowly defined set of beliefs who were diverging from the historical identity of the church. This argument set the tone for the entire report.[89]

After the report was read, opponents offered several amendments but all were defeated. In fact, very little opposition to the report surfaced at the assembly. Dr. Machen seemed to be one of the few, however, who understood the report's significance for the conservative wing of the church. At the convention he told a friend, "If the evangelical party votes for this report its witness bearing is gone and all the sacrifices of the past few years will go for nothing."[90] Overall, however, the report was enthusiastically supported throughout the church. According to Weston, "When the General Assembly of 1926 embraced this tolerant and constitutional understanding of the Presbyterian church, the tide turned in favor of pluralism in the church."[91]

Fundamentalism and Modernism

In Matthews's own report to his own congregation regarding the commission's work, he argued otherwise. He made great efforts to assure his flock that the results of the 1926 General Assembly, and specifically the report of the commission, would not adversely affect the conservative forces within the church. "There is not a line in that report that could give comfort to the modernistic or rationalistic forces of the world."[92] He agreed that the majority elements within the Presbyterian church demonstrated sound belief. "It does seem, to some of us who have been fighting so long, that the conservative forces of the Church should learn that the clanking bells of modernism are rung by just a few ecclesiastical bell-ringers, but, the majority of the Church is marching to the tune of 'Onward Christian Soldiers of the Cross.'"[93] But Matthews must have privately acknowledged that the forces of toleration had clearly prevailed over the more conservative voices.

The final report was delivered at the 1927 General Assembly, but the essence of what was said mirrored the conclusions delivered the previous year. In that same assembly, Robert Speer, the moderate who had exercised considerable influence over the substance of the commission's report, was elected moderator. Many historians have regarded the report as one of the most important developments within the modern history of the Presbyterian church. Lefferts Loetscher called it the "major turning point in the theological history of the Church" since the reconciliation of the Old and New School Presbyterians in 1869.[94] Essentially, the commission sanctioned a policy of toleration and rejected Machen's position that liberal Presbyterians had to leave the church. In a direct criticism of the five-point doctrinal standard of 1910, the report asserted that the General Assembly did not have the constitutional power to render binding definitions of the church's essential faith.[95]

The question remains of why Matthews moved to a position of moderation and abandoned Machen's views. On the surface it appears that the two had much in common. Machen, like Matthews, was raised a Southerner and was heavily influenced by Old School Presbyterian theology. As late as 1924, there was no indication that Matthews had any desire for moderation. In fact, it was in that year that Matthews came out with a collection of sermons in book form entitled *Gospel Sword Thrusts*. Strongly attacking modernism and the cultural decadence Matthews perceived, the sermons solidified his conservative reputation.[96]

Fundamentalism and Modernism

The key difference between Matthews and Machen, however, is found in the latter's intense conviction that the great battleground was theology. Machen had studied the adherents of Schleiermacher firsthand in Europe and had returned to America convinced that the church must fight to prevent any introduction of modernistic thought. Matthews, on the other hand, came to fundamentalism through a combination of his evangelical background, Old School Presbyterian theology, and a frustration with the lack of progress in establishing righteous communities. But Matthews always remained committed to keeping the community together, and he must have seen how wrenching this conflict had become for the Presbyterian church.

It is likely that Matthews's change in position resulted from his acute political perception. He may have sensed that the tide had turned in 1924 with the two critical defeats for the conservative faction; rather than be left behind by the change, he might have decided to be a part of that change. Matthews also might have been influenced by his good friend Robert Speer, a leading advocate for compromise on the special commission. Whatever the reasons, Matthews was part of one of the most significant theological developments in the twentieth-century Presbyterian church.[97]

Another indication of Matthews's more moderate views by 1925 was his response to the Scopes Monkey Trial. The courtroom clash between William Jennings Bryan and Clarence Darrow over the theory of evolution seemed to exemplify the larger struggle in the minds of many Americans between the Biblical account of creation and the new scientific explanation. Historians have often used this event to symbolize the split between modernists and fundamentalists. Although Matthews expressed his conviction that the Bible be taught in the schools, he said little in public about the Scopes trial. One can only speculate, but perhaps Matthews was uncomfortable with Bryan's attack on the validity of science, or perhaps, after the General Assembly of 1925, he felt he needed to tone down his rhetoric. The daily newspapers and his collected sermons offered no harangue against Clarence Darrow or advocacy of an antievolution law in Washington but rather included general statements about the need for moral education. "Common school education, even superficial as it is," Matthews wrote, "must have a moral foundation if we are to save the youth of this land."[98] On another occasion he chastised those who sought to "remove God" from the schools, but he also suggested that specific denominational doctrine should be avoided. "We will never permit our educational institutions to make an attack on God, upon the Bible, upon the faith of our children," Matthews said in a radio address, "neither will we allow them to teach denominational doctrine."[99]

Matthews's moderating role also surfaced in a small way in the controversy that swept Princeton Seminary in the late twenties. Princeton had been dominated by faculty who held to Old School Presbyterianism, and the influence of Charles Hodge remained strong. The majority of the faculty favored the extreme conservative position, opposed Fosdick, and thus strongly objected to the report by the Special Commission.[100]

Controversy at the seminary was exacerbated in 1926 when, in May, the seminary's board of directors elected J. Gresham Machen to the chair of apologetics and ethics and his election was subsequently confirmed by the board of trustees. The boards had sharply divided opinions, and the vote on Machen's appointment was extremely close. A number of dissatisfied directors and trustees requested that the General Assembly of 1926 investigate conditions in the seminary; in response, the assembly recommended the appointment of a committee to study the situation. President J. Ross Stevenson took the floor of the assembly and explained that the divisiveness related to the report of the Special Commission of 1925. Stevenson wanted Princeton to represent not a particular faction but both Old and New School positions. After a debate centering on whether or not orthodoxy and toleration were compatible, the assembly decided to delay action on Machen's appointment.[101]

The investigating committee's report to the General Assembly in 1927 stressed that the root of the problem seemed to be in the plan of governance by two boards; the majority report proposed that a single Board of Control be established and that approval of Machen's appointment as well as any others be withheld until reorganization could be completed. After the General Assembly, Matthews reported to his congregation that he opposed dissolving the two boards. "There is grave danger in smashing this dual system because of the great financial trusts involved. The legal difficulties are far greater than have as yet been pointed out."[102] But Matthews also opposed the efforts on the part of the conservative faculty at Princeton, who were in the majority, to control the direction of the seminary. "The faculty does not and should not control the Seminary," preached Matthews to his congregation in 1927. "It is not in the jurisdiction of the members of the faculty nor is it their

Fundamentalism and Modernism

right to govern the Board of Trustees or the Board of Directors."[103]

At the 1928 General Assembly, the proposal to dissolve the boards underwent extensive debate until Mark Matthews proposed a substitute resolution "that the further consideration of said Reports be postponed for one year, and that the Board of Directors of Princeton Seminary be and hereby is instructed to proceed immediately to compose the differences at the Seminary and to make a full report on these instructions to the next General Assembly."[104] The motion may have been designed to give conservatives more time to reverse the majority report or simply as a way of ending rancorous debate so that a compromise could be reached. Matthews hoped somehow to maintain a bridge between the conservative and moderate wings. As a result, the board of directors at Princeton attempted "to compose the differences," but that proved impossible. The assembly of 1929 finally settled the Princeton issue by adopting the majority report of the previous year and establishing one board of control.[105]

This desire to maintain a modicum of Presbyterian unity while still advocating fundamentalist principles was reflected in Matthews's activities both in Presbyterian politics and in his pulpit during the late 1920s. At one point, his mediating efforts were even interpreted by some ultraconservative critics as aiding the modernists.[106] Perhaps it was in response to this criticism that Matthews used his sermons to reassure his conservative supporters. Hoping to erase any remaining doubt concerning his fundamentalist assumptions, Matthews repeatedly placed an emphasis on "the whole Gospel and the premillennial coming of Christ."[107] However, out of the pulpit, he expressed his belief that J. Gresham Machen's threat to split from the church was unacceptable.[108]

In 1929, extreme conservatives, led by Machen, decided to form Westminster Seminary in order to preserve the Old School tradition. Machen hoped to train "soldiers of orthodoxy," as one historian phrased it.[109] In 1936, Machen decided to split from the Presbyterian Church U.S.A. and form the Presbyterian Church of America. In 1939, the name was formally changed to the Orthodox Presbyterian Church. Matthews, though sympathetic to Machen, believed that this schism would be counterproductive. Matthews took the view of Clarence Macartney, another conservative, who believed that it was better for Machen and conservative theologians to stay within Princeton than to abandon it to more moderate forces.[110]

The new split within Presbyterianism affected Matthews's own congregation. By one estimate, more than 100 people left First Presbyterian in 1936 and 1937 over the issue of premillennialism, believing that Matthews should be even stronger in his advocacy of this doctrine. Matthews, however, remained consistent in his belief that the forces of modernism were best fought by trying to keep the Presbyterian church as united as possible.[111]

Throughout his life, Mark Matthews had kept much of his focus on the building of his version of a righteous community. And though his methods and strategies evolved over the years, his ultimate goal remained largely unchanged. His religious views, however, underwent a much greater metamorphosis. Throughout much of his early career, he identified himself as evangelical but broadly tolerant of denominational differences. Like many evangelicals in the early twentieth century, however, Matthews gradually became more militant in his defense of orthodoxy. He came to believe very fervently that Christianity required adherence to a specific set of beliefs. He was convinced that the challenges presented by modern intellectual movements as well as liberal theology threatened the very core of Christianity. He also came to believe that the authors of *The Fundamentals*, the doctrinal deliverance of 1910, and the pronouncements of J. Gresham Machen were on the right track. Yet, as he witnessed the fragmentation within the Presbyterian church, he drew back from the extreme militancy expressed by Machen. Matthews reached the conclusion that compromise provided more promise than did secession.

The historian Ernest Sandeen, upon reflecting on the course of fundamentalism in the 1920s, found a peculiar irony: "Whether one views it as fortunate or unfortunate, it is apparent that the iron-hard schism-before-compromise policy typical of the nineteenth-century millenarians had lost its appeal among some of the most able descendants of those patriarchs," wrote Sandeen. "The decade looked upon as the zenith of militant censoriousness actually witnessed a striking degree of compromise."[112] Mark Matthews perhaps had as much to do with that spirit of compromise as anyone.

⌒ CHAPTER 10 ⌒

Screenitis and the Radio

*This is the amusement age. The craze for amusements fore-
tells the doom of present day civilization. . . . Principles
are being abandoned, and character sacrificed in the mad
rush to reach the Beach of Frivolity and Pleasure. . . . Ba-
bies are born in the mad house of Jazz and are being rocked
in the cradle of indecency.*
— Mark Matthews (1922)

Mark Matthews's power was at its zenith
during the second decade of the twentieth century. An important figure within the national Presbyterian church, the preacher often advised
Seattle mayors, and his relationship with Woodrow Wilson brought
him into contact with national political leaders at the highest level.
Nevertheless, his hope for a righteous community remained unfulfilled.
The events of the war, the labor disputes in his own city, and the struggle
between fundamentalists and modernists made that dream seem less
attainable by the 1920s. Like many Americans, Mark Matthews faced
the modern age with a combination of fear and hope. He embraced
most of the technological advances, although he never hesitated to
blame them for making churchgoing less attractive. He loved the radio as a means of mass communication, and he and his wife, Grace,
became motoring enthusiasts. At the same time, he feared the rising
popularity of movies. Horrified by the advent of the flapper, he lashed
out at the revolution in sexual attitudes and expressed concern about
the changing role of women in American society and within the church.

Compared with statements from his early career, Matthews's pronouncements during the twenties seem markedly less optimistic. Absent from his sermons was the sense of progress that had marked his prewar views. And though at times he argued that Seattle could still fulfill a vital role in national and religious affairs, his exhortations to city residents to change behavior or support specific civic improvements came less frequently. Matthews spent much of his time responding to immediate problems. Walter Lippmann's 1929 observation "Whirl is King" seemed applicable to Matthews's own situation. In the process of trying to make sense of the cultural and social changes occurring in the twenties, Matthews, like many Americans, grew anxious about the current state of American society.

Yet throughout the decade, Matthews seemed to grow in esteem in the eyes of many, if not most, Seattleites. He remained the most visible of Seattle's religious leaders, and he found himself in the midst of a number of public issues. Certainly, his stature can be attributed to his association with a variety of worthy causes, but it also may have been a result of the particular social-psychological needs of Seattle residents in the decades between the two world wars. Although few people in Seattle understood it at the time, the city began to stagnate economically and socially after World War I. The population grew much more slowly than it had previous to the war, and after the building boom in 1919-20, Seattle manufacturing lagged. The historian Roger Sale points out that in 1940 there were fewer industrial workers in the entire Seattle-Tacoma area than there had been in Seattle alone in 1920. Sale's interpretation of Seattle's socioeconomic climate rests largely on his observation that the middle class had created a very pleasant environment in which to live: parks, neighborhoods, and excellent schools contributed to a sense of security that wrapped itself in conservatism. Outside of being the first major city to elect a woman to the office of mayor (Bertha K. Landes in 1926), Seattle experienced few political controversies during the decade.[1]

However, at the national level, the twenties witnessed significant changes in American society, and historians frequently point to an increased anxiety concerning the perils of the modern age. The automobile, the radio, and the sexual revolution each had an impact on the values of middle-class urbanites. The debate over the teaching of evolution, the Red Scare, and the rise of the Ku Klux Klan reflected a nervousness about the possible demise of traditional values. Matthews continued to preach conservative Christian orthodoxy and embody

Screenitis and the Radio

middle-class values. Many Seattleites probably took a certain comfort in the fact that Matthews walked the streets. The affairs of the world may have seemed more manageable as long as there was still a preacher whom everybody knew. Matthews nurtured that image of being the city's pastor, and he was still motivated by a vision of righteousness. He continued to express his opinions and to work on many fronts; from foreign affairs and presidential politics to hospital drives and labor disputes, he hoped to retain his influence in Seattle and realize his dream of a righteous community.[2]

The events in Europe following the First World War continued to occupy Matthews's attention; he followed the peace talks in Paris very closely and supported Wilson with unflinching loyalty. The war reaffirmed Matthews's belief in the sinfulness and selfishness of human nature. For many Americans in the 1920s, the war encouraged a belief in political isolation. In fact many conservative Christians believed that the United States should remove itself from foreign alliances of every kind. The historian Joel Carpenter notes how fundamentalists in general were quite suspicious of the League of Nations.[3] Matthews took the opposite point of view. He concluded that America needed to be involved in world affairs in order to check the naturally evil tendencies of other nations. He firmly believed that America should accept the Treaty of Versailles and participate in the League of Nations.

In March and April of 1919, Americans debated the merits of Wilson's proposed League of Nations. The Seattle daily newspapers often editorialized about the treaty.[4] The chamber of commerce decided to provide its own forum for the opposing positions and asked Matthews to present the affirmative side in a debate with Judge Cornelius Hanford. The request underscores the preacher's stature in the area of public policy. Matthews argued that the nation had to be involved in the world in order to prevent further armed conflict. "Shall the United States refuse to become a member of the proposed League," Matthews asked, "and thereby make it impossible to create an agency that will hold in check the infamous powers of the earth?" America, Matthews asserted, had to hold to the "doctrine of conciliation and arbitration."[5]

When the Senate finally rejected the Treaty of Versailles, Matthews expressed his outrage in a letter to the editor of the *New York Times*. The Seattle preacher accused the United States Senate of fostering "famine, pestilence, disease, poverty, anarchy, and bolshevism."[6] Not realizing the extent of Wilson's illness, Matthews urged the president to resubmit the treaty and force the Senate to accept it. "Expose the influences and motives behind the defeat of the treaty," Matthews telegrammed Wilson.[7] But of course this had no effect. Ultimately resigned to the defeat of the treaty and the nonparticipation of the United States in the League of Nations, Matthews continued to argue for an interventionist policy in the face of growing public sentiment for isolationism. In early November 1921, he spoke out against the Harding-sponsored Washington Disarmament Conference. The Seattle preacher argued that Americans should not naively believe that Europe's problems could be solved by the destruction of the instruments of war. "If [the nation] were to disarm, it would be impossible for her to be reconstructed," Matthews said. "Superficial people are talking about prohibiting war. That cannot be done unless human nature can be changed."[8]

Matthews's interest in foreign policy drew him to comment on the future of Germany. Matthews believed that the U.S. needed a more realistic foreign policy in regard to Germany. He urged Congress to assist the defeated nation in finding ways to pay its reparations or risk being responsible for more serious economic complications. "I am not so much interested in the amount of the indemnity as I am in the fact that the indemnity ought to be fixed finally both in amount and in method of payment," Matthews wrote. "The uncertainty is disastrous to world peace. . . . England and America should endorse the bonds, underwrite that amount of money, and permit Germany to begin her commercial existence with credit and honor to herself, and with assistance and confidence from the two greatest powers on earth."[9] Running counter to prevailing public opinion, Matthews's visionary perspective seems remarkable given his virulent anti-German sentiments only four years earlier.

He consistently blamed isolationists for being overly naive and contributing to further problems in world affairs.

> The doctrine of isolation is being preached by politicians but not by statesmen. They misinterpret and give a wrong construction to the utterances of Mr. Washington, in which he advised that America in her inception avoid entangling herself with foreign alliances. . . . We are the superior power in the world. We are in the world. We are a part of the world. . . . It is criminal to preach or practice isolation.[10]

Although Matthews remained confident about America's general strength and virtue, he expressed less optimism about the amelioration of the world's problems than he had before the war. Unlike millions of Americans who wanted to retreat from responsibility in the postwar world, Matthews vigorously argued that the United States shouldered a major role for securing the future peace.

If the First World War illustrated for Matthews the depravity of human nature, popular culture of the 1920s only reinforced his pessimistic view of the human condition. The decadence of society became a consistent sermon theme as the preacher attacked almost every cultural symbol from the flapper and bathtub gin to the automobile and Al Capone. Historians agree that the decade witnessed a proliferation of technological breakthroughs and social changes that affected virtually all Americans. Henry Ford made the automobile readily available, and the radio brought instant mass communication and entertainment to millions of people. Motion pictures combined with the popularity of jazz music and a booming fashion and cosmetics industry to present a lifestyle that celebrated freedom, sexuality, and pleasure.[11] As early as 1910, Matthews began railing against the broader social effects of the automobile and a consumer culture. Even before the assembly line came into existence, Matthews began to fight against the psychology of consumption and pleasure.

> The automobile is responsible for an insane competition in extravagance. With the use of this convenience, which will eventually become a commercial necessity in the transaction of business, has come a desire for all of its accompanying evils. Men aren't satisfied with a machine within their income, but, they must have a machine that competes with their neighbor's, and must do the things their neighbors do with their machines, must buy the things their neighbors buy, give the functions, dinners, parties and outings their neighbors give. Consequently, there has arisen in society this insane competition for show, sham, and extravagance until men are leaping into the vortex of bankruptcy every day.[12]

On another occasion Matthews railed against what he believed was the impact of the automobile on church attendance. "The gasoline mania causes thousands to take the family, the dog, and the lunch baskets into the automobile early Sabbath morning," Matthews preached, "when they begin to break the Ten Commandments, the speed laws, the rules of domestic tranquillity and Sabbath observance."[13] Actually, Matthews, himself, came to enjoy driving an automobile, and his wife,

Grace, received publicity for being one of the first women in the city to possess a Washington State driver's license.

But in general, most aspects of popular culture displeased him. He lamented the amount of money being spent on vaudeville entertainment instead of being offered to the collection plate at church.[14] Not surprisingly, in the postwar decade, Matthews continued to fight for restrictive legislation against everything from horseracing to card-playing and was greatly disturbed by the tendency in American culture to embrace more freedom of expression. He attacked the explosion of cinema on many occasions and frequently attempted to make his audience feel guilty regarding their church attendance. "Screenitis sends thousands into the motion picture houses when they make a pagan attack upon God's Holy Day," Matthews railed.[15] Though a member of the Seattle Golf Club, Matthews expressed little sympathy with the Sunday golfer. "Tomorrow, 200,000 golfers and 30,000 caddies will break the Ten Commandments on the links of the nation, pleading that they need the fresh air," Matthews told a Denver audience. "They might well get it, for some day the idiots are going to need it," he said implying that they would end up in hell.[16]

Throughout the decade, Matthews never tired of attacking the "amusement mania or pleasure insanity [that] seems to have afflicted eighty-five percent of the population."[17] He often compared the decadence of contemporary America with ancient Greece and Rome.

> This is the amusement age. The craze for amusements foretells the doom of present day civilization. . . . Properties are being shattered, principles are being abandoned, and character sacrificed in the mad rush to reach the Beach of Frivolity and Pleasure. . . . Babies are born in the mad house of Jazz and are being rocked in the cradle of indecency.[18]

Matthews and many others hoped that prohibition would be the answer to many of these social problems. But clearly as the decade wore on, Matthews grew impatient over the issue of enforcement and the manner in which politics seemed to play a role in its overall social effect. He often preached about the necessity of enforcing the law as well as obeying the letter of the law. Increasingly he sought to exercise his own political power and find a way to influence the enforcement of prohibition within the state. Like many dry Democrats, Matthews became a Hoover supporter after the Democrats nominated Al Smith, who called for the repeal of the Eighteenth Amendment.[19] The Seattle preacher campaigned for Hoover and consistently offered his support to the president during his term in office.

Matthews was more closely involved with another Republican, Senator Wesley Jones. Jones's moral beliefs coincided closely with Matthews's; he did not smoke, drink, or gamble, and he was devoted to the American middle-class ideal.[20] Frequently, the two men discussed specific legislation, particularly if it related to prohibition. However, Matthews's propensity to use his political contacts in strange ways affected his relationship with Jones. As he had done with other political figures, Matthews attempted to ingratiate himself further as Jones's personal confidant and to use Jones's influence to achieve greater power for himself.

In a letter reminiscent of some sent to Wilson during the war years, Matthews told Jones that he knew of a conspiracy that threatened to bring the senator down and that, if Jones approved, he could expose the conspirators before they did any harm. "Give me the authority that I have asked for and I may be able to clear the situation," Matthews wrote Jones. "Make people sign on the dotted line, resign, and perhaps save a great upheaval."[21] The senator replied that he did not know what Matthews was talking about, and in any event he had nothing to hide; apparently the matter was dropped.[22] But Matthews continued to seek personal power through Jones. In this case, his quest involved a fairly bizarre controversy between Matthews and the Anti-Saloon League. In 1929, Matthews dropped a bombshell on the state's dry forces by seriously attacking the Anti-Saloon League. In a sermon to his congregation, he argued that "fanatical stress" had been placed on the enforcement of one law—prohibition—at the expense of other crimes, such as murder. He cited national statistics that suggested that of 13,000 murders in 1928, only 100 suspects were prosecuted. "What we need in this country is a League that will prevent the establishment of leagues for specific purposes," Matthews preached, "and which will bring the American people back to a sense of their responsibility to the government and to law."[23]

Greeted largely with approval from those who opposed prohibition, Matthews's urgings seemed to convince many people that the time had come for a reassessment of the Volstead Act. "Coming from such a source the attack was remarkable," the Seattle Star observed. "It shows pretty plainly that people in general are tired of fanaticism and hypocrisy."[24] But clearly, supporters of the Anti-Saloon League were stunned. State Prohibition Director Bernard Hicks had no comment, and the *Aberdeen Daily World* charged Matthews with hypocrisy. "If Dr. Matthews be not giving aid and comfort to violators of federal prohibition laws," the editorialist asked, "in all reason just what is he doing?"[25]

Matthews's actions might be interpreted as a simple shift in position in response to political realities if it were not for his request in February 1930 to Wesley Jones that the senator nominate him for the office of United States Prohibition Commissioner. "I would like to give Prohibition a real enforcement test," Matthews wrote Jones, "and if they will let me organize it I can do it."[26] Jones tried to dissuade Matthews from seeking the position, apparently successfully.[27] Norman Clark is apparently correct in concluding that Matthews was actually trying to split the dry leadership with his attack on the Anti-Saloon League and assume direction himself. This was certainly what State Prohibition Administrator Roy Lyle believed when he wrote to Senator Jones that Matthews was "deliberately betraying us."[28]

Matthews accomplished very little with his attack on the Anti-Saloon League. By 1930, there was a nationwide review of prohibition, and, according to Clark, "the egomania of Dr. Matthews had weakened the unity with which prohibitionists might face such an ordeal."[29] If Clark somewhat overstated the importance of Matthews's one sermon on the ability of the drys to continue the fight, he accurately pointed out the lack of sensitivity Matthews displayed for his fellow supporters of prohibition. The Seattle pastor envisioned himself as a key leader in the movement, but his political manipulation, designed to secure greater power for himself, did more harm than good.

If Matthews found himself frustrated regarding prohibition, he also ran against the prevailing social tide regarding the role of women in American society and in the Presbyterian church. Unquestionably, the decade did much to transform, if not eliminate, the vestiges of a Victorian code of dress and behavior for women. "The most conspicuous sign of what was taking place," Frederick Lewis Allen noted, "was the immense change in women's dress and appearance."[30] He found it significant that during the decade of the twenties the cosmetics industry experienced explosive growth.[31] Short skirts became fashionable, and the term "flapper" symbolized the liberation of women, all of which greatly upset Matthews. "The flapper is not condemned per se because she is a flapper," he wrote. "But she is to be criticized because of the methods she uses to become a flapper. . . . She is using the cosmetics that destroy her skin, and rob her of the distinctive features that belong to the sweet girl."[32]

But Matthews expressed other concerns regarding the possibility that women's roles were changing throughout American society. Most specifically, he emerged as a significant voice in opposition to the movement within the Presbyterian church to extend the principle of equality and allow women greater voice and responsibility in positions of ecclesiastical leadership. His views regarding women continued to reflect his conservative assumptions and, perhaps, to a certain extent, his larger concerns that the issue could further divide the Presbyterian church. Despite the seeming complexity of his motives, however, he must be regarded as a major voice in opposition to the extension of equality for women.

During the 1920s, the Presbyterian church entered into the national debate over the changing role of women. Presbyterians, including those at First Presbyterian Church in Seattle, had not allowed women to preach or serve as ruling elders. During the middle part of the decade, a number of women began to push the General Assembly to adopt policies that would open up positions of leadership within the church. Specifically, it was urged that the church should ordain women as ruling elders and that all language that implied or acknowledged sexual inequality be removed from constitutional documents.[33] However, Matthews, as one might expect, vigorously opposed any effort to change the status of women in the church, and he did all that he could to at least delay the implementation of any reforms that would allow women to assume greater authority.

Perhaps one of the reasons contributing to Matthews's resistance was his fear that this issue, in combination with the fundamentalist-modernist controversy, would simply rip the church apart. But Matthews's vitriolic views toward the possibility of women becoming preachers clearly express opposition that went well beyond a simple desire to hold the church together. In an article published in *The Presbyterian* entitled "Why Women in the Pulpit?" he declared that women who desired to preach were not Presbyterians but members of a "freak class" usually found in denominations that were heretically inclined or mentally unsound. He noted that the "female pulpitress" was an unscriptural monstrosity, arguing that Jesus did not choose a woman to be among the twelve apostles. He also expressed fear that ordaining women would drive thousands of men out of the ministry and replace them with those who were constitutionally unfit for such work. With dogmatic certainty, Matthews proclaimed that God had never meant for a woman to preach.[34]

In the spring of 1930, presbyteries throughout the country began voting on several initiatives that would, if passed, allow women much greater authority in the church. Specifically, one overture proposed that women be allowed to become ordained as ministers and elders; a second proposal would only allow for women to become ruling elders, and a third would permit women to become licensed evangelists. When the voting was finally tallied, the first proposal regarding women ministers failed, as did the third one, which would have permitted women to become licensed evangelists. But the second overture, permitting women to become ordained as ruling elders, passed. The historians Lois Boyd and Douglas Brackenridge see the election results as indicative of middle-class Presbyterian values in the late 1920s. They convincingly argue that there are a number of explanations for the defeat of full ordination, among which was the absence of significant support from women at the local level, as well as the strength of opposition from people like Matthews. "The middle-class constituency of the Presbyterian church in good conscience defeated Overture A in the name of conservatism," wrote Boyd and Brackenridge, "and in the same good conscience approved Overture B [ordination as elders] in the name of progressivism."[35] Unlike his stand on the Special Commission of 1925, in which he displayed surprising moderation and toleration, Matthews clearly reflected a reactionary perspective regarding the role of women in the church. His harsh language and unflinching conviction that women should not be allowed to serve in positions of leadership exemplified not only his traditional Southern values but also his heightened anxiety over the state of American society in the 1920s.

If Matthews clearly opposed most of the new cultural forces and trends in American society during the decade, he offered less resistance to the booming culture of speculation in land, stocks, and oil. Millions of Americans attempted to make easy money in ventures such as the Florida land boom and, of course, on Wall Street. The prospect of greater wealth appealed to Matthews, too. In 1922, with eight others, he invested in an oil business near Tulsa, Oklahoma. Reasonably successful during the latter part of that year, the business developed serious cash-flow problems in early 1923.[36] Matthews had to find an immediate source of capital or face losing the oil lease. In February 1923, he wrote his friend and fellow Georgian William McAdoo, former secretary of the treasury under Wilson, and asked if he knew anyone who could invest $10,000 in the company. McAdoo replied that he did

Screenitis and the Radio

have a friend in the area, but evidently this lead did not result in any new investment.[37]

Matthews's plight apparently moved him to attempt to deceive his friend Henry Wellcome in July 1923. In an effort to conceal the real reason for needing the money, Matthews explained to Wellcome that his battles for the cause of righteousness had resulted in serious financial difficulties.[38] But again the appeal did not result in additional capital, and Matthews's group lost the lease. How much money Matthews forfeited is not known; he seems to have suffered comparatively little and probably lamented most the missed opportunity to strike it rich. However, the incident does suggest the vulnerability of many Americans, including Matthews, to temptations of easy riches in the decade.

One other aspect of mass culture in the 1920s, however, that turned out more favorably for Matthews was the advent of radio. By the beginning of the decade, creative minds had begun experimenting with this remarkable means of mass communication. Matthews had always believed in the power of the media and quickly apprehended that this invention could enhance his popularity. His first radio sermon came in late 1921 over a broadcast station in the offices of the *Seattle Post-Intelligencer*. It proved so successful, he began weekly radio sermons.[39] Evidently received with great enthusiasm, Matthews's weekly radio sermons inspired him to have First Presbyterian build its own radio station. Chiefly responsible for construction and operation were J. D. Ross, the very powerful head of Seattle City Light, and James G. Priestley, city chemical engineer and licensed radio operator. Costing approximately $15,000, the radio station, with the call letters KTW, began broadcasting in the spring of 1922 and was reportedly the first church-built, church-owned radio station in the world. Matthews frequently bragged that his station came into existence before there was any federal regulatory agency in the field.[40]

A stunning success, the radio station drew attention from the press across the country. Its broadcasts reportedly could be heard as far east as Indiana, as far south as Mexico, as well as throughout much of western Canada, because there were so few other stations on the air. In a letter to the *Boston Evening Transcript*, Matthews proudly described the technological accomplishment:

> Excellent modulation has been accomplished in the speaking, and the magnetic transmitters lie at the front of the platform eight or ten

feet from the speaker. Not the slightest hum from the motor genera-
tor or from the 250 volt direct current commercial circuits or from the
alternating filament circuit can be heard, these having been absolutely
cleared from the background.[41]

Campers all over Washington reportedly sang hymns together as
they gathered around receiving sets listening to services from First
Presbyterian. On one occasion, a group met in a vacant lot in the north
end of Seattle and listened to a receiver that had been placed on the
ledge of a window in an adjacent apartment. The broadcasts seemed
so realistic that when Matthews requested the women to remove their
hats, several in the vacant lot responded.[42] For a short time, Matthews
hoped that he could reach the entire North American continent from
his radio station. He envisioned the expansion of his ministry into logging camps, coal mines, and a host of other venues that had been previously inaccessible.

Yet the world of early radio was fluid; for the next two decades,
Matthews and J. D. Ross, the chief engineer, attempted to protect their
position on the dial. Countless times, Matthews wrote the governmental official responsible for regulatory action or the Federal Communi-
cations Commission directly over issues related to the radio. As the
airwaves became more crowded, the privileged position for KTW diminished. In retrospect, some of the incidents appear quite humorous,
although surely Matthews did not find them nearly so amusing. One
person wrote to the pastor describing the following:

By the most careful adjustment during your morning service I was
able to get a mixture of your service and Dr. Weyer's [pastor of Tacoma
Presbyterian Church] and it sounded very comical at times. When
you folks were asking for the offering the local operator here advised
the world that it was the First Presbyterian Church of Tacoma with
Dr. Clarence Weyer as pastor, and almost immediately your operator
tried to drown him out by saying it was the First Presbyterian church
of Seattle with Dr. M. A. Matthews as pastor. The most comical thing
was when both choirs got into the action at the same time. Of all the
racket I ever heard in my life that seemed the worst. However, when
Weyer with his stentorian voice got started he took up just one-third
of my dial and I gave up in despair. Same condition prevailed in the
evening, according to my wife, with First Christian Church of Tacoma
drowning you out.[43]

Matthews collected letters and sent them all to Washington, D.C., in an effort to prove that his radio was being drowned out illegally. And at one level, in retrospect, this concern seems out of perspective, but at another level it needs to be measured against the hope that he and many radio enthusiasts had that they would be able to reach millions of people through this new technology.

By 1929, Matthews felt beleaguered by a popular culture and complained to Ross that "the government must give us relief. These jazz hounds must not interfere with our station."[44] In the same year, a local radio executive asked Matthews if he might take his Bible study program off the air on Thursday evenings or move it to another place on the dial because advertisers did not think that a religious audience would lead to satisfactory ratings for their program.[45] Matthews surely must have felt that all his warnings regarding the decline in moral values in the larger society were evident in such requests. By 1933, First Presbyterian entered into a formal agreement with Washington State College in Pullman whereby the two institutions shared the 1220 spot on the dial. First Presbyterian had total control of the spot on all Sundays, holidays, and Thursday evenings from 7:30 to 10:30 P.M. Periodically both Washington State College officials and Matthews would raise objections to the possibility of new stations interfering with the range of their transmission.[46]

Overall the success of the radio focused renewed attention on the accomplishments of First Presbyterian in the 1920s. Throughout the decade, the church supported Matthews and four assistant ministers. By 1926, twenty-eight branch Sunday schools were operating throughout the greater Seattle area, and total church membership exceeded 7,000 members.[47]

First Presbyterian reflected the general prosperity of the 1920s, and in gratitude for Matthews's leadership, the congregation provided its pastor and his family with the gift of a three-month vacation to the Holy Land. Matthews, his wife, Grace, their twenty-year-old daughter, Glwadys, and their sixteen-year-old son, Mark, Jr., made plans for their first major family vacation. They left for Europe on January 26, 1925, and did not return until April 15.[48] Traveling by ocean liner, the Matthews family stopped in Madeira, where they met George Bernard Shaw and Rudyard Kipling. They made port on the northern African coast, in Greece, and in Constantinople before visiting various places from the Sea of Galilee to Jerusalem in the Holy Land. According to a 1979 interview with Gwladys, the Matthewses were among the first

American families to visit the tomb of Tutankhamen.[49] Incapable of assuming a low profile, Matthews served as master of ceremonies for a fencing tournament on board the ocean liner. According to his daughter, except for a terrible bout of seasickness on the return voyage, Matthews thoroughly enjoyed himself.

In general, the Matthews family seems to have been a close-knit group. The extant correspondence reveals their interest in each other's activities, humorous anecdotes, requests for advice, and open affection. "I am crazy because I cannot hear from your mother," father wrote son on the occasion of Grace's traveling abroad.[50] "It's not just a thousand times that I wished for you in the last week, but a million, if not more than that," sixteen-year-old Mark, Jr., wrote to his father.[51] According to the wife of Mark, Jr., humor cemented the relationship between father and son, and this humor was frequently reflected in their correspondence. "You made a bum effort at forging my name when you took your four sweethearts down to lunch," needled father in a letter to his son. "Or did you have two boys and two girls? Well next time you forge my name do a better job."[52]

Matthews enjoyed his children; he derived great pleasure from discussing their career goals and even some of his own problems. He often provided fatherly advice in a humorous manner. Once, he made an exaggerated attempt to assure his son's survival on his first camping trip. "Another thing in which you must obey me: keep your clothes buttoned; sleep in your underwear," wrote father to son. "Remember that I am not there to tuck you in. You must do the tucking. And you had better sleep in a night cap, so your head will not get cold."[53]

According to his daughter, both children enjoyed playing Parcheesi and dominoes with their father. Following the morning service on Sundays, the Matthews family would gather with guests around a sumptuous meal that featured Southern cooking and rich desserts. Light, fluffy waffles were usually on the menu following the Sunday evening service. In this manner, Matthews and his family relaxed and enjoyed each other's company.[54]

The affection among the members of Matthews's family stands in some contrast to his cooler relations with his father and sister. It is difficult to say for certain how close Mark Matthews was to his father. There is no extant correspondence between the two, and, according to Gwladys, her father spoke infrequently of her grandfather, who died in 1915. She did remember that Matthews's father did not fully support his son's decision to go into the ministry and that there was some tension between the two concerning the elder Matthews's views on alcohol. Matthews's daughter also sensed that her father did not have a particularly warm relationship with his sister, Laura. Gwladys believed that Laura had difficulty hiding her jealousy of Grace.[55]

Matthews's wife and children apparently tolerated what must have been a very busy schedule. Unable to discuss freely the intricacies of his political involvement or even the daily matters of the church with his friends, he confided in his family. Matthews once described Grace as the best friend he ever had, and Gwladys felt that it was only at home that her father felt free to unburden himself of the day's events.[56]

Finally, the Matthews clan rallied together because of the intense publicity focused upon the family and the actual physical threats to their persons. Gwladys remembered that in about 1910, someone threw two small bombs into the nursery of the Matthews home. Sleeping upstairs, the children escaped injury, but the experience deeply impressed upon Gwladys the family's vulnerability. Anonymous threats of physical harm and kidnapping plagued Matthews's daughter throughout her childhood, and, at one point, police escorted her to and from school. Gwladys recalled that on one occasion her father discovered that someone had been hired either to threaten him or possibly to kill him. According to his daughter, Matthews sent for the man to come to his office, and upon the man's arrival the preacher opened his desk drawer and took out one of two pearl-handled revolvers and placed it on the table in front of the man and demanded that he use it or be on the next train back to Chicago.[57] It is difficult to tell how true the story is, but Gwladys believed that this experience bound the family more tightly together. Wife, son, and daughter loyally supported Matthews.

If the family vacation to the Holy Land allowed Matthews to enjoy his family in a way that he had not previously, it did not symbolize a basic retreat from the world. Typical of the role he played and the power he continued to wield was his involvement in the affairs of Whitworth College in Spokane. Having served as a Whitworth trustee since 1902, Matthews, according to the college historian, influenced the hiring and firing of faculty members.[58] After the First World War, the college faced enormous hardships, due primarily to low enrollment. On several occasions, merger with another denominational college seemed likely. Matthews, however, vehemently opposed the idea on the grounds that it would destroy the Presbyterian identity of the institution. He successfully urged Presbyterians throughout the state to support the college. Matthews deserves a large part of the credit for helping Whitworth remain Presbyterian. "His stubbornness on this matter," the historian Al Gray wrote, "was to save the college more than once."[59] While less involved than at Whitworth, Matthews also served as a trustee at Whitman College in Walla Walla, Washington, as well as on the board of the San Francisco Theological Seminary, a Presbyterian institution.[60]

Matthews's national reputation reached a new level in 1924, when he appeared on a list of the twenty-five most influential ministers in America. Selected in a poll of 25,000 clergymen, Matthews was increasingly identified as one of the nation's leading spokesmen for religious fundamentalism.[61] At the same time, he still influenced the affairs of the city of Seattle. His style in civic matters continued to reflect a combination of pragmatism and skillful organization. He promoted tourism for the city, served on the chamber of commerce, urged occasional civic reforms, and spearheaded the drive for a major new hospital. Without question, he was regarded as the most influential cleric in the city.

Matthews continued to challenge businessmen and bankers to embrace better ethical conduct. "The banking business of America is rotten at the core," he preached. "It has largely fallen into the hands of a class of men who believe that the end justifies the means."[62] He advocated committed citizenship: "The country is not suffering from bad citizens. No country ever suffered from such. Our country is suffering from the bad citizenship of good citizens," he told a group of businessmen. "The business man and the banker use every possible means to escape jury duty. They are traitors to good government."[63]

One of Matthews's major civic coups came in 1925 as a result of his connection with Freemasonry. Matthews had been a Mason since his days in Georgia when he had written columns for a Masonic publication. In 1925, Seattle played host to the Triennial Conclave of the Grand Encampment for the Knights Templar in North America, a national convention that brought thousands of visitors to Seattle. Hosting the Grand Encampment had been a personal dream of Matthews's for nearly ten years, and he deserved the major credit for its coming to Seattle. But, as was typical with him, it was the manner in which Matthews achieved this goal that reveals something about his personality.

As early as 1916, at a state convention of the Knights Templar, Matthews first suggested that Seattle should seek the 1922 Grand Encampment. Apparently, most of his brother Masons believed it would be impossible, but in deference to Matthews they passed a motion favoring an effort to secure the national convention. By 1919, Matthews was forced to try to sell the idea once again, and this time he organized a publicity committee that made a serious effort to secure the convention. However, at the Grand Encampment of 1919, the Committee on Time and Place awarded the 1922 convention to New Orleans.[64]

With his typical persistence in such matters, Matthews insisted that the city make an even greater effort to secure the 1925 convention. In New Orleans, the choice for the next encampment was between Indianapolis and Seattle. However, since the most eminent grand master–elect was from the Indiana state capital, the Committee on Time and Place awarded the 1925 convention to Indianapolis. Reportedly, Matthews rose immediately to speak in opposition. He moved to replace Indianapolis with Seattle and then made an impassioned plea for the merits of the Pacific Northwest. Praising its geographic location and climate, Matthews argued that the time had come to recognize his section of the country. "As I understand it this Grand Encampment is 106 years old," Matthews said. "You have never visited the northwest section of this country. . . . In the name of Templarism, in the name of Americanism, come to us and put the imprint of your presence and power upon a band of Knights as chivalrous as you can find in the world."[65] Greeted with great applause, Matthews's speech forced the Indiana representative to respond. The mood had shifted, and Seattle won by a vote of 199 to 173.[66]

Seattle played host to the Grand Encampment between July 25 and July 31, 1925, and the convention ranked as one of the major events of the year for the city. Reputedly the largest parade in Seattle history, comprising more than 8,000 Masons, marched through downtown before a crowd of approximately 200,000 people. Organizers bestowed upon Matthews the title of Grand Prelate, the highest honor of the encampment.[67]

During the following year, Matthews found himself once again in the thick of Seattle politics with his involvement in the complex debate over the nature of Seattle's city government. For the previous two decades, debate had regularly surfaced over a variety of proposals intended to reform the structure of government. Typical of most cities across the country, Seattle debated the merits of different structures from the strong mayor and commission form of governments to the city-manager configuration. Matthews had weighed in periodically and had long been a member of the Municipal League of Seattle. Beginning in 1922 and continuing for the next four years, the Municipal League advocated for the city-manager form of government. Complicating the issue of the particular form of city government were issues involving the enforcement of vice laws by the mayor and the ongoing debate between advocates of the private ownership of utilities and supporters of public ownership. In the middle of this conflict stood the head of Seattle City Light, J. D. Ross, a member of First Presbyterian and, because of his work on the radio, one of the parishioners with an exceptionally close relationship to Matthews. By 1925, Matthews felt compelled to issue a statement in which he laid out his proposal for a new concept of city government. Specifically Matthews advocated the merger of city and county governments in order to increase efficiency. He argued that the council should consist of five or seven members elected from the city at large and that they should serve without compensation. He proposed that the mayor serve only in a ceremonial capacity and that the city council be vested with the power to elect a city manager at a salary of $25,000 per year. According to Matthews's proposal, the city manager could serve seven to nine years and not be subject to removal for political reasons. Matthews further suggested that the manager appoint a police commission with full authority over the police force. And finally Matthews argued that the city council should have the power to select the superintendents of lighting, water, and street railways. Each of the superintendent's terms would run concurrently with the city manger. Possibly in deference to Ross, Matthews stated that the "light and water systems are successful. They are revenue-producers, and they are creating enormous assets for the city. It would be an easy matter to destroy them by putting their enemies in power; therefore, no City Council, no Mayor, nor any department ever should be vested with power to destroy by seductive methods such enormous productive assets."[68]

How much of Matthews's proposal was formulated with Ross in mind is not clear; it appears as if he was straddling the fence in attempting to find a way of protecting Ross's position at City Light and at the same time moving to a city-manager concept that would diminish the power of the mayor and the police chief. Given his long-standing struggle with Hiram Gill, this seems understandable. In any event, the waters surrounding proposals became increasingly muddied in 1925 and 1926. The Municipal League's proposal for a city-manager system was defeated in March 1925, but another proposal continued to gain momentum. Voters were given the opportunity to elect a slate of freeholders for the purpose of writing a new city charter. Whether Matthews had thought about running for a freeholder position himself is not clear, but in January 1926, he received a letter from J. D. Ross asking him to run for one of the fifteen positions.[69] Clearly Ross wanted to insure that any proposal would be as friendly as possible to City Light, and he lobbied for several other candidates as well. Matthews must have liked Ross's idea, because he decided that he would stand for election as a freeholder.

The city election of March 1926 was quite complicated. Seattle voters were asked to consider approving another proposal for a city-manager system sponsored by the Municipal League and also were asked to vote on a proposal to revise the city charter by electing fifteen freeholders to revise the city charter, which would also require later voter approval. In any event, in the March 1926 election, the city-manager proposal was defeated but the charter revision amendment passed, and Matthews was elected with the second-highest vote total of all the freeholders.[70] In late April, the freeholders presented their plan for a revision of the charter, and apparently the proposal both surprised and disappointed a great many people. Ross vigorously opposed the revision because he believed that the charter would prohibit the council from issuing public utility bonds that Ross believed were necessary for the future development of City Light. Others, including former mayor George Cotterill, attacked provisions that would have made the police commissioner an unsalaried position. Still other critics voiced concern that the proposal seemed elitist in nature and was dominated by business interests.[71] Perhaps most difficult to explain is the fact that Matthews and Ross eventually ended up on opposite sides of the proposed new charter. In the few weeks leading up to the election in October, Ross openly opposed the revision. Matthews, on the other hand, far from slipping out of public sight, came out strongly in favor of the new charter. "We have written a lot of good American government into the charter," he said, "and it is by far the best ever offered to the people of this city."[72] Just days before the election, Matthews went on the radio and vigorously defended the charter as a document that safeguarded the interests of all Seattle citizens. He took on all critics; he attacked those who claimed that the charter simply reflected the interests of Seattle's business elite. "Big business had no more to do with the writing of the charter . . . than the most innocent babe that sleeps in its mother's lap." In an apparent reference to Ross's claim that the primary issue of contention was over the future of the city's utilities, Matthews firmly stated:

You would infer from the remarks of these people that this whole question now before us was a controversy between the private power company and our municipal light plant. I have no interest in the power company and I would defend the city light plant to the last minute and every member of the charter commission did defend it all the way through the writing of the charter, and we are defending it yet.[73]

Matthews defended the proposal regarding the police commissioner and other city departments. "We have written into this charter a police commission which will lift your police powers and departments out of politics. . . . We have written a welfare department into this charter which ought to appeal to every lady in the city." Matthews further attacked the Municipal League critics who were complaining that the proposal did not have as strong a city manager as needed:

> The Municipal League crowd say that we have not written a business manager plan into this charter. I am sorry for them, for they talk in the terms of a dictator. They appointed themselves and wrote a charter which we rejected on two different occasions. They wrote a dictatorial plan that made their manager a czar! The city of Seattle will never submit to a czar, whether he comes out of the Municipal League clique or from any other indescribable land of mystery.[74]

In the end, Matthews failed to persuade Seattle voters. The charter went down to a resounding defeat by a three-to-two margin. Perhaps the best explanation for Matthews's advocacy of something other than what Ross wanted was the fact that Matthews probably played a significant role in crafting the charter proposal. Why he did not check more closely with Ross is not clear; the charter proposal of 1926 reflected many of the same ideas that Matthews had previously articulated in 1925. Perhaps having put so much effort into the charter, Matthews felt compelled to defend it until the bitter end. The Seattle preacher continued to believe that civic righteousness required civic governmental structures that could shape behavior. With characteristic boldness, he stated, "If the good citizens have a standard of absolute righteousness for the government and if they hold the manager to the strictest account in the discharge of the duties, such a government would eliminate all pettiness, all antiquated methods, all discourtesies, all idleness and laziness."[75] Perhaps even at the risk of alienating his friend and parishioner, J. D. Ross, Matthews battled for what was clearly an unpopular position. And when the dust settled, Ross was still attending First Presbyterian, and the tall preacher had once again demonstrated a considerable public presence in a way that set him apart from most of his ministerial colleagues across the country.

In one other situation, Matthews played something of a dramatic public role, in late 1925 and early 1926 during a serious labor dispute. It was then that Matthews first met and worked with Dave Beck, who later assumed immense power in the Pacific Northwest as head of the Teamsters Union.[76] In October 1925, it became apparent that initial attempts to reach an agreement between the laundry owners and the various laundry unions had met with failure. Matthews, aware of the possibility of a strike, convinced William Short, president of the Washington State Federation of Labor, that Matthews's pastoral and political skills might be of assistance in mediating between the two parties. "In line with our conversation yesterday," Short wrote Matthews, "I am herewith urging you to use your good offices to bring about arbitration of the existing differences between Laundry Owners and the Unions."[77] Within three days, Matthews helped achieve agreement on a plan for negotiations: each side would select one representative who, in turn, would select a third member agreeable to both sides.[78]

Problems developed, however, in the attempt to select a third member, and another formula had to be agreed upon. The parties reached accord regarding the process of arbitration, but negotiations bogged down with owners' fears that labor agitators were at work in their plants. The fact that William Short, the labor representative, could not participate until January 1925 also hampered the discussion. Matthews worked to appease the owners and served as the contact between the two factions. Dave Beck, then secretary for the Laundry Drivers Union, later recalled in an interview how Matthews was thoroughly trusted by both sides.[79]

After much work, the owners association and the laundry unions announced on February 20, 1926, that the strike had been averted. William Short publicly acknowledged Matthews's role in the settlement. "Particularly must a great deal of credit go to Dr. Matthews," Short told the press, "who threw himself wholeheartedly into the threatening situation for several months, devoting the major portion of his time to it and never letting up until both sides had put their feet under the table in joint conference."[80]

Screenitis and the Radio

For the next thirteen years, Matthews, according to Dave Beck, served as labor's principal contact with the business community. In an interview, the former Teamster leader recalled how he had relied on Matthews on numerous occasions to facilitate a conversation or begin a negotiation. Matthews's correspondence reveals that he played a minor role in labor negotiations at the *Seattle Post-Intelligencer* in 1936 and at the *Seattle Star* in 1938.[81]

Perhaps Matthews's most lasting legacy to the city involved his work on behalf of the King County Medical Society. In the spring of 1926, the medical society requested that Mark Matthews head efforts to secure a site and funds for a major new hospital. Throughout 1927, the Matthews-led committee discussed various options and finally decided that a new facility should be built on the University of Washington campus in order to assist the university's development of a medical school—an idea that Matthews had offered as early as 1902.[82] However, the university turned down the proposal in February 1928, when a dispute over the actual ownership of the hospital made its construction on university property not feasible.[83] Matthews, however, kept arguing the idea that the new hospital should be associated with the university. "We are anxious to build such a hospital near our university, and ultimately establish a medical school in the northwest," he wrote to a variety of possible contributors. "We are more than anxious to make this hospital a clinical laboratory second to none in the country and ultimately second to none in the world."[84] However, a second site near the university also had to be abandoned.

Finally, King County voters passed a $2,750,000 hospital bond issue on November 6, 1928.[85] The cornerstone was laid at the site on Ninth and Terry Avenues, not far from First Presbyterian, on July 10, 1930, and after a citywide contest to name the facility, hospital administrators selected "Harborview." Dedicated before 3,000 people on February 27, 1931, the hospital fulfilled a thirty-year-old dream of Matthews's; the hospital indeed developed a close relationship with the university and served as the principal training center for the University of Washington's nursing program—another idea suggested by Matthews.[86]

One final event from this period suggests the complex nature of Matthews's public role in city affairs. Beginning in 1924, tensions between the governor of the state, Roland Hartley, and the president of the University of Washington, Henry Suzzallo, began to grow. Hartley resented Suzzallo's power and began to move to challenge the president by replacing the university's board of regents with his own supporters.[87] This conflict finally culminated in 1926 when Hartley fired Suzzallo. Much of the Seattle community came to Suzzallo's defense, including Matthews. Local headlines read, "Rhodes, Dr. Matthews and Eckstein in closed parley with the Governor," as the three tried to convince Hartley to rescind his decision to terminate Suzzallo.[88] Matthews went on the radio to condemn the political meddling with the affairs of the university. He defended the right of the university to operate in a manner unimpeded by the governor's office.[89]

In general, Matthews became increasingly nervous regarding a number of intellectual trends that he discerned to be a part of the growing secularization of American higher education. "I'll admit there are blasphemous, psychological perverts, such as Mr. Jordan of your California university," Matthews wrote, "and some others in your Chicago universities and other eastern schools who say sin is a matter of experience."[90] In a sermon entitled "Our Children's Kidnappers," he criticized a number of academics at leading universities across the country for various positions regarding marriage, miracles in the Bible, and universal moral truths.[91] And yet Matthews refrained from taking on the growing number of scholars at the University of Washington who were gaining national recognition for their research. He rallied to Suzzallo and he remained steadfast in his support for an institution that Matthews believed would be vital to the future greatness of the city.

Mark Matthews's vision of a righteous city had taken different expressions during the decade of the 1920s, but he still wielded a great deal of influence in the city. Whether as fundraiser for a hospital or as freeholder for the charter revision, the preacher remained a very visible figure in Seattle public life. Controversy within the Presbyterian church troubled him a great deal, and he attempted to mitigate the pain of division. But by the end of the decade, he could still claim that he was Seattle's preacher. His harangues against cultural decadence and his general association with conservative values seemed to be in step with the desires of much of Seattle's middle class. "In this jazz-mad age—this day of mental, moral and religious chaos," reported one weekly newspaper, "a church such as the First Presbyterian Church of Seattle, is a mighty comforting fortress to contemplate."[92] In 1924, shortly before the General Assembly met, a reporter for the *New York Sun* noted Matthews's appeal to those who cherished traditional values in an age of rapid cultural change. "Even his style of dress—the long frock coat and low turnover collar, with black bow tie—seems to

Screenitis and the Radio

be part of his personality," the reporter wrote, "and [seems] to relate him to earlier Americans, men who were sturdily independent and yet conservative, and were not to be swept away by every passing whim in thought and fashion."[93] In spite of his success and the stability that he embodied for so many who knew him, Mark Matthews experienced a great deal of anxiety as he entered the last decade of his life and ministry. From the increasing evidence that prohibition was failing to have the desired effect and the myriad signs that America's youth were embracing values at odds with a Christian worldview, to the unpredictability of Seattle politics and the unforeseeable consequences of the stock market crash, Matthews looked to the decade of the thirties with significant uncertainty.

CHAPTER 11

The Final Years

There is no man in the city of Seattle who is more familiar with its shortcomings than Dr. M. A. Matthews. . . . He knows men, and knows how to make them work. He is a born organizer. He is not narrow minded. . . . There is no man in this city who could do more for it in the capacity of mayor than Dr. Matthews.

— *Seattle Argus* (1931)

In July 1937, Art Hunt, the leading home-run hitter in the Pacific Coast League, made sports headlines by getting married on the pitcher's mound prior to one of the Seattle Indians' home games. Hunt also decided that the presiding minister should be Mark Matthews. Never one to avoid a public ceremony or spectacle, Matthews approached the event with the spirit of a master showman. "Then came the Rev. Dr. Mark A. Matthews, who arrived in a limousine at third base. From there, he solemnly walked to the altar, his black string tie flowing on every breeze."[1] Even though Matthews was then sixty-nine years old, his voice boomed over the microphone as he conducted the service. In front of 9,272 fans, Matthews pronounced Hunt and his new bride husband and wife. As Mr. and Mrs. Hunt exited, they walked under an archway of crossed bats held by the members of the two teams.[2]

In 1937, Matthews still had a flair for the dramatic, and most Seattleites, including Art Hunt, still saw him as their pastor. During the 1930s, the last decade of his life, Matthews never seriously considered retiring. He remained active on a variety of fronts, from his efforts to convince Hitler to resign to his fight against communist influence within the city to his continued involvement in civic affairs. The quest for a righteous city, country, and world continued to motivate and drive him. Yet in some ways Matthews was seen as increasingly anachronistic by both his supporters and his detractors. To his followers, he represented the best of traditional America. He stood for those nineteenth-century Victorian ideals that seemed to be slipping away with the growth of cities, the coming of the automobile, and the onset of the Jazz Age. On the other hand, many of Matthews's critics viewed the preacher as an annoying figure from a Puritan past who was always interfering in other people's business.

Matthews's final decade in the pulpit at Seattle's First Presbyterian Church saw him continue his general pattern of ministry and political activity until the week before his death in February 1940. The decade was extraordinarily difficult for him and most Americans: the Great Depression shattered the economic prosperity of the previous decade; the storm clouds in Europe and Asia grew increasingly ominous; the social changes in the 1920s continued to threaten an older world of Victorian values, and finally the Christian church continued to face internal division over a number of issues. Through it all, Matthews attempted to exercise leadership and influence. Without question, his powers of persuasion as well as his seemingly indefatigable energy began to wane. Yet even in his last decade, Matthews continued to be a significant force locally and nationally. He continued to reflect the currents of his day as well as to respond to the historical forces in his life. And his search for a righteous society continued unabated.

As Matthews aged, he also continued to command respect throughout the city. On the occasion of his twenty-fifth anniversary at First Presbyterian, in 1927, and nearing his sixtieth birthday, even the *Seattle Times*, with its history of criticizing the minister, admitted that Matthews had contributed greatly to the city's welfare.

> It is likely that Dr. Matthews is known to more persons in Seattle than any other man. We have grown to regard him almost as an institution—certainly as an interesting and magnetic personality. His shrewd common sense, his business acumen and his civic wisdom have helped Seattle upon many an occasion. While he has ministered to his growing flock as spiritual adviser, he also has served this growing city as elder counselor and civic guide.[3]

The Final Years

In April 1929, when Matthews seriously considered leaving the Northwest for Philadelphia and Bethany Presbyterian Church, many Seattle residents poured out their affection for him. "Dr. Matthews is more than a pastor," the *Seattle Post-Intelligencer* reminded its readers. "He is an institution, it might almost be said a national monument."[4] A Seattle weekly newspaper simply said that the city would not be the same without him.

> It is hardly an exaggeration to say that Dr. Matthews has been the greatest single influence for good that this city has known. Dr. Matthews is a Seattle institution. He is an essential part of Seattle, an indispensable factor in its community life, an indefatigable worker for its welfare and progress. We look up to him, we follow him, we are proud of him and we love him—even when he chastens us, as sometimes he deservedly does.[5]

Somewhat surprisingly, given all of the political controversies of the past, Matthews's name still surfaced for possible political leadership. In late 1931, one newspaper suggested that he run for mayor.

> In the opinion of *The Argus*, there is no man in the city of Seattle who is more familiar with its shortcomings than Dr. M. A. Matthews. . . . He knows men, and knows how to make them work. He is a born organizer. He is not narrow minded. . . . There is no man in this city who could do more for it in the capacity of mayor than Dr. Matthews.[6]

In 1932, city council members publicly charged Matthews with exercising too much influence over Mayor John Dore's appointments.[7] And as late as December 1935, Matthews again surfaced as a serious mayoral candidate. The group considering the Seattle minister was the New Order of Cincinnatus, founded in 1933. Concerned with municipal reform during the New Deal, the order pushed for cleaner and more efficient government. Its adherents also conducted inspections of the Tenderloin (Seattle's red-light district) and sought to eliminate gambling and prostitution. Not surprisingly, Matthews's long concern with these issues and the respect he commanded in Seattle made the preacher a likely choice. However, the minister, at age sixty-eight, respectfully declined to run for office.[8] Yet all of this public discussion about whether Matthews would consider running for public office, or whether he still exercised significant political influence, testifies to the unusual way in which this conservative minister had established himself in the mind of the Seattle public.

In the last decade of his life, Matthews continued to dodge local political minefields and to look for calculated opportunities to win public support. For example, in 1936 the preacher distanced himself from John Dore when the mayor, with great indiscretion, called the Women of Washington, a group fighting for women's rights, "fur-clad perfumed hussies."[9] Meeting in the civic auditorium, 5,000 women were addressed by various people including Mark Matthews, who perhaps hoped to redeem himself in the eyes of many women who had never forgiven him for opposing woman suffrage. Speaking over a telephone projected over a microphone, Matthews addressed the group from Chicago. "No one has a right to cast aspersions on a woman," he told the group in reference to Dore's remark. "No one has a right to criticize her because she takes an interest in her home and city. That is the duty of a woman."[10] Appreciative of his support, the women responded to the preacher's remarks with a hearty round of applause. But it would be wrong to suggest that Matthews had experienced a conversion to the cause of women's rights; he remained clearly on the conservative end of the spectrum on this issue.

In the same year that Matthews tried to present himself as a friend to women, a long chapter involving another controversial matter began to come to an end. Matthews delivered to a Congressional subcommittee what he described as an independent report on matters related to a mission in Metlakahtla (sometimes spelled Metlakatla), Alaska. Often times referred to simply as "The Case," the report detailed events that stretched back for decades and exemplified the type of incident that attracted Matthews's attention as well as the lengths that he would go to try and effect an outcome to his liking.

The case involved an Episcopalian missionary by the name of William Duncan. In 1857, the Church Missionary Society of England sent Duncan, an unordained Anglican minister, to Fort Simpson in British Columbia to work among the Tsimshian Indians. A large tribe with a highly developed culture, the Tsimshian were known to be warlike and, according to some reports, cannibalistic. Duncan learned to speak their language and brought a simplified Gospel to these tribal people. In 1862, he relocated his community of believers and mission to a place called Metlakahtla, approximately twenty miles south of Fort Simpson on a passage leading to the site of present-day Prince Rupert. Over the next few years, Duncan helped develop a settlement based on Christianity and capitalism.[11]

By the 1880s, the Church Missionary Society had established a diocese at Metlakahtla in order to bring Indians closer to the practices of the Church of England. Duncan objected, arguing that the Tsimshians' cannibalistic past and propensity for alcoholism would make celebration of the Eucharist extremely problematic. After a futile protest, Duncan decided to move the mission and 800 followers again, this time to Annette Island in Alaska Territory, and there he successfully rebuilt the community. Duncan became something of a legend; here was someone who had walked away from considerable personal wealth, gone to the wilds of the Pacific Northwest, and built a successful Christian community.[12]

Over the next two decades, Metlakahtla continued to develop commercially. However, a split developed between the native council and Duncan. The latter owned the major industries in the town. The Indians worked in the cannery and sawmill but were paid meager wages in the form of coupons redeemable at Duncan's store. Tribal leaders believed that the school inadequately prepared the Indians to manage the businesses, and therefore the council desired that the United States Bureau of Education build a government school. Duncan, now over eighty years old, had grown increasingly alienated from tribal leaders, and Bureau of Education agents expressed frustration with his intransigence.[13]

As a consequence of the feud, the American government finally stepped in and established a school at Metlakahtla in 1913. Duncan maintained that just a very few Indians objected to his practices, and he claimed that the school only further divided the community. In 1914, Duncan, in retaliation, dismantled the pipeline that provided a source of fresh water to the community. The native council complained, and the government announced that it would intervene and take control of all major operations, arguing that Duncan, in fact, did not own these commercial operations. In fact, Secretary of the Interior Franklin Lane believed Duncan to be demented and ordered the government to seize control. The seizure occurred on August 5, 1915, and was abrupt by any standard. Bureau of Education agents, apparently frustrated from months of disputes with Duncan, moved into the cannery, schoolhouse, sawmill, warehouse, carpentry shop, and town hall. Agents smashed windows, broke doors, and removed various articles.[14] Duncan continued to hold services on the island, but the bureau, out of apparent vindictiveness, held dances across the road from his prayer meetings. Government authorities dropped the restrictions on alcohol and gambling, and lawlessness increased.

Duncan sought help from a longtime friend and supporter, Sir Henry Wellcome, and it was Wellcome who involved Mark Matthews. Wellcome had known Duncan since 1878 and had written a book about Duncan's work at Metlakahtla. Something of a philanthropist, Wellcome had attained his wealth as a manufacturer of chemicals and pharmaceutical products in England. He supported medical research, world exploration, archeology, and Christian missionary activity.[15]

Wellcome met Matthews in 1917, and the philanthropist provided the preacher with money for his work at First Presbyterian. Wellcome informed Matthews of Duncan's plight and asked for assistance.[16] The Seattle pastor wrote Duncan in 1917: "It is an honor and a compliment to be hated by the enemies of Christ, and to be persecuted and killed by those who would again persecute and kill Christ if He were here."[17] But in 1918, Duncan died. In his last will and testament he expressed his desire that his estate be used to regain and perpetuate the Metlakahtla mission.

Even before Duncan's death, Matthews had sent Bert Thompson, a worker in his Sunday school, to Metlakahtla to investigate the situation. Thompson's report convinced Matthews that Duncan had been greatly wronged. "I am now convinced that the conspiracy between government officials . . . to establish different commercial companies, etc., was for the purpose of destroying Mr. Duncan, getting all commercial interests of this section of Alaska into their own hands in order that they might make fortunes," Matthews wrote to Wellcome. Matthews further suggested that an "operator" be sent back to Metlakahtla in order to buy stock in the Metlakahtla Commercial Company, which was formed after the ousting of Duncan. Matthews hoped that this individual would be able to review the company's records. "When we get in we will not only save Mr. Duncan, but we will be able to expose a well laid plot to exploit the government in Alaska."[18]

Wellcome tried to temper some of Matthews's sweeping conclusions, but he also established an office in Washington, D.C., in the early 1920s for the primary purpose of gathering information and preparing legal briefs relative to "The Case."[19] In 1926, Wellcome's office produced a lengthy document that argued in great detail the conspiracy theory against Duncan. The situation was further complicated by the introduction of a Presbyterian mission on the island shortly after

The Final Years

Duncan's death. Matthews opposed this intrusion; he believed that it would make returning the mission to the Duncan estate more difficult. Matthews wrote extensive reports to the secretary of the interior, met with President Hoover on at least two occasions, and appeared before the U.S. Senate subcommittee on Indian affairs as a witness in the dispute.[20]

Matthews's work began in earnest when he testified before the secretary of the interior in August 1926 that he believed Duncan had been severely mistreated. For the next ten years, Matthews worked off and on with Wellcome and his office to prepare a comprehensive report that would persuade the government to compensate Duncan's estate.[21] Throughout these years, Matthews and Wellcome remained in close contact. Matthews frequently asked Wellcome for money to assist him in his various crusades at home, particularly those against communist influences in Seattle.[22]

The "Independent Report," which bore Matthews's name, was first delivered in 1936 and consisted of more than 1,800 pages, with 300 photographic plates. The report presented in detail not only Matthews's opinion of what happened, based mostly on the documents provided by Wellcome's office, but also specific criticisms of church and government officials. Often hyperbolic and unsupported by facts, the report reflects Matthews's tendencies to charge his opponents with conspiratorial behavior.[23]

Matthews essentially restated from Wellcome's earlier document the arguments that certain individuals had conspired to gain control of the mission and deliver it to the Bureau of Education. He spent much of the report trying to undermine the credibility of witnesses who had testified against Duncan. He argued that the government needed to acknowledge the unjust manner in which bureau agents had mistreated Duncan and ruined the mission. Matthews demanded that the government compensate the trustees of Duncan's will for every mission building. In addition, Matthews argued that the government should honor Duncan's life with a national monument. The U.S. government did not follow these recommendations. It did pay for the publication of the report in 1939, as a part of the general survey of conditions of Indians in the United States, but that was all.

Henry Wellcome died in 1936, leaving $1,000 to Matthews.[24] With Wellcome's death, and the government's refusal to compensate the Duncan estate, "The Case" came to an end. Perhaps Matthews wearied of the effort. The episode does reflect Matthews's loyalty in regard

The Final Years   213 to certain adopted causes or individuals; in the midst of a very busy schedule, he seems to have devoted significant time to the problem of Duncan's estate. Yet, the Metlakahtla incident also reflects what can, at best, be termed his questionable judgment, as well as his fascination with conspiracy, investigation, and exposure of persons or institutions he believed were either corrupt or criminal.

The last decade of Mark Matthews's life was marked by work that reflected his ongoing commitment to the well-being of the community. He continued his involvement with the Red Cross and, for the last fifteen years of his life, worked on the board of the White Cross, the antinarcotics society, serving for a number of years as its national president. Matthews remained steadfast in his belief that most convicted criminals could be rehabilitated. His papers contain numerous references to the parolees for whom he took responsibility, and he always made sure that he and other clergy held religious services at the local jails.[25]

But the last decade of Matthews's life proved exceptionally difficult for a variety of reasons. His sister, Laura, died of a heart attack in 1934, and though he was not particularly close to her, this tragedy surely took him by surprise and caused him to reflect on his own mortality. There is no written record of his reaction to Laura's death, but he must have felt deeply saddened at the passing of his only sibling, who had followed him from Georgia to Seattle.[26]

The severity of the Depression not only stunned Matthews, as it did so many Americans, but it also proved to be a challenging political situation. He initially responded by giving all of his support to Herbert Hoover. "He is conscientious and sincere . . . ," Matthews said of Hoover in a sermon, "sacrificing every ounce of strength and employing every one of his consecrated talents to serve you faithfully. . . . Awake to your responsibilities! Arise and perform your duty. Render to your President unqualified sympathetic support."[27]

On a number of occasions, Matthews called for a national revival and maintained that, if people would turn to Christ, conditions in the country could be greatly improved. "The legislation of human statutes cannot instill principles, change hearts, or build character," he preached in 1931. "We are not helping our brothers by simply furnishing a soup table for the passing bread line. Why haven't we evangelized and Christianized?"[28] In 1932, Matthews fondly quoted the *Wall Street Journal*, which argued that what the country needed was "a revival of piety, the kind mother and father used to have."[29]

Matthews stressed the virtues of patience, but there were moments when his own frustration became almost overwhelming, and, in almost poetic form, he described the pervasive sense of fear and confusion:

Today we are in the presence of plenty, and yet suffer; today we stand before coffers bulging with gold, and yet have empty purses; we stand before barns and bins filled with produce asking for transportation to places of suffering and want, and yet we are without bread.[30]

Matthews had always been known for his compassion for the poor and the suffering. Beginning in Georgia and extending to the final years of his life, he made a constant practice of tending to many of the oppressed in his community. "I have known him, in recent years," one reporter wrote, "to willingly preach the funeral sermon over the remains of a fallen man and fallen woman when other preachers hesitated or refused. I have known him to go down into the very dregs in an effort to salvage a human wreck."[31]

But the Great Depression must have rocked him to the core. Matthews must have been shaken by the overwhelming needs of the poor, and he responded to the growing economic crisis on a number of levels. Countless people called him and asked for his help. Evidence suggests that he used all his available contacts to assist in any way that he could. He often entreated his friend J. D. Ross, head of Seattle City Light, to use his influence to employ someone or to keep the lights turned on for people with overdue bills.[32] Typical of the many requests Matthews received was the plea for the preacher's help in obtaining a job. "We are asking Dr. Matthews to help us," wrote one person to a Matthews assistant, "because we feel he is in a position to contact Mr. Ross, and his understanding of the difficulties of others makes him ever ready to help those in distress."[33]

But Matthews also realized that personal influence on individual cases would not be enough to improve the general condition. By 1932, he had begun to advocate laws that would prevent the confiscation of property due to a late mortgage payment. More radical, Matthews suggested in a letter to his old friend George Cotterill that the Populist solution of remonetizing silver should be attempted, and he supported Senator C. C. Dill's call for an international silver conference. He further suggested to Cotterill that the government should provide unused land for unemployed workers.[34]

However, Matthews seemed hesitant to support publicly Franklin Roosevelt in 1932. He certainly disagreed with Roosevelt's position on prohibition. After the election, Matthews continued to play it safe with rather uncontroversial pronouncements, such as his reminders of the sanctity of the Constitution. "Legislation by administrative edict is unconstitutional," Matthews argued. "But legislation by judicial decision is equally unconstitutional."[35] The Seattle preacher hardly charted new ground when in 1937, along with most Americans, he expressed criticism of Roosevelt's plan to change the structure of the Supreme Court. "They seem to forget," he wrote to Montana Senator Burton Wheeler, "that if one executive can thus fix a Court, or pack a Court, or bring a Court under subjection by intimidation, flattery, or anything else, then any future executive could do the same."[36]

But privately, by the mid-thirties Matthews had begun to favor the public employment programs of the New Deal. In 1934, the Seattle minister supported Washington Senator Homer T. Bone's effort to create a major public employment project, the National Employment Cooperative Association.[37] In the late thirties, Matthews asked various senators for their support for public employment agencies, such as the Works Progress Administration.[38]

Matthews also kept a watchful eye on the deteriorating world situation. Openly condemning pacifism, he advocated America taking an active role in world affairs and being ready to intervene on behalf of its interests. "This nation should have the largest, best, most perfect, and highly equipped navy in the world," he insisted in 1937.[39] Throughout the decade, the Seattle minister expressed increasing concern over the rise of fascism.

Matthews followed Hitler's movements in Europe with a keen eye. And he expressed significant anxiety when Germany attempted to move into Czechoslovakia. Accordingly, he bitterly denounced the western nations' response to Hitler, in the form of the Munich agreement. "The compact signed by the four powers was a compact born in fear and cowardi[c]e," Matthews wrote. "It did not avert war; it simply postponed it. It was the most infamous diplomacy the world has ever seen."[40] In a letter to Neville Chamberlain, Matthews did not hesitate to remind England's prime minister that, in the preacher's opinion, the politician had made a "mistake at the Munich Conference."[41]

Two months after Munich, Matthews wrote Franklin Roosevelt and urged him to take more specific action against both Japan and Germany by imposing a total economic boycott.

The Final Years

I heartily commend, endorse and support your stand, protesting Germany's infamous, hellish brutality. Delighted you have recalled our Ambassador, and I hope you will isolate Germany, put a boycott around her, quarantine her and make her eat her own hatred and malice. I hope you will urge Congress to repeal that infernal, so-called Neutrality Law. It is the biggest piece of legal bunk that was ever put on the statute books.[42]

In public, Matthews supported the president fully. In one sermon, he urged everyone to "suspend criticism" of Roosevelt. "It is silly, unpatriotic, disloyal, and disreputable to criticize the President while he is leading the forces for the stability of the nation," he wrote. "Mr. Hitler is a madman."[43] In an article published in the *Post-Intelligencer*, he supported Roosevelt's policy of neutrality. He maintained that the Cash and Carry Act was clear "evidence of our impartiality and of our desire to stay out of the conflict."[44]

Much to his credit, Matthews also raised publicly the plight of the European Jews. Unlike the famous radio priest from Detroit, Father Charles Coughlin, who fanned anti-Semitic feeling in the late thirties, Matthews consistently criticized the German persecution of the Jewish people. "The idea of confiscating the properties of Jews," Matthews preached, "then herding them like cattle across the borders of a country is indescribably corrupt and hellish."[45] He repeatedly chastised Germany for its treatment of Jews and warned of God's eternal judgment concerning behavior designed "to persecute and cause to suffer unmentionably the Israelite people. . . . Germany shall suffer for her presumption and for her presumptive actions against Israel."[46] In an article in 1938 for *The Presbyterian*, a national journal, Matthews wrote, "America should never tolerate racial prejudice or religious prejudice." He attacked Hitler and predicted that "the persecution of Jews and Christians is only the beginning of greater atrocities. It is impossible for the Jews to fight this battle alone. It is a battle that must be fought by the Christian Church."[47] Here again, Matthews should be distinguished from most religious fundamentalists or conservatives of his day. The historian Joel Carpenter noted that "the Jewish people held a rather low priority on fundamentalists' agenda."[48] And some religious conservatives, such as William Bell Riley from Minnesota, were slow to reject anti-Semitic views. But Matthews kept up a regular barrage against Nazi policies and specifically the Hitler regime.

In a fit of frustration, just three months before he died, Matthews wrote a letter to Adolf Hitler. "I wrote you regarding the Munich Conference and told you frankly that you were moving as a madman, a paranoiac, that you were seeking something by wrong methods. Eliminate yourself, abdicate your seat of power and authority, retire from the scene of action."[49] It is not clear whether he expected to receive a response or even if he believed Hitler would ever receive the letter, but writing it must have been satisfying.

Matthews's concern with fascism was nearly matched by his fear of communism. In this case, the Seattle preacher seems to have reflected a perspective more consistent with the religious right's. Carpenter found that "the conspiratorial specter had returned," by the 1930s and "for many fundamentalists, as for other American conservatives, it was 'international communism.'"[50] Since the Seattle General Strike of 1919, Matthews believed that the United States was vulnerable to covert action on the part of left-wing conspirators. He frequently cautioned his congregation to be vigilant against any suspected subversives. "Seattle will be one of the first points of attack in the intended communistic attempt to throw our country into the chaos of revolution," he declared. "Traitorous communist professors and teachers have invaded our schools and universities to preach treason to our children."[51] He often warned that communism was "knocking at the doors of the colleges and at the doors of American public schools," and, therefore, parents needed to exercise great care when choosing an institution for their children.[52] In 1936, his fear of communism was reinforced by his frustration over the fight to keep his radio broadcasts free from interference from other stations. "Isn't it rather strange that people should spontaneously spring up in Philadelphia and ask for our own wave length at the same time that Santa Barbara spontaneously asks for our wave length?" he wrote a government official. "Who is behind this spontaneous attempt upon our rights? Are the communists behind it? Is there some prejudiced religious issue behind it?"[53] In the following year, the *Seattle Star* invited him to write a front-page editorial on the dangers of communism. Entitled "Americanism versus Communism," the piece lashed out at those who believed communism was compatible with the free world. "Communism logically and inevitably leads to atheism and anarchy," Matthews wrote. "We will not tolerate Communism in this country."[54]

The rise of totalitarianism and the renewed fears of communism at home seemed to increase the Seattle preacher's already well-developed penchant for legalized authority. He had always been proud of his association with the Seattle Police Department, and he continued to lead services for prisoners. But during the 1930s, he thought he should have even more formal authority. In 1934, he asked United States Attorney General Homer Cummings, whom he knew personally, for a special badge, presumably for the purpose of officially identifying himself with the U.S. Department of Justice. Though appreciative of Matthews's support, Cummings respectfully turned down the minister's request.[55] Not to be denied, Matthews pursued legal authority elsewhere, and in that same year he succeeded in becoming bonded as a special officer in the Washington State Patrol. Giving him a book of traffic tickets, state authorities told him to use it with great discretion.[56] Matthews's zest for law enforcement remained undiminished, and, at the age of seventy, he still filed occasional reports with the Seattle Police Department on illegal gambling operations.[57]

From 1936 to 1939, Matthews carried on a fairly regular correspondence with J. Edgar Hoover, head of the Federal Bureau of Investigation. On more than one occasion, the Seattle minister requested that he be named a special agent or have special authority given to him in order to assist his pursuit of spies. Hoover encouraged Matthews to help the F.B.I., but, like Cummings, he could not comply with Matthews's request. Frequently, however, Hoover sent Matthews copies of speeches that he had given and expressed appreciation for the Seattle minister's support.[58]

In one other interesting piece of correspondence, Matthews was urged in 1937 by Harry Chandler, president of the *Los Angeles Times*, to rally Seattle voters to elect new leaders. In a letter, Chandler alluded to graft and the phenomenon of "Davebeckism" on the West Coast that needed to be rooted out. Matthews, in return, asked Chandler for a list of people outside Seattle who would fund another private investigation similar to the Burns investigation of Gill and Wappenstein. Apparently, nothing came of Matthews's request, but two observations might be made: first, Matthews obviously never abandoned his interest in exposing civic corruption, and second, he was not alone. The 1930s were still a time when many people perceived issues in black and white. Anticommunism provided a focal point for a great many people's energies during the decade.[59]

Matthews's quest for authority underscored his belief that he was not ready for retirement. He never liked to share the spotlight, and he refused to admit that he had lost any of his abilities. He served throughout the decade on the editorial board of *The Presbyterian* and frequently contributed articles. And in the last three years of his life, Matthews continued to exhibit the passion and enthusiasm for issues that had marked his entire career. His themes remained the same as he challenged the clergy and laity alike to work harder to evangelize on behalf of Christ's kingdom. Just four months before his death, Matthews published one of his classic diatribes:

> The ministers waste too much time, have too many days off for play. It is the life of seclusion, of meditation, of incessant study and prayer, that makes the minister a prophet, a preacher, and a master of the situation. You cannot spend your time playing tiddledywinks or golf and thereby conquer Satan or evangelize a nation. If every minister in America who knows how, would preach on the sovereignty of God, on effectual calling and election, on regeneration, and the perseverance of the saints, for the next six months, the face of America's corrupt life would be changed and the spiritual life of the churches would be increased. Sinners would tremble before the consciousness of the judgment bar.[60]

Matthews continued to be active in his role as pastor at First Presbyterian. The Monday night Bible school in 1938 reported 125 students in attendance, with Matthews serving as dean. The curriculum included Greek, French, English, stenography, current events, music, public speaking, and the Bible. Matthews led the Bible study while he had Dr. G. O. Vikan, pastor of the Greek Orthodox Church, teach the class in Greek. Two local attorneys led the course in current events.[61] In that same year, Rachel McDowell, religious news editor of the *New York Times*, published a pair of articles reporting her visit to several Presbyterian churches on the Pacific Coast. She fondly recounted her visit to Matthews's home, his warm hospitality, his good-natured kidding, and his limitless energy as he "jumped up from where we were sitting" in order to drive her down to the church so that she could speak on his afternoon radio program.[62]

Though at moments age did seem to take its inevitable toll, Matthews seemed only to fight harder to prove that he was capable of continuing his pastoral role. More than a few people were concerned about the future of First Presbyterian—particularly about what would happen after Matthews's death.[63] In mid-November 1939, less than three months before he died, Matthews reiterated his position that he

The Final Years

would not share his pulpit with an associate pastor who was not directly responsible to him. He continued to maintain that he alone was accountable for every act of every assistant and staff worker. However, increasing numbers of parishioners expressed unhappiness with Matthews's lack of effort to secure a successor, as well as what seemed to be a deteriorating youth program. "Doctor, won't you please heed this warning," one elder wrote Matthews in late 1939. "These are contributing reasons for the present low ebb of spiritual life in the church; for the great number of withdrawals in membership and support of the work; for the seemingly indifferent attitude of the young people." The elder reminded his pastor that "the American people, including your own congregation, are in no mood for dictatorships and therefore your star of hope is setting, not rising."[64] Matthews's response was cordial, and he did indicate the extensive efforts that the church had made to secure a youth pastor. But clearly he had no intention of sharing authority.[65]

Years later, Mark Koehler, one of the candidates for the position of youth pastor, recalled his own interview with Dr. Matthews in 1939. After several questions regarding the nature of the job, Koehler asked Matthews what he would like him to do. Matthews rose from his desk, leaned over and said, "Take orders! Take orders! Take orders!" Koehler concluded that he should seek employment elsewhere.[66]

Publicly, Matthews refused to give any indication that the possibility of death or even retirement had entered his mind. In his 1939 annual message, he spoke of possible fortieth and fiftieth anniversaries of his work in Seattle. Privately, however, Matthews must have sensed that his time was growing short; he made arrangements for his pension to be turned over to his wife, and certainly the idea of his own epitaph must have occurred to him when, in mid-January 1940, he was asked to write an inscription for the grave of William Duncan, the missionary for whose interests Matthews had fought for so many years.[67]

In that last year of his life, Matthews delivered a sermon entitled "The Growth of Christianity in the Northwest." In some respects, the sermon reflected many of his consistent themes, although it had a rambling character about much of it. He began with kudos to the Whitmans, Spaldings, and Whitworths who came west and "fought wild forests, conquered the beasts, evangelized the Indians, and planted the church, the school, and the home." He praised the pioneers for their efforts at establishing a Christian civilization. Touching on a number of themes, Matthews reminded parents to establish family altars in their homes, and made one more effort to convince his audience, and perhaps himself, that true science and the Bible were not in conflict. But finally, he returned to the theme that marked so much of his ministry—the pursuit of righteousness. "Righteousness must prevail—personal righteousness, civic righteousness, domestic righteousness, [and] commercial righteousness" if Christians remained attentive to God's calling. Rhetorically, Matthews finished by asking, "Will we do it?" And he answered his own question with a statement that he had made many times in his life, dating back to his time in the hills of Georgia. "We will if we go back to the church. America cannot be saved unless she comes back to the pews of the church, to the Cross of Jesus Christ, to the infallibility of the Bible and to fundamental Christianity. Let us lead the way and demonstrate the truthfulness of these words."[68] With remarkable consistency, Matthews had preached this message from the beginning of his ministry to the very end.

A short time later, on January 29, 1940, Matthews, suffering from pneumonia, entered Seattle General Hospital. On February 1, his condition deteriorated, and his daughter, Gwladys, and son, Mark, Jr., flew from southern California to be at his bedside. Whether it was the presence of family or the fact that the following day would mark the thirty-eighth anniversary of his pastorate in Seattle, Matthews rallied briefly. However, on February 2, the day of the anniversary, he suffered a stroke that paralyzed his left side and severely reduced his chance of recovery. The following evening, First Presbyterian members held a special prayer service; hundreds of people throughout the city kept vigil and awaited news about Matthews. But on Monday, February 5, at 7:40 A.M., Matthews died.[69]

The outpouring of grief and affection for a minister in a city of nearly 400,000 people was indeed remarkable. Flags flew at half-mast at the County-City Building and at the office of the chamber of commerce. Seattle civic leaders filled the newspapers with eulogies for the seventy-two-year-old transplanted Southerner. Virtually every paper in the state offered editorial praise for Matthews's work, and James Wood, associate editor for the *Seattle Times*, paid the following tribute:

> Far beyond the limits of his own congregation . . . the death of Mark
> Allison Matthews is deeply mourned. The shadow falls upon the
> whole country, for he was personally known in many parts of it, and
> known by name and reputation in all. Here in the city where he had
> lived and labored for thirty-eight years, there is a keen sense of com-

The Final Years

munity bereavement of irreparable loss. Dr. Matthews was unique; Seattle has never known, nor is likely to ever know again, a pulpit personality so vigorous and vivid. . . . Dr. Matthews was a fighter from the beginning to the end of his life's work. . . . And it was with no cessation of that fight that he also fought, through all those years, for the general welfare of his fellow-men; for the physical and economic health of the people; for community decency and civic righteousness.[70]

The *Seattle Post-Intelligencer* maintained that Matthews's name would be indelibly etched on the pages of Seattle's history. "He had a far greater hand in shaping the destinies of Seattle during the thirty-eight years he lived in the city than any other single man," said the paper.[71] The Jewish community praised Matthews's stand against the persecution of European Jewry. "Dr. Mark A. Matthews did at every opportunity raise his voice in protest against the anti-Semitism of European countries," according to the Seattle chapter of B'nai B'rith, "and did introduce and cause to be passed at the General Assembly of the Presbyterian Church of the United States, resolutions denouncing the Nazi regime."[72]

Matthews's body lay in state at First Presbyterian while more than 5,000 people, after lining up in wind and rain, passed by the coffin to pay their final respects. Countless civic leaders participated in the tribute, including Governor Clarence Martin and Mayor Arthur Langlie. When the service ended, the family followed Matthews's request that his body be cremated.[73]

Residents throughout the city seemed to sense that they had lost someone unique. Beginning on the day he died, the *Seattle Star* ran nine consecutive days of articles on Matthews's life, coverage that probably has not been repeated for any other local figure in Seattle history.[74] From the early days in Georgia to his battles with Hiram Gill, Matthews's life was reviewed. Matthews had brought a part of the South and a particular brand of Presbyterianism to the Pacific Northwest. But he also reflected many of the most important values of the late nineteenth and early twentieth centuries—the belief in absolute values, rugged individualism, religious vision—and it was this element that Seattle residents most closely identified with Matthews. The preacher from Calhoun, Georgia, had sought to lead his people to a vision of righteousness and, by an act of personal will, to hold on to that nineteenth-century outlook for as long as possible.

The Final Years

During the years between the two world wars, Matthews continued to exercise his influence in the Seattle community. They were, however, years of struggle against the social and cultural currents of the 1920s, the problems of the Depression, and the threat of war from Europe and Asia. At times, Matthews had manipulated people and grasped for power in questionable ways. But in February 1940, most of the city recalled only those moments when he had expended his limitless energy and employed his power for the good of individual people and the general improvement of his adopted city.

≈ Conclusion ≈

On February 8, 1942, a large gathering of people, including city officials, met in Seattle's Denny Park to dedicate a bust of Mark A. Matthews. Looking down on Seventh Avenue toward First Presbyterian Church, the bust of Matthews served to remind the city of Seattle of the Southern-born Presbyterian's remarkable life and career. With the words "Preacher of the Word of God and Friend to Man" engraved on its base, the monument testified to the deep feelings of his congregation and the willingness of the city to cooperate in such a tribute. But the monument also reflected an attempt by some of Matthews's contemporaries to offer an assessment of his ministry and contribution to the city.

It has been most common among Seattle historical circles to see Matthews as an anachronistic figure who seemed more at home with the Salem witch trials than the twentieth century. And there is much that supports this general impression. He dressed in an unusual fashion with his long waistcoat, and his height, of course, set him apart. He made arresting and sometimes wild pronouncements on myriad subjects, from the dire consequences of woman suffrage to the evils of playing bridge. His involvement with mayors, private investigators, the Billingsley brothers, and presidents of the United States distinguished him from most other preachers, both before and since. To focus exclusively on these facets of the Seattle minister's career, however, diverts attention from not only a more complete understanding of Mark Matthews, but also from the historical value of such a person.

It is easy to overlook the fact that the life of the Georgia-born minister provides an excellent lens through which to view the years between the Civil War and the Second World War. Rather than being seen as a total anachronism, Matthews should be viewed as having had much in common with significant numbers of white Anglo-Saxon Protestant males who lived in the last half of the nineteenth and first half of the twentieth centuries. Born when Andrew Johnson was president and long-lived enough to see Hitler's invasion of Poland, Matthews witnessed an enormous number of social and political events. The interplay of his life with major historical forces sheds light not only on the nature of his activities but also on those events and periods.

Clearly, the relationship between Matthews and the major historical currents was distinctly shaped by attitudes and assumptions formed during his years in Georgia. As a member of a family and a community directly affected by the Civil War, Matthews grew up in an environment that strongly influenced his basic outlook. Religion and politics mixed freely in his part of the South. Imbued with a Protestant ethic, he grew up believing that he knew just exactly what constituted proper moral behavior. He came to believe that Christian and democratic principles would triumph throughout the world. The God-ordained destiny of greatness for the United States was etched in young Matthews's mind. In Georgia and Tennessee, he began to formulate the roots of his vision to create a righteous urban environment, and it was this vision that gave his ministry such a dynamic quality.

Politically and socially, Matthews's life provides insight into a number of major historical movements. Through him, one can witness the frustrations of the poor and powerless in the South after the Civil War. As a result, one can feel the lure of Populist ideas to the citizens of the hills of northwestern Georgia. Similarly, one can sense the appeal of Progressivism to the middle class through Matthews's embrace of the movement's quest for consumer protection, penchant for efficiency, moral optimism, and attempt to regain management of city government for the middle class. The power of nationalism and the troubling effect of propaganda on many Americans can be observed in Matthews's response to the First World War. The overwhelming fear of communism and radical politics can be seen in his anguish over the Seattle General Strike and the activities of the I.W.W. The anxiety that millions of Americans experienced in regard to the Roaring Twenties was demonstrated in his injunctions against "screenitis" and the automobile. And the uncertainty and fear of the depression and apprehensions about world affairs in the 1930s can be read in his letters and felt in his sermons.

As a representative of mainline Protestantism between the Civil War and Second World War, Matthews engaged many of the most important historical forces and movements of his era. The complexity of the nineteenth-century Southern Presbyterian experience was manifested in his acceptance of revivalism in the context of Old School Presbyterianism and common-sense realism. The appeal of social Christianity throughout the country to young ministers who desired to make Christianity a vital part of the urban environment was exemplified in Matthews's ministry in Jackson, Tennessee. His early years in Seattle typified the widespread lure of the Orient for Christians and the great sense of hope and progress associated with the spread of Christianity. Matthews's vision of a "City on a Hill" reflected a confidence, shared by many, that American society could fully exemplify divine principles and be fully redeemed.

Similarly, the fears of the many proponents of orthodoxy can be seen in Matthews's articulation of fundamentalist doctrine shortly before the First World War. Threatened as much by liberal theologians within the denomination as by scientific naturalists, Matthews, along with millions of Americans, fought for the preservation of basic principles and what they believed were common-sense truths. Likewise, his struggle to weave his way through the extreme positions in the debate between fundamentalists and modernists after World War I reflected the anxiety of many Christians in the face of an increasingly complex society.

The thrust of this biography has been to attempt to understand him as a man deeply immersed in and very much the product of his historical circumstances. But questions remain about how we should evaluate the ways in which he differed from many of his contemporaries as well as the nature of his contribution to the world in which he lived—the answers continue to be complex.

As a good Calvinist, Matthews set out to redeem the world; like many late-nineteenth- and early-twentieth-century Christians, he centered his efforts in the communities in which he lived, although he remained fascinated and committed to the overseas missionary efforts in Asia. His peculiar background in Georgia blended frontier religion, Princeton theology, and radical farmers' politics. These influences, in combination with his confident and at times egotistical personality, allowed him to emerge as a leader when many of his peers did not. Matthews's desire to redeem his communities led him directly to the strategies and tenets associated with the Social Gospel. For a Southerner, this was unusual. Many of his fellow Christians below the Mason-Dixon line resisted political involvement and social reform for a number of reasons, but not Matthews. Captured by the vision of a more just and a more righteous society, he effected more change in the towns in which he lived than the typical Southern preacher. Proper education, adequate health care, just government, better working conditions, and an invigorating physical environment were all the responsibility of Christians, according to Matthews, and this is the agenda that he brought to Seattle. His personal investment in these issues was remarkable; sermon after sermon challenged his parishioners as well as all of Seattle's residents to pursue this vision. Like a whirling dervish, Matthews seemed to be everywhere at once. His critique of capitalism, his attack on conspicuous consumption along with his condemnation of traditional vice and popular culture encouraged his various audiences to apply their Christianity to the world around them. He never stopped elaborating on the ways in which he believed a Christian should be in but not of the world. And the impact of this message and his organizational efforts seems significant by any standard. Whether it was in Calhoun, Dalton, Jackson, or Seattle, Matthews should be credited with the establishment of an array of social services and institutions that affected thousands of people's lives. His churches always engaged difficult social problems within the community; from unemployment bureaus, kindergartens, and day care facilities, to community hospitals, soup kitchens, and night schools, members of Matthews's churches attempted to make their communities more humane.

Yet Matthews's fears, anxieties, and prejudices, while also being very reflective of the times in which he lived, seemed to limit his effectiveness. His life reminds us of how troubled many Americans were in the late nineteenth and early twentieth century over the state of American society and the prospects for the future. Although his world was one that twentieth-century Americans might find attractive because of its moral commitments, stable social moorings, and healthy communities, Matthews's world harbored a deep unrest concerning the nature of modernity. The combination of his Southern background, his religious worldview, and uncertainty about the changing role for males in an urbanized world led to a number of ideas and behaviors that were often extremely hostile toward individuals and movements with which he disagreed. Matthews was particularly vexed over the prospect of any new role for women in either the church or society as a whole. His attacks against woman suffrage and his plea for male authority, while not altogether contrary to the sentiments of many Americans of his day, nevertheless seem at odds with some of his other more progressive views. Although Matthews should be commended for his support for Asian-Americans in the 1920s and European Jews in the 1930s, he harbored deep suspicions of southern and eastern European immigrants. While he often supported elements of the labor movement, particularly in his early years, Matthews, like many of his fellow middle-class Seattleites, feared radical labor movements in the Pacific Northwest. Combined with the anxieties accompanying the First World War, Matthews's hatred of the I.W.W. led him to encourage his parishioners to despise a number of groups with a vehemence that seems quite unfortunate eighty years after the fact. Perhaps the only thing that can be said in his defense is that he was not alone. Prejudice against immigrants and fear of what was considered radical political ideology permeated American culture during Matthews's life. And all of those fears limited his ability to embrace a broader view of social justice.

Like many Americans of his day, Matthews had great difficulty embracing any concept of political and social life that might be described as pluralistic. Victorian America encouraged a view of society that was quite homogeneous in character, and certainly Matthews accepted this premise throughout his life. As a consequence, he failed to impress many people as a Christian with a gracious and humble spirit; he alienated many Seattleites because of his penchant for hyperbole, judgment, and apparent egotism. At a time when many Americans were struggling with the role of the pastor and Christianity in public life, Matthews's authoritative approach certainly presented problems for a significant number of people.

If Matthews failed to grasp any notion of a future America that might be more pluralistic in character, he did believe in a vision of America that has been the subject of increasing reflection on the part of many sociologists in the late twentieth and early twenty-first centuries. Matthews may strike the student of American society as an interesting example of a person who fostered the development of local institutions and community authority. Robert Bellah and other sociologists have pointed to the gradual shift in American society over the last two centuries. According to Bellah, Americans have abandoned local communities and forsaken obedience in any manner to the authority of the church, the family, the local government, and even the local school in favor of a radical individualism in which ultimate sovereignty over the most important questions resides with the self.

Matthews fought that trend his entire life. He believed in establishing authority outside of the self and dedicated himself to building institutions at all levels within the society, including the family, the school, the local government, the health-care community, and of course the church. He created institutional connections for his parishioners at a remarkable number of levels. In the midst of a culture that was moving rapidly toward the celebration and affirmation of individual choice, and a culture that fostered a consumer mentality when it came to everything from entertainment to religion, Matthews did everything in his power to counteract these tendencies. His demands for obedience and loyalty seem in the late twentieth century to be limited by his middle-class perspective and virtually dictatorial in nature. But most of the members of First Presbyterian did not see it that way. For them, Matthews's strength was his conviction that each Christian must commit to a life of service and sacrifice to the Seattle community. First Presbyterian members were constantly exhorted to minister to the broader society in all sorts of ways. Matthews believed that human beings needed local institutional connections in order to provide the social, intellectual, and spiritual moorings for a healthy life. While nervous about many of the intellectual trends in secular universities, he supported the University of Washington. He promoted the chamber of commerce; he believed in the local union hall and in the possibilities of local government; and he ardently championed the Presbyterian church. He could never bring himself to abet the fragmentation and division of the church along doctrinal lines. For as much as he believed in "the fundamentals" of orthodox Christianity, he planted his stake on the side of unification and cooperation because he understood the power of the church as institution.

In the end it must be said that Matthews failed to redeem the city in quite the ways that he had hoped. He failed to build a righteous community in the way in which he had dreamed. He alienated a great many people in his lifetime who thought him too intolerant, judgmental, and obsessed with his own personal power. However, Matthews's life stands as a testimony to the willingness of Christians in the twentieth century to try and make their faith and lives relevant to the problems of their day. Anxious, fearful, and judgmental about trends and issues of modern America, Matthews and others like him make the contemporary reader nervous about identifying with him too closely. And yet for many, Matthews might still be seen as a courageous individual who tried to live out his Christian convictions in a world that was often hostile and intolerant itself of people like him.

Perhaps even more remarkably, the drama of Matthews's life played out on the stage of the Pacific Northwest. From the perspective of the twenty-first century, his accomplishments seem even more noteworthy given the fact that the region remains the least churched in the country. Geographical distance from denominational headquarters, increased social mobility among its residents, and perhaps a natural desire to be free from institutional obligations have seemingly marked the religious experience of most people who have come to the region. Yet Matthews achieved his many successes in spite of these obstacles. His vision, energy, and persistence paid many dividends.

Mark Matthews remains for us, at the dawn of a new millennium, a complex figure from a remarkably complex period. He reminds us how difficult it is to sort out the most powerful forces that shape an individual's life, and how difficult it is to state with certainty the impact of a person on the communities in which he or she lives. Yet in his day, Matthews's contemporaries had no doubt about his significant influence on the city. Friend and foe believed that this minister had left a lasting mark. Sixty some years after his death, few contemporary Seattle residents know much of his life. Fewer still remember him in his pulpit or walking the streets of the city. But the continuing presence of First Presbyterian at Seventh and Spring and the weathered bust in Denny Park testify to his vision that a Southern-born preacher could come to the Pacific Northwest with hopes of redeeming Seattle in pursuit of civic righteousness for all of the world to see. And the story of his life reminds us of the strengths and weaknesses of just such a dream.

Notes

Chapter 1: The Hills of Georgia

1. The bulk of Matthews's papers consists of typescript sermons. This unpublished material hereafter will be referred to as *Sermonettes*, the name given to them in the collection. Matthews collected clippings and memorabilia throughout his life. The Mark A. Matthews Papers (97-2), at the University of Washington Libraries, Seattle (hereafter cited as Matthews Papers), include more than twenty scrapbooks, most unpaginated. Biographical information can be found in Matthews Scrapbook #15; a brief reference to Matthews's father and grandfather is found in *Memoirs of Georgia* (Atlanta: Southern Historical Association, 1895), p. 1039; additional biographical information on Matthews's early life can be found in Mark A. Matthews to Edwin Camp, Editor, *The Georgian* (Atlanta, Ga.), Sept. 27, 1910; *Sermonettes*, July 1910–January 1911.

2. Report, "Memorial to Mark Lafayette Matthews," box 6, Matthews Papers.

3. Ezra P. Giboney and Agnes M. Potter, *Life of Mark A. Matthews* (Grand Rapids, Mich.: William B. Eerdmans Publishing Co., 1948), pp. 14-15; William T. Sherman, *"War is Hell!" William T. Sherman's Personal Narrative of His March through Georgia*, ed. Mills Lane (Savannah: Beehive Press, 1974), p. 18.

4. *Calhoun (Ga.) Times*, Sept. 23, 1886; Giboney and Potter, *Life of Mark A. Matthews*, pp. 16-17.

5. Anne Firor Scott, *The Southern Lady: From Pedestal to Politics, 1830-1930* (Chicago: University of Chicago Press, 1970), p. 17.

6. David D. Hall, "The Victorian Connection," in *Victorian America*, ed. Daniel W. Howe (Philadelphia: University of Pennsylvania Press, 1976), p. 83.

7. Matthews, "Sketch of Mark Matthews' Life," *Sermonettes*, 1906.

8. *Ibid.*

9. Conway Gregory, Jr., *A Presbytery Called Chattanooga* (Alpharetta, Ga.: W. H. Wolfe Associates, 1994), p. 625.

10. Ben Barrus, Milton Baughn, and Thomas Campbell, *A People Called Cumberland Presbyterians* (Memphis: Frontier Press, 1972), pp. 88-95; Randall Balmer and John R. Fitzmier, *The Presbyterians* (Westport, Conn.: Praeger, 1994),

pp. 61-65; Bradley J. Longfield, *The Presbyterian Controversy: Fundmentalists, Modernists, and Moderates* (New York: Oxford University Press, 1991), pp. 60-62.

11. Longfield, *The Presbyterian Controversy*, p. 61.

12. Barrus, Baughn, and Campbell, *A People Called Cumberland Presbyterians*, pp. 177-78, 253-58.

13. Longfield, *The Presbyterian Controversy*, p. 62.

14. *Ibid.*

15. Lulie Pitts, *History of Gordon County, Georgia* (Calhoun, Ga.: Calhoun Times Press, 1933), p. 145.

16. *Ibid.*, pp. 327-28.

17. Matthews, "Letter to *Georgian*," *Sermonettes*, July 1910–January 1911.

18. Matthews, "Sketch of Mark Matthews' Work," *Sermonettes*, 1906.

19. Theodore Bozeman, *Protestants in an Age of Science* (Chapel Hill: University of North Carolina Press, 1977), pp. 116-31; Sydney Ahlstrom, "The Scottish Philosophy and American Theology," *Church History*, Vol. 24 (September 1955), 257-72; E. Brooks Holifield, *The Gentlemen Theologians: American Theology in Southern Culture, 1795-1860* (Durham, N.C.: Duke University Press, 1978).

20. Bozeman, *Protestants in an Age of Science*, pp. 116-31.

21. Charles Hodge, *Systematic Theology*, Vol. 1 (Grand Rapids, Mich.: William B. Eerdman's Publishing, 1970), p. 1; E. David Willis-Watkins, "Systematic Theology," *American Presbyterians*, Vol. 66, no. 4 (Winter 1988), 270-72.

22. Hodge, *Systematic Theology*, Vol. 1, p. 10.

23. Giboney and Potter, *Life of Mark A. Matthews*, p. 20.

24. *Calhoun Times*, June 30, 1887.

25. Pitts, *History of Gordon County*, p. 255; *Calhoun Times*, Jan. 30, 1890.

26. *Ibid.*

27. *Dalton (Ga.) Argus*, April 24, 1894.

28. *Calhoun Times*, April 24, 1890, June 25, 1891.

29. *Calhoun Times*, Oct. 7, 1889.

30. Alex Arnett, *The Populist Movement in Georgia* (New York: Columbia University Press, 1922), p. 34; Stephen Hahn, *The Roots of Southern Populism: Yeoman Farmers and the Transformation of the Georgia Upcountry, 1850-1890* (New York: Oxford University Press, 1983), pp. 226-37.

31. Alex Arnett, *The Populist Movement in Georgia*, p. 34.

32. *Ibid.*; Hahn, *Roots of Southern Populism*, pp. 226-37; see correspondence between Matthews and Felton's son in Matthews Scrapbook #5; *Calhoun Times*, Aug. 25, 1892.

33. Robert McMath, Jr., *Populist Vanguard* (Chapel Hill: University of North Carolina Press, 1975), p. 62.

34. *Southern Mercury*, Aug. 20, 1891; S. K. McGowan quoted in Theodore Mitchell, *Political Education in the Southern Farmers' Alliance, 1887-1900* (Madison: University of Wisconsin Press, 1987), p. 89.

35. Mitchell, *Political Education*, p. 89.

36. T. J. Stone quoted in Mitchell, *Political Education*, p. 89.

37. Isom Langley quoted in Mitchell, *Political Education*, p. 90.

38. *Ibid.*, p. 88.

39. Jewell B. Reeve, *Climb the Hills of Gordon* (Atlanta: L. A. Lee Publishing Co., 1962), p. 65; *Calhoun Times*, July 24, 1890 (qtn).

40. Matthews Scrapbook #4.

41. Matthews Scrapbook #9.

42. Matthews Scrapbook #4.

43. William Jennings Bryan, *The First Battle: A Story of the Campaign of 1896* (Chicago: Conkey Company, 1896), p. 199.

44. *Calhoun Times,* March 12, 1891.

45. Matthews quoted in Reeve, *Climb the Hills of Gordon,* p. 74.

46. *Calhoun Times,* July 14, 1892; Jan. 5, 12, 1893; Feb. 23, 1893.

47. *Today and Tomorrow Became Yesterday* (Dalton, Ga.: Bicentennial Commission, 1976), p. 23.

48. Matthews Scrapbook #2.

49. "The First Presbyterian Church," *Whitfield-Murray Historical Quarterly,* Vol. 7 (April 1984), 7.

50. *Dalton Argus,* Dec. 8, 1894.

51. L. L. Bemis to *Seattle Times,* Feb. 1, 1905, box 3, Matthews Papers.

52. Matthews Scrapbook #2.

53. *Dalton Argus,* Aug. 18, 1894.

54. *Dalton Argus,* Nov. 17, 1894.

55. C. Vann Woodward, *Tom Watson: Agrarian Rebel* (New York: MacMillan Company, 1938), pp. 269-71; *Dalton Argus,* Nov. 17, 1894.

56. *Dalton Argus,* Aug. 31, 1895.

57. *Ibid.*

58. *Ibid.*

59. *Dalton Argus,* Dec. 14, 1895.

60. *Memoirs of Georgia* (Atlanta, Ga.: Southern Historical Association, 1895), p. 1040.

61. *North Georgia Citizen* (Dalton), Dec. 26, 1895.

62. *Ibid.,* Jan. 2, 1896.

Chapter 2: Social Gospel in Tennessee

1. Edward L. Ayers, *The Promise of the New South: Life after Reconstruction* (New York: Oxford University Press, 1992), pp. 160-86; Timothy Smith, *Revivalism and Social Reform: American Protestantism on the Eve of the Civil War* (New York: Abingdon Press, 1957); John Lee Eighmy, "Religious Liberalism in the South during the Progressive Era," *Church History,* Vol. 38 (1969), 359-72; Ferenc Morton Szasz, *The Divided Mind of Protestant America, 1880-1930* (Tuscaloosa: University of Alabama Press, 1982), pp. 42-67; Hugh C. Bailey, *Liberalism in the New South: Southern Social Reformers and the Progressive Movement* (Coral Gables, Fla.: University of Miami Press, 1969); Hugh C. Bailey, *Edgar Gardner Murphy: Gentle Progressive* (Coral Gables: University of Miami Press, 1968); John P. McDowell, *A Social Gospel in the South: The Woman's Home Mission Movement in the Methodist Episcopal Church, South, 1886-1939* (Baton Rouge: Louisiana State University Press, 1982); Elizabeth Hayes Turner, "Women's Culture and Community: Religion and Reform in Galveston, 1880-1920" (Ph.D. dissertation, Rice University, 1990), pp. 130-33; Henry F. May, *Protestant Churches and Industrial America* (New York: Harper & Brothers, 1949); Aaron Abell, *The Urban Impact on American Protestantism, 1865-1900* (Cambridge: Harvard University Press, 1943).

2. General correspondence to Mark Matthews, Feb. 8, 1905, box 1, Matthews Papers.

3. *Jackson's Business: A Chronology of Business Enterprise in the Jackson Area of Western Tennessee*, ed. Laurie Mercier and Clint Daniels (Jackson, Tenn.: Business History Project, Jackson/Madison County Library, 1981), p. 4.

4. Roger Hart, *Redeemers, Bourbons, and Populists* (Baton Rouge: Louisiana State University Press, 1975), p. 223.

5. Matthews Scrapbook #2.

6. Matthews Scrapbook #4.

7. Matthews Scrapbook #1.

8. *Ibid.*

9. Matthews Scrapbook #2.

10. Matthews Scrapbook #1.

11. *Ibid.*

12. Matthews Scrapbook #2; Norris Magnuson, *Salvation in the Slums: Evangelical Social Work, 1865-1920* (Metuchen, N.J.: Scarecrow Press, 1977), pp. 26-27; *Memoirs of Georgia* (Atlanta: Southern Historical Association, 1895), p. 1040.

13. Matthews Scrapbook #2; C. Howard Hopkins, *The Rise of the Social Gospel in American Protestantism, 1865-1915* (New Haven: Yale University Press, 1940), pp. 142-44.

14. Matthews Scrapbook #1.

15. *Ibid.*

16. Matthews Scrapbook #4; Samuel Stanworth, *History of First Presbyterian Church of Jackson, Tennessee* (Jackson, Tenn., ca. 1924), pp. 11-12.

17. Matthews Scrapbook #5.

18. *Ibid.*

19. *Ibid.*; Emma Williams, *Historic Madison: The Story of Jackson and Madison County, Tennessee* (Jackson: Madison County Historical Society, 1946), p. 378.

20. Matthews Scrapbook #7.

21. Williams, *Historic Madison*, p. 261; Matthews Scrapbook #7; Letters, Mobil and Ohio R.R. to Presbyterian Hospital, Aug. 26, 1897, and Illinois Central R.R. to Presbyterian Hospital, Oct. 28, 1897, box 6, Matthews Papers.

22. Matthews Scrapbook #1.

23. Matthews Scrapbook #4.

24. *Ibid.*

25. Matthews Scrapbook #5; interview with Mrs. Jane Ward, Jan. 29, 1980.

26. Matthews Scrapbook #5.

27. Matthews Scrapbook #19.

28. Matthews Scrapbook #5.

29. *Ibid.*

30. Matthews Scrapbook #4.

31. *Ibid.*

32. Matthews Scrapbook #5.

33. Matthews, "Christianity's Life and Growth," *Sermonettes*, 1907; Keith Hardman, *Charles Grandison Finney, 1792-1875: Revivalist and Reformer* (Syracuse, N.Y.: Syracuse University Press, 1987).

34. Henry F. May, *Protestant Churches and Industrial America* (New York: Harper & Brothers, 1949).

35. Matthews Scrapbook #4.

36. *Ibid.*

37. Matthews Scrapbook #1.

38. Matthews Scrapbook #14; bar certificate to Mark Matthews, passed bar exam March 3, 1897, box 3, Matthews Papers. Matthews continued to be a member of the state bar after he came to Seattle. According to an early biographer, Matthews was admitted to practice before the United States Supreme Court after passing an examination before Chief Justice William H. Taft. Giboney and Potter, *Life of Mark A. Matthews*, p. 21.

39. Matthews Scrapbook #1.

40. C. Vann Woodward, *Tom Watson: Agrarian Rebel* (New York: MacMillan Company, 1938), p. 335.

41. Matthews Scrapbook #4.

42. Matthews Scrapbook #1; *Nashville Banner*, Oct. 28, 1900.

43. Matthews Scrapbook #1.

44. *Ibid.*

45. Matthews Scrapbook #1.

46. Matthews Scrapbook #5.

47. *Ibid.*

48. Matthews Scrapbook #1.

49. *Ibid.*

50. Matthews Scrapbook #5; "Clippings," box 2, Matthews Papers.

51. Matthews Scrapbook #4.

52. Matthews Scrapbook #5.

53. *Ibid.*; Matthews Scrapbook #14.

54. Matthews Scrapbook #5.

55. *Ibid.*

Chapter 3: Building Seattle's First Church

1. Matthews Scrapbook #5.

2. T. J. Jackson Lears, *No Place for Grace: Antimodernism and the Transformation of American Culture, 1880-1920* (New York: Pantheon Books, 1981), pp. 4-58; Susan Curtis, *A Consuming Faith: The Social Gospel and Modern American Culture* (Baltimore: Johns Hopkins University Press, 1991), pp. 1-15; Herbert Gutman, *Work, Culture, and Society in Industrializing America* (New York: Vintage, 1976); Philip Rieff, *The Triumph of the Therapeutic* (New York: Harper, 1966); John Higham, "The Reorientation of American Culture in the 1890s," in *Writing American History: Essays on Modern Scholarship* (Bloomington: Indiana University Press, 1970); Warren Susman, *Culture as History: The Transformation of American Society in the Twentieth Century* (New York: Pantheon Books, 1973).

3. Richard C. Berner, *Seattle 1900-1920: From Boomtown, Urban Turbulence, to Restoration* (Seattle: Charles Press, 1991), pp. 8-9.

4. *Ibid.*, p. 9.

5. Roger Sale, *Seattle Past to Present* (Seattle: University of Washington Press, 1976), p. 53.

6. *Ibid.*, p. 54.

7. *Ibid.*, p. 52.

8. Morgan, *Skid Road*, p. 75; *Seattle Argus*, Feb. 15, 1902; *Seattle Times*, May 11, 1902.

9. Jan Reiff, "Urbanization and the Social Structure: Seattle, Washington, 1852-1910" (Ph.D. dissertation, University of Washington, 1981), pp. 256-57.

10. Alfred O. Gray, *Not by Might: The Story of Whitworth College, 1890-1965* (Spokane: Whitworth College Press, 1965), p. 20.

11. *Ibid.*, pp. 11-22.

12. Matthews Scrapbook #5.

13. *Seattle Argus*, May 31, 1902.

14. Report, "Program of the First Presbyterian Church Twenty-fifth Anniversary of Matthews' Seattle Pastorate" (Seattle: First Presbyterian Church Press, 1927), p. 14, in First Presbyterian Church Archives, Seattle, Washington.

15. Matthews Scrapbook #5.

16. *Seattle Mail and Herald*, May 31, 1902.

17. *Seattle Times*, May 19, 1902.

18. Clippings 1884–1948, box 2, Matthews Papers; Matthews Scrapbook #9, p. 81.

19. Matthews, "First Presbyterian Church, Seattle, Wash.," *Sermonettes*, Jan.–July 1910.

20. Matthews Scrapbook #10, p. 19; #9, p. 25; *Pacific Building and Engineering Record*, July 28, 1906, pp. 3-4.

21. Matthews, "Pastor's Annual Report and Message," *Sermonettes*, Jan.–June 1911; Matthews Scrapbook #10, p. 178; *Seattle Post-Intelligencer*, Jan. 3, 1911; *Minutes of the General Assembly of the Presbyterian Church U.S.A.* (Philadelphia: Office of the General Assembly, 1915-39), 1915, p. 885; 1920, p. 888; 1923, p. 882; 1930, p. 879; 1935, p. 812; 1939, p. 811; Jonathan Jones, "Glimpses of New Presbyterian Statistics," *The Continent*, Sept. 18, 1924.

22. *Seattle Argus*, March 7, 1908.

23. Robert K. Churchill, *Lest We Forget* (Philadelphia: The Committee for the Historian of the Orthodox Presbyterian Church, 1985), p. 23.

24. *Seattle Argus*, Aug. 6, 1910.

25. *Ibid.*, Feb. 21, 1903.

26. Matthews Scrapbook #10, p. 256.

27. *Ibid.*, p. 257.

28. *Seattle Argus*, March 7, 1908.

29. *Ibid.*, Aug. 31, 1907.

30. *Seattle Times*, Nov. 30, 1908; Paul Dorpat, *Seattle Now & Then*, Vol. 3 (Seattle: Tartu Publications, 1989), p. 119.

31. Robert Wiebe, *The Search for Order, 1877-1920* (New York: Hill and Wang, 1967); Gabriel Kolko, *The Triumph of Conservatism* (New York: Free Press, 1963).

32. Burton Bledstein, *The Culture of Professionalism: The Middle Class and the Development of Higher Education in America* (New York: W. W. Norton, 1976), p. 27.

33. Matthews, "Pastor's Annual Report and Message," *Sermonettes*, Jan.–June 1911.

34. *Ibid.*

35. *Ibid.*; Matthews, "The Organization and Execution of the Work of the First Presbyterian Church of Seattle," *Sermonettes*, Jan.–June 1911.

36. "Program of First Presbyterian, 25th Anniversary of Matthews' Pastorate, 1927," p. 38.

37. Matthews, "Fellowship Dinner," *Sermonettes*, Jan.–July 1910.

38. Giboney and Potter, *Life of Mark A. Matthews*, p. 66.

Notes to Chapter 3

39. *Ibid.*, p. 58.

40. *Ibid.*, p. 59.

41. *Ibid.*

42. *Ibid.*, p. 64.

43. *Ibid.*, pp. 64-65.

44. *Ibid.*, pp. 66-74; Robert Boyd, *History of the Synod of Washington of the Presbyterian Church in the United States of America* (Seattle: Synod Office, 1909), pp. 48-49; nineteen branches became independent churches: Ravenna Boulevard 1911, University 1911, Georgetown 1911 (merged into New Hope), West Side 1912, Central 1914 (Wallingford), Boulevard Park 1941 (now PCA), Lake City 1941 (now Southminster), Mount View 1944, Magnolia 1946 (Lawton), Japanese 1947, Wedgwood 1947 (Morningside), South Park 1948 (New Hope), Lake Burien 1951, Lake Forest Park 1951, Rose Hill 1951. Four former churches are no longer part of the Presbytery of Seattle: Greenwood (1946-1963 now closed), Hillcrest (now PCA), Boulevard Park (now unaffiliated Presbyterian) and Van Asselt (1947-1953 then closed).

45. Matthews, "Sunday and Bible Classes of the First Presbyterian Church of Seattle," *Sermonettes*, 1910.

46. Matthews, "The First Presbyterian Church Sunday School," *Sermonettes*, 1922.

47. *Ibid.*

48. Giboney and Potter, *Life of Mark A. Matthews*, p. 76.

49. Lears, *No Place of Grace*, p. 4

50. *Ibid.*, pp. 4-5; for an excellent discussion of the issues surrounding the effect of effeminacy on religion and gender relations, see Gail Bederman, "'The Women Have Had Charge of the Church Work Long Enough': The Men and Religion Forward Movement of 1911-1912 and the Masculinization of Middle-Class Protestantism," *American Quarterly*, Vol. 41 (September 1989), 432-65.

51. Lears, *No Place for Grace*, p. 4; Ann Douglas, *The Feminization of American Culture* (New York: Alfred Knopf, 1977).

52. Robert Scott to Matthews, March 12, 1907, in *Sermonettes*, 1907.

53. Matthews, "Wanted: More Man in Men," *Sermonettes*, 1907.

54. Matthews, "The Manhood of Seattle's Churchmen Mortgaged," *Sermonettes*, Jan.–June 1909; see also Matthews, "The Young Man as Suitor, Husband, and Father," *Sermonettes*, Sept. 1906–Jan. 1907; Matthews, "The Young Man in Business, in Society and in Church," *Sermonettes*, Sept. 1906–Jan. 1907.

55. Matthews, "Organization and Execution of the Work of First Presbyterian," *Sermonettes*, Jan.–July 1911.

56. Matthews, "Homeless Man," *Sermonettes*, Jan.–July 1909.

57. Matthews, "Friendless Man," *Sermonettes*, Jan.–July 1909.

58. Matthews, "Penniless Man," "Heartless Man," "Conscienceless Man," "Childless Man," and "Christless Man," *Sermonettes*, Jan.–July 1909.

59. Dale E. Soden, "Men and Mission: The Shifting Fortunes of Presbyterian Men's Organizations in the Twentieth Century," in *The Organizational Revolution: Presbyterians and American Denominationalism*, ed. Milton J. Coalter, John M. Mulder, Louis B. Weeks (Louisville: Westminster/John Knox Press, 1992), pp. 233-53.

60. Bederman, "'The Women Have Had Charge of the Church Long Enough,'" pp. 432-41.

61. Lears, *No Place for Grace,* p. 15

62. Matthews, "The Cafe Girl," *Sermonettes,* 1907.

63. Matthews, "The Evolution of a Model Girl," *Sermonettes,* Sept. 1906–Jan. 1907.

64. Matthews Scrapbook #2.

65. Matthews, "The Marriage Ring," *Sermonettes,* 1911; Russell, "Mark Allison Matthews," p. 456.

66. Matthews, "The Face Beautiful," *Sermonettes,* 1906.

67. Matthews, "The Young Man as a Suitor, Husband, and Father," *Sermonettes,* 1906.

68. Matthews, "Why Women in the Pulpit?" *Sermonettes,* 1930.

69. Susan Curtis, *A Consuming Faith: The Social Gospel and Modern American Culture* (Baltimore: Johns Hopkins University Press, 1991), p. 76.

70. *Ibid.,* p. 77.

71. *Ibid.*

72. Matthews, "Society's Crime against Children," *Sermonettes,* 1906; see also Matthews, "The Boy—The Greatest Institution in the World," *Sermonettes,* Sept. 1906–Jan. 1907.

73. Matthews, "Childless Homes: Empty City Homes," *Sermonettes,* Jan.–July 1910.

74. *Seattle Argus,* July 25, 1908.

75. *Seattle Argus,* March 12, 1904.

76. *Ibid.,* Aug. 6, 1904.

77. Lears, *No Place for Grace,* p. 5.

78. "Luxury: The Enemy of Character, Personal, and National," April 24, 1904, Matthews Scrapbook #8.

79. Matthews, "Extravagance is Criminal," *Sermonettes,* Jan.–July 1912.

80. Matthews, "Making a Life, Making a Living, or Making a Failure," Dec. 17, 1905, *Sermonettes,* 1905.

81. Matthews, "Are There More Kinds of Blood Money than Mr. Rockefeller's?" *Sermonettes,* 1906.

82. Matthews, "Are the Foundations of Society Rotten?" *Sermonettes,* 1906.

83. Matthews, "Three Essentials to Success," *Sermonettes,* 1906.

84. Matthews, "Digging up Business Skeletons," *Sermonettes,* 1906.

85. Curtis, *A Consuming Faith,* pp. 1-15.

86. Matthews, "The Clergyman in Politics," *Sermonettes,* July–Dec. 1908.

87. Wiebe, *The Search for Order;* Bledstein, *The Culture of Professionalism;* Thomas Haskell, *The Emergence of Professional Social Science* (Urbana: University of Illinois Press, 1977); Paul Starr, *The Social Transformation of American Medicine* (New York: Basic Books, 1984).

Chapter 4: The Church Is My Force, the City My Field

1. Matthews quoted in *Seattle Times,* Feb. 3, 1902, p. 7.

2. For another significant Seattle religious leader, see Jan Dawson, "A Social Gospel Portrait: The Life of Sydney Dix Strong, 1860-1938" (M.A. thesis, University of Washington, 1972).

3. Philip S. Foner, *A History of the Labor Movement in the United States,* 4 vols.

(New York: International Publishers, 1947-64); Robert Heilbroner and Aaron Singer, *The Economic Transformation of America* (New York: Harcourt Brace Jovanovich, 1977); Herbert Gutman, *Work, Culture, and Society in Industrializing America: Essays in American Working Class and Social History* (New York: Alfred Knopf, 1976); Carlos Schwantes, *Radical Heritage: Labor, Socialism, and Reform in Washington and British Columbia, 1885-1917* (Seattle: University of Washington Press, 1979).

4. Paul Boyer, *Urban Masses and Moral Order in America, 1820-1920* (Cambridge, Mass.: Harvard University Press, 1978).

5. W. T. Stead, *If Christ Came to Chicago* (Chicago: Laird and Lee, 1894); Edward Everett Hale, *If Jesus Came to Boston* (Boston: J. S. Smith, 1894); Charles M. Sheldon, *In His Steps: What Would Jesus Do?* (New York: Hurst and Company, 1897).

6. Paul T. Phillips, *A Kingdom on Earth: Anglo-American Social Christianity, 1880-1940* (University Park: The Pennsylvania State Univerity Press, 1996), p. 60.

7. Matthews Scrapbook #1.

8. Matthews, "The Internal Kingdom," *Sermonettes,* 1906.

9. Keith Hardman, *Charles Grandison Finney, 1792-1875: Revivalist and Reformer* (Syracuse, N.Y.: Syracuse University Press, 1987), pp. 254-55.

10. Matthews, "The Internal Kingdom," *Sermonettes,* 1906.

11. Gregory Conway, Jr., *A Presbytery Called Chattanooga: Tracing the History of Chattanooga Presbytery, Cumberland Presbyterian Church from 1842-1989* (Alpharetta, Ga.: W. H. Wolfe Associates, 1994), p. 626.

12. Phillips, *A Kingdom on Earth,* p. 5

13. Matthews, "The Fight of Fights," *Sermonettes,* July–Jan. 1911.

14. *Ibid.*

15. Matthews, "The Tramp of the Ages," *Sermonettes,* Jan.–July 1908.

16. *Ibid.*

17. Matthews, "The New City—Newly Discovered Seattle," *Sermonettes,* Jan.–June 1911.

18. Matthews, "What is Seattle's Moral Sentiment?" *Sermonettes,* July–Dec. 1910.

19. Matthews, The New City—Newly Discovered Seattle," *Sermonettes,* Jan.–June 1911.

20. Matthews, "The Manhood of Seattle's Churchmen Mortgaged," *Sermonettes,* Jan.–July 1910.

21. Matthews, "Practical Christianity," *Sermonettes,* 1907.

22. Matthews, "Christian Socialism," *Sermonettes,* Sept. 1906–Jan. 1907.

23. *Ibid.*

24. *Ibid.*

25. Charles H. Hopkins, *The Rise of the Social Gospel in American Protestantism, 1865-1915* (New Haven: Yale University Press, 1940).

26. Matthews Scrapbook #8.

27. Matthews, "The Emancipation of the Laboring Classes," *Sermonettes,* Jan.–July 1910.

28. Matthews, "Song of the Saw," *Sermonettes,* Sept. 1906–Jan. 1907.

29. Matthews Scrapbook #1.

30. Matthews, "The Bondage of the Pawn Shop," *Sermonettes,* 1906.

31. Matthews, "Three Sources of Wealth Neglected by Seattle Men," *Sermonettes*, Sept. 1906–Jan. 1907.

32. *Ibid.*

33. Matthews, "The Inconsistencies of Capital in Light of the Golden Rule," *Sermonettes*, 1906.

34. Matthews, "The Practical Church," *Seattle Mail and Herald*, March 11, 1905.

35. Matthews Scrapbook #3.

36. Matthews, "Seattle's Unemployed Church Forces," *Sermonettes*, 1906.

37. Matthews, "Should the Aged Be Turned Out to Graze?" *Sermonettes*, June–Dec. 1911.

38. Matthews Scrapbook #5.

39. Matthews Scrapbook #10, p. 230; Giboney and Potter, *Life of Mark A. Matthews*, p. 28.

40. Matthews Scrapbook #10, p. 169.

41. *Red Cross News*, Oct.–Nov. 1971, p. 3, copy in Special Collections, University of Washington Libraries.

42. Matthews, "Help, Help, Help Dying Italy," *Sermonettes*, 1907.

43. Matthews, "To All Horse Lovers," *Sermonettes*, 1907.

44. Matthews Scrapbook #7.

45. Matthews, "Future Seattle," *Sermonettes*, Sept. 1906–Jan. 1907.

46. "A Church of International Significance," *The Westerner*, Vol. 13 (December 1910), 10.

47. Report from Sara Van Wagener, "Oriental Night School," *Sermonettes*, 1916. One missionary in Montana wrote, "I also learned that about half of them [approximately nine Chinese] were converted . . . in the Presbyterian Mission of Seattle, Washington, sustained by the First Presbyterian Church, of which Reverend M. A. Matthews, D.D., is pastor."

48. Matthews, Scrapbook #10, p. 40; Giboney and Potter, *Life of Mark A. Matthews*, p. 78.

49. *Ibid.*

50. Matthews, "Pastor's Annual Report and Message," *Sermonettes*, Jan.–June 1911; First Presbyterian heavily supported a mission in Soochow, China.

51. Matthews Scrapbook #10, p. 222.

52. Matthews, "Racial Prejudice Un-American," *Annals of the American Academy of Political and Social Science*, Vol. 93 (January 1921), 69-72.

53. Willard Straight to Matthews, March 16, 1914, and Committee on Japanese Presbyterian Mission to Matthews, Oct. 21, 1913, box 1, Matthews Papers.

54. Matthews, "The Lifters and the Leaners," *Sermonettes*, 1907; C. Allyn Russell, "Mark Allison Matthews: Seattle Fundamentalist and Civic Reformer," p. 459.

55. Matthews, "First Presbyterian Day Nursery," *Sermonettes*, Jan.–July 1910. First Presbyterian is often credited with establishing the first kindergarten in the city, but according to Thomas Prosch, the original kindergarten in Seattle was established in 1888. See Thomas Prosch, "A Chronological History of Seattle from 1850 to 1897," typescript, 1900-1901, Special Collections, University of Washington Libraries, p. 299.

56. Matthews, "The First Presbyterian Day Nursery," *Sermonettes*, Jan.–July 1910.

57. Matthews Scrapbook #16.

58. Matthews Scrapbook #9; Giboney and Potter, *Life of Mark A. Matthews*, p. 28; Austin Griffiths, "Great Faith: Autobiography of an English Immigrant Boy in America, 1863-1950," typescript, 1950, Special Collections, University of Washington Libraries, pp. 157-58.

59. Giboney and Potter, *Life of Mark A. Matthews*, p. 29.

60. Matthews Scrapbook #9.

61. Bernard Weisberger, *They Gathered at the River* (Boston: Little, Brown, and Company, 1958), p. 167.

62. For a more complete analysis of the revival, see Dale E. Soden, "Anatomy of a Presbyterian Urban Revival: J. W. Chapman in the Pacific Northwest," *American Presbyterians: Journal of Presbyterian History*, Vol. 64, No. 1 (Spring 1986), 49-57; William G. McLoughlin, Jr., *Modern Revivalism: Charles Grandison Finney to Billy Graham* (New York: Ronald Press, 1959); Weisberger, *They Gathered at the River*; Lefferts Loetscher, "Presbyterian Revivals Since 1875," *Pennsylvania Magazine of History and Biography*, Vol. 68 (January 1944), 54-92.

63. *Seattle Times*, April 14, 1905.

64. *Seattle Post-Intelligencer*, April 12, 1905.

65. *Ibid.*

66. *Seattle Times*, April 18, 1905.

67. *Seattle Post-Intelligencer*, April 19, 1905.

68. *Seattle Times*, April 16, 1905.

69. Charles Stelzle, *A Son of the Bowery* (New York: George Doran, 1926), p. 215; see also Curtis, *A Consuming Faith*, pp. 259-65; Phillips, *A Kingdom on Earth*, pp. 143-46.

70. Stelzle quoted in *Seattle Times*, April 17, 1905.

71. *Ibid.*, April 14, 1905.

72. *Ibid.*, April 18, 1905.

73. *Seattle Mail and Herald*, March 18, 1905.

Chapter 5: *Progressive Impulses*

1. Matthews, "The Clergyman in Politics," *Sermonettes*, July–Dec. 1908.

2. Matthews, "The Sleeping Forces in Our Civic Government," *Sermonettes*, 1907.

3. *Seattle Post-Intelligencer*, Sept. 18, 1911.

4. John D. Hicks, *The Populist Revolt* (Minneapolis: University of Minnesota Press, 1931); Norman Pollack, *The Populist Response to Industrial America* (Cambridge: Harvard University Press, 1962); and Benjamin P. DeWitt, *The Progressive Movement* (New York: Macmillan, 1915).

5. Richard Hofstadter, *The Age of Reform: From Bryan to F.D.R.* (New York: Alfred Knopf, 1955); George E. Mowery, "The California Progressive and His Rationale: A Study in Middle Class Politics," *Mississippi Valley Historical Review*, Vol. 36 (September 1949), 239-50.

6. Gabriel Kolko, *The Triumph of Conservatism: A Reinterpretation of American History* (New York: Free Press of Glencoe, 1963); Samuel P. Hays, *Conservation and the Gospel of Efficiency: The Progressive Conservation Movement, 1890-1920* (Cambridge: Harvard University Press, 1959); Robert H. Wiebe, *Business-*

men and Reform: A Study of the Progressive Movement (Cambridge: Harvard University Press, 1962); Robert Wiebe, *The Search for Order 1877-1920*; for an excellent discussion of the historiographical problems associated with Progressivism, see Daniel T. Rodgers, "In Search of Progressivism," in *The Promise of American History Progress and Prospects*, ed. Stanley Kutler and Stanley Katz (Baltimore: Johns Hopkins University Press, 1982), pp. 113-32.

7. Robert M. Crunden, *Ministers of Reform: The Progressives' Achievement in American Civilization, 1889-1920* (New York: Basic Books, 1982); Paul Boyer, *Urban Masses and Moral Order*, pp. 189-292; Susan Curtis, *A Consuming Faith*, pp. 128-46.

8. Matthews Scrapbook #10.

9. Matthews, "The Spirit of the Hour Is Responsible for Statutory Lawlessness," Matthews Scrapbook #7.

10. Matthews, "How to Enforce the Law," *Sermonettes*, 1907.

11. Matthews, "The Dynamics of Gratitude," *Sermonettes*, Sept. 1906–Jan. 1907.

12. Matthews, "Lifters and Leaners," *Sermonettes*, 1907.

13. Matthews, "Municipal Reform," *Sermonettes*, 1913.

14. Boyer, *Urban Masses and Moral Order*, p. 196.

15. *Ibid.*, pp. 196-97.

16. Frederic Howe quoted in *ibid.*, p. 197.

17. Matthews, "Short Beds and Narrow Covers," *Sermonettes*, 1906.

18. Matthews, "What the Census Man Saw and Got, or the Moral Value of the Census," *Sermonettes*, Jan.–July 1910.

19. Matthews, "The Cost of Civic Indifference," *Sermonettes*, Jan.–July 1910.

20. Boyer, *Urban Masses and Moral Order*, p. 175.

21. Matthews, "Our Citizens," *Sermonettes*, Jan.–July 1908.

22. Matthews, "The Internal Kingdom," *Sermonettes*, 1907.

23. Matthews, "Our Disposition of the Future," *Sermonettes*, 1907.

24. Matthews, "The Young Man in Politics," *Sermonettes*, 1911.

25. Boyer, *Urban Masses and Moral Order*, p. 175.

26. James H. Timberlake, *Prohibition and the Progressive Movement, 1900-1920* (Cambridge: Harvard University Press, 1963), pp. 1-2.

27. Boyer, *Urban Masses and Moral Order*, p. 191 (qtn.); Timberlake, *Prohibition and the Progressive Movement*, pp. 1-2.

28. Boyer, *Urban Masses and Moral Order*, p. 165.

29. Berner, *Seattle, 1900-1920*, p. 59.

30. *Ibid.*, pp. 59-60.

31. Matthews, "Society's Crimes Due to a Diseased Nervous System," *Sermonettes*, 1907.

32. Matthews, "The Liquor Conspiracy," *Sermonettes*, Jan.–July 1910.

33. *Ibid.*

34. Vice committee to Matthews, May 21, 1910, in *Sermonettes*, Jan.–July 1910.

35. Lowell S. Hawley and Ralph Bushnell Potts, *Counsel for the Damned: A Biography of George Francis Vanderveer* (Philadelphia: J. B. Lippincott Company, 1953), pp. 129-30; Murray Morgan, *Skid Road*, (New York: The Viking Press, 1951), pp. 3-10; Gordon Newell and Don Sherwood, *Totem Tales of Old Seattle* (New York: Ballantine Books, 1956), p. 162.

36. Matthews Scrapbook #10, p. 147.

Notes to Chapter 5

37. *Seattle Post-Intelligencer*, Sept. 19, 1910.

38. Berner, *Seattle, 1900-1920*, pp. 112-13.

39. Matthews, "Tolerated Graft on the Increase," *Sermonettes*, Jan.–July 1909.

40. Matthews, "Society's Crimes Due to a Diseased Nervous System" (qtn.), and "The Christian View of Sin," *Sermonettes*, Jan.–July 1909.

41. Matthews, "Society's Crimes Due to a Diseased Nervous System," *Sermonettes*, 1907.

42. Matthews, "Roses for Seattle's Children," *Sermonettes*, 1906.

43. Matthews, "Society's Crimes Due to a Diseased Nervous System," *Sermonettes*, 1907.

44. Matthews, "Convict Citizens," *Sermonettes*, 1906.

45. Matthews, "Coffee or Coffin House–Which?" *Sermonettes*, 1907.

46. Matthews, "Roses for Seattle's Children," *Sermonettes*, 1906.

47. Matthews, "Society's Crimes Due to Diseased Nervous System," *Sermonettes*, 1907.

48. Matthews, Scrapbook #9, p. 243.

49. Matthews, "City Grafters and the Eighth Commandment," Scrapbook #7.

50. *Seattle Times*, Sept. 16, 1905.

51. James William Donnen, "Personality and Reform in the Progressive Era: An Interpretation of Five Washington State Careers" (M.A. thesis, University of Washington, 1974); Lee Pendergrass, "Urban Reform and Voluntary Association: A Case Study of the Seattle Municipal League, 1910-1929" (Ph.D. dissertation, University of Washington, 1972); Robert Saltvig, "The Progressive Movement in Washington" (Ph.D. dissertation, University of Washington, 1966); Mansel Blackford, "Reform in Seattle during the Progressive Era, 1902-1916," *Pacific Northwest Quarterly*, Vol. 59 (1968), 177-85.

52. Mattthews Scrapbook #9, p. 222.

53. Matthews, "Three Outrages," *Sermonettes*, Jan.–July 1910.

54. *Ibid.*

55. *Ibid.*

56. Matthews, "Rest Rooms for Workingmen," Matthews Scrapbook #7; *Seattle Times*, Sept. 4, 1905.

57. *Seattle Union-Record*, May 12 and 19, 1906.

58. Matthews, "Song of the Saw," *Sermonettes*, Sept. 1906–Jan. 1907.

59. Matthews, "The Birth of a New Force in the Settlement of All Problems," *Sermonettes*, 1906.

60. Matthews, "Song of the Saw," *Sermonettes*, Sept. 1906–Jan. 1907.

61. Matthews, "The False Label and Its Consequences," *Sermonettes*, 1906.

62. Report, "History of the Milk Commission," June 1911, box 1, Matthews Papers.

63. Matthews, "Interview on Female Suffrage," *Sermonettes*, July 1910–Jan. 1911.

64. Matthews, "Be Liberal to the University," *Sermonettes*, Jan.–June 1911.

65. Matthews, "Fellowship Dinner," *Sermonettes*, Sept. 1906–Jan. 1907.

66. Matthews, "The Blue-Pencil Campaign," *Sermonettes*, Sept. 1906–Jan. 1907.

67. Matthews Scrapbook #10, p. 116.

68. Matthews, "Enemies of Progress," *Sermonettes*, Jan.–July 1908.

69. Alaska-Yukon-Pacific Exposition Scrapbooks, June 28, 1907, and

April 5, 1908, Special Collections, University of Washington Libraries.

70. Blackford, "Reform Politics in Seattle," pp. 177-85.

Chapter 6: The Great Feud

1. Morgan, *Skid Road*, pp. 164-93; Blackford, "Reform in Seattle, 1902-1916," 177-89.

2. *Seattle Times*, Jan. 5, 1904.

3. Matthews Scrapbook #10, pp. 98-99.

4. *Seattle Post-Intelligencer* and *Seattle Times*, Jan. 31, 1905.

5. *Ibid.*

6. *Seattle Post-Intelligencer*, Jan. 31, 1905.

7. *Seattle Star*, Jan. 31, 1905.

8. *Seattle Post-Intelligencer*, *Seattle Times*, and *Seattle Star*, Jan. 31–Feb. 2, 1905.

9. Saltvig, "The Progressive Movement in Washington," p. 92.

10. *Ibid.*, p. 94.

11. Matthews Scrapbook #9.

12. *Seattle Times*, Sept. 1-8, 1906.

13. Berner, *Seattle, 1900-1920*, p. 112.

14. *Ibid.*, pp. 113-14; Matthews, "Segregation of Vice," *Sermonettes*, July–Jan. 1910.

15. Matthews Scrapbook #10, p. 144.

16. *Ibid.*

17. *Ibid.*

18. *Seattle Times*, Feb. 21, 1910.

19. Berner, *Seattle, 1900-1920*, p. 115.

20. Matthews, "Seattle Needs the Sword for Tuesday," *Sermonettes*, Jan.–July 1910.

21. Berner, *Seattle, 1900-1920*, pp. 115-16; *Seattle Times*, Feb. 9, 1910.

22. *Seattle Times*, Oct. 23, 1910.

23. Sharon A. Boswell and Lorraine McConaghy, *Raise Hell and Sell Newspapers: Alden J. Blethen and The Seattle Times* (Pullman: Washington State University Press, 1996), p. 156; *Seattle Times*, Oct. 23, 1910; Wappenstein's biographical description is found in Dorothy Miller Kahlo, *History of the Police and Fire Departments of the City of Seattle* (Seattle: Lumbermen's Printing Company, 1907), pp. 75-76.

24. Boswell and McConaghy, *Raise Hell and Sell Newspapers*, pp. 158-59.

25. *Ibid.*, p. 159.

26. *Ibid.*, p. 160; Clarence Bagley, *History of Seattle From the Earliest Settlement to the Present Time*, Vol. 2 (Chicago: S. J. Clarke Publishing Company, 1916), p. 555.

27. Saltvig, "Progressive Movement," p. 107; Morgan, *Skid Road*, p. 173.

28. *Seattle Post-Intelligencer*, Oct. 17, 1910.

29. *Ibid.*, Dec. 3, 1910.

30. Matthews, "What I Would Do If I Were Mayor of Seattle," *Sermonettes*, July 1910–Jan. 1911.

31. Only Matthews's reply to Brainerd is preserved in the files; letter, Mark Matthews to Erastus Brainerd, Jan. 24, 1911, box 3, Erastus Brainerd Papers, University of Washington Libraries.

32. *Ibid.*

33. Matthews to Hiram Gill, Jan. 24, 1911, *Sermonettes*, Jan.–June 1911.

34. *Seattle Post-Intelligencer*, Jan. 27, 1911.

35. *Seattle Post-Intelligencer*, Jan. 28, 1911.

36. *Seattle Times*, Jan. 28, 1911.

37. Matthews to Hiram Gill, Jan. 24, 1911, *Sermonettes*, Jan.–June 1911.

38. Report to Mark Matthews from Burns agent, July 19, 1911, box 2, Matthews Papers.

39. Matthews to Brainerd, Jan. 24, 1911, box 3, Erastus Brainerd Papers.

40. Burton J. Hendrick, "The 'Recall' in Seattle," *McClure's*, Vol. 37 (October 1911), 660-63; Boswell and McConaghy, *Raise Hell and Sell Newspapers*, p. 160.

41. William R. Hunt, *Front-Page Detective: William J. Burns and the Detective Profession, 1880-1930* (Bowling Green, Ky.: Bowling Green State University Popular Press, 1990), pp. 76-77.

42. *Seattle Post-Intelligencer* and *Seattle Times*, Feb. 13–15, 1911.

43. *Ibid.*

44. *Seattle Times*, Feb. 26, 1911.

45. *Seattle Town-Crier*, Feb. 25, 1911.

46. *Ibid.*, April 8, 1911.

47. *Seattle Post-Intelligencer*, May 7, 1911; Matthews, "An Account of My Stewardship," *Sermonettes*, Jan.–June, 1911.

48. *Seattle Argus* and *Seattle Town-Crier*, May 13, 1911.

49. *Seattle Post-Intelligencer*, May 25, 1911.

50. Report to Matthews from Burns agent, May 25, 1911, box 2, Matthews Papers.

51. *Seattle Post-Intelligencer*, May 26–27, 1911.

52. *Seattle Post-Intelligencer*, May 30, 1911.

53. *Seattle Post-Intelligencer*, July 4, 1911.

54. *Seattle Post-Intelligencer*, Sept. 15, 1910.

55. *Seattle Argus*, March 7, 1908.

56. Blackford, "Reform in Seattle," 177-89.

57. Sale, *Seattle Past to Present*, p. 86.

58. Bledstein, *The Culture of Professionalism;* Haskell, *Emergence of Professional Social Science.*

59. Charles Gates, *History of the University of Washington* (Seattle: University of Washington Press, 1961), p. 117; Thomas McClintock, "J. Allen Smith and the Progressive Movement: A Study in Intellectual History" (Ph.D. dissertation, University of Washington, 1959), pp. 159-61.

Chapter 7: "Shall Matthews Run the City?"

1. Peter Clarke MacFarlane, "The Black-Maned Lion of Seattle," *Collier's Magazine*, Vol. 50 (December 28, 1912), 21-23.

2. *Ibid.*, 21.

3. *Ibid.*, 22.

4. *Seattle Post-Intelligencer*, May 24, 1911.

5. Boswell and McConaghy, *Raise Hell and Sell Newspapers*, pp. 161-65; *Seattle Times*, May 25, 1911; Operative C Reports, June 5, 1911, box 2, Matthews Papers.

6. *Seattle Times*, May 28, 1911.

7. *Seattle Argus*, Aug. 12, 1911.

8. Matthews, "Committee on Civic Righteousness Report," *Sermonettes*, 1912.

9. *Seattle Argus*, March 9, 1912.

10. Matthews to Austin Griffiths, Dec. 3, 1912, box 6, and Jan. 10, 1913, box 7, Griffiths Papers; Charles Byler, "Austin E. Griffiths: Seattle's Progressive Reformer," *Pacific Northwest Quarterly*, Vol. 75 (1985), 26.

11. *Seattle Town-Crier*, May 24, 1912.

12. Matthews, "To the Ministers Regarding Voting Recommendations," *Sermonettes*, Jan.–July 1912.

13. *Seattle Town-Crier*, Sept. 14, 1912; *Seattle Post-Intelligencer*, Sept. 9, 1912.

14. Matthews, "Letter to Ministers' Federation," *Sermonettes*, 1914.

15. Matthews, "King County Evangelical Ministers' Congress," *Sermonettes*, July–Dec. 1912.

16. *Seattle Post-Intelligencer*, Dec. 20, 1913.

17. Morgan, *Skid Road*, p. 183.

18. Matthews, "The Plot of the Enemy," *Sermonettes*, July–Dec. 1912.

19. *Seattle Times*, July 18, 1913.

20. Matthews Scrapbook #16.

21. Matthews, "Free Speech and Its Possibilities," *Sermonettes*, 1913.

22. *Seattle Sun*, July 21, 1913.

23. *Seattle Times*, July 23, 1913.

24. *What's Doing* (Tacoma), Dec. 18, 1915.

25. Matthews, "God Ordered Steps," *Sermonettes*, 1913.

26. Matthews, "Our City's Needs," *Sermonettes*, July–Dec. 1912.

27. Berner, *Seattle, 1900-1920*, p. 348.

28. Matthews, "Our Charter Perils," *Sermonettes*, 1914.

29. *Seattle Post-Intelligencer*, March 27 and 29, 1914.

30. Pendergrass, "Urban Reform and Voluntary Association," p. 31.

31. Norman Clark, *The Dry Years*, p. 68.

32. Matthews quoted in Clark, *ibid.*, p. 69.

33. *Ibid.*, p. 133.

34. *Ibid.*, p. 66.

35. Matthews to Austin Griffiths, July 2, 1914, box 7, Griffiths Papers, University of Washington Libraries.

36. *Seattle Times*, Jan. 31, 1916; Matthews Scrapbook #17.

37. Clark, *Dry Years*, p. 69.

38. *Seattle Times*, Aug. 14, 1916.

39. Lowell S. Hawley and Ralph Bushnell Potts, *Counsel for the Damned* (New York: Lippincott, 1953), p. 169.

40. Matthews, "In Re: Graft Situation," *Sermonettes*, 1917; *Seattle Post-Intelligencer*, March 18, 1917.

41. *Seattle Post-Intelligencer* and *Seattle Times*, March 18–April 1, 1917.

42. Report, Burns agents to Mark Matthews, Nov. 12, 1916, box 2, Matthews Papers.

43. *Seattle Post-Intelligencer*, June 23–28, 1917; *Seattle Argus*, June 30, 1917.

44. Matthews to William H. Taft, Sept. 13, 1910, William Howard Taft Presidential Papers.

Notes to Chapter 7

45. *Seattle Argus*, March 1, 1913.

46. Secretary of Mayor Hanson to Matthews, July 17, 1918, box 3, Matthews Papers. Indicative of Matthews's power was the fact that Hanson sought the preacher's endorsement in February 1918. "I am very anxious to secure your support in the mayoralty campaign," Hanson wrote Matthews. "I stand for a sane, constructive administration, an administration free from chaos, trouble, petty quarrels and bickering." Hanson to Matthews, Feb. 22, 1918, box 3, Matthews Papers.

47. William Short and Robert Proctor to Woodrow Wilson, Feb. 27, 1919, box 5, Matthews Papers.

48. Franklin Lane to A. Mitchell Palmer, Dec. 8, 1919, box 3, Matthews Papers.

49. Woodrow Wilson to Matthews, Aug. 15, 1914, box 4, Matthews Papers.

50. Woodrow Wilson to T. W. Gregory, Oct. 9, 1914, Woodrow Wilson Papers.

51. Woodrow Wilson to Matthews, Jan. 25, 1915, box 4 , Matthews Papers.

52. Matthews and William Parry, Jan.–Feb. 1915, box 2, Matthews Papers; Matthews to Wilson, Jan. 12, 1915, Woodrow Wilson Papers.

53. Matthews to W. B. Wilson, Feb. 11, 1915, Woodrow Wilson Papers.

54. *Seattle Post-Intelligencer*, Aug. 23, 1916.

55. Matthews to Wilson, June 12, 1916, box 4, Matthews Papers.

56. Matthews to Thomas Marshall, Oct. 18, 1917, box 5, Matthews Papers.

57. Matthews to Thomas Marshall, Nov. 26, 1917, box 5, Matthews Papers.

58. Franklin Lane to Matthews, Aug. 22, 1919, box 3, Matthews Papers.

59. Woodrow Wilson to Newton Baker, June 21, 1918, Woodrow Wilson Papers.

60. Matthews to Wilson, Oct. 9, 1920, box 5, Matthews Papers.

61. Matthews to Wilson, Oct. 29, 1920, box 5, Matthews Papers.

Chapter 8: The Great War and the General Strike

1. Woodrow Wilson quoted in John F. Piper, Jr., *American Churches in World War I* (Athens: Ohio University Press, 1985), p. 9.

2. *Ibid.*, p. 11.

3. Matthews, "Birth of the Prince of Peace," *Sermonettes*, 1913.

4. Matthews Scrapbook #16, p. 225.

5. Matthews Scrapbook #17.

6. William Jennings Bryan to Mark Matthews, Feb. 2, 1916, box 1, Matthews Papers.

7. Matthews to William H. Taft, Jan. 18, 1916, William Howard Taft Presidential Papers; Matthews, "Washington Branch of the National League to Enforce the Peace," *Sermonettes*, 1916. In June 1916, Matthews was named as the delegate to the National Conference of the League to Enforce the Peace in Washington, D.C.; *Seattle Post-Intelligencer*, June 3, 1916.

8. Matthews Scrapbook #17.

9. Matthews, "Interview in Re. Our National Duty," *Sermonettes*, 1917.

10. Matthews, "The Supernatural Church," *Sermonettes*, 1917.

11. Matthews Scrapbook #17.

12. Matthews to Wilson, June 26, 1918, box 4, Matthews Papers.

Notes to Chapter 8

13. Matthews, "The Morale of America in the War," *Sermonettes*, 1918.

14. Wesley Jones to Matthews, July 24, 1918, and Oct. 4, 1918, box 2, Matthews Papers.

15. Billy Sunday quoted in Ray Abrams, *Preachers Present Arms* (Scottsdale, Pa.: Herald Press, 1969), p. 106.

16. Abrams, *Preachers Present Arms*, p. 109.

17. Matthews to Wilson, Dec. 8, 1917, box 4, Matthews Papers.

18. Matthews to Thomas W. Gregory, Jan. 29, 1918, Department of Justice File RG 60-186701-49-52, National Archives, Washington, D.C.

19. William Preston, Jr., *Aliens and Dissenters: Federal Suppression of Radicals, 1903-1933* (Cambridge: Harvard University Press), p. 167.

20. Matthews to Wesley Jones, Feb. 13, 1918, and Jones to Matthews, April 26, 1918, box 2, Matthews Papers.

21. Matthews Scrapbook #17.

22. *Ibid.; New York Times*, Aug. 26, 1918.

23. *The Nation*, Vol. 107, No. 2776 (Sept. 14, 1918), p. 294.

24. Matthews Scrapbook #17; *New York Times*, Aug. 27, 1918.

25. Matthews to Wilson, March 8, 1918, box 4, Matthews Papers.

26. Matthews to Wilson, Oct. 7, 1918, box 4, Matthews Papers.

27. Matthews to Wilson, Nov. 14, 1918, and Matthews to Wilson, Oct. 7, 1918, box 4, Matthews Papers.

28. Norman Clark, *Mill Town: A Social History of Everett, Washington, from Its Earliest Beginnings on the Shores of Puget Sound to the Tragic and Infamous Event Known as the Everett Massacre* (Seattle: University of Washington Press, 1970); Robert E. Ficken and Charles P. LeWarne, *Washington: A Centennial History* (Seattle: University of Washington Press, 1989), p. 86.

29. Matthews, "Our Damnable Enemies," *Sermonettes*, 1917.

30. Matthews to Wilson, Aug. 4, 1917, box 4, Matthews Papers.

31. Matthews to Wilson, Aug. 17, 1917, box 4, Matthews Papers.

32. Matthews to Wilson, April 27, 1918, box 4, Matthews Papers.

33. Wilson to Matthews, May 4, 1918, box 4, Matthews Papers.

34. Matthews to Thomas Marshall, Dec. 10, 1918, box 5, Matthews Papers.

35. Matthews to Wilson, Aug. 20, 1919, box 4, Matthews Papers.

36. Joel A. Carpenter, *Revive Us Again: The Reawakening of American Fundamentalism* (New York: Oxford University Press, 1997), pp. 102-103.

37. Robert Murray, *Red Scare* (Minneapolis: University of Minnesota Press, 1955), p. 12.

38. *Ibid.*, p. 13.

39. Robert Friedheim, *The Seattle General Strike* (Seattle: University of Washington Press, 1964), pp. 55-80.

40. *Ibid.*, pp. 66-68.

41. Matthews to Wilson, Nov. 14, 1918, box 4, Matthews Papers.

42. Matthews to Wilson, Nov. 18, 1918, box 4, Matthews Papers.

43. Wilson to Matthews, Nov. 20, 1918, box 4, Matthews Papers.

44. Friedheim, *Seattle General Strike*, p. 96; Murray, *Red Scare*, pp. 58-59.

45. Friedheim, *Seattle General Strike*, pp. 95-96.

46. *Ibid.*

47. Murray, *Red Scare*, p. 60.

48. *Seattle Union-Record*, Feb. 4, 1919.

Notes to Chapter 8

49. Matthews, "An Appeal to the Patriots of Seattle," *Sermonettes*, 1919.

50. *Seattle Star*, Feb. 11, 1919.

51. *Seattle Argus*, Feb. 22, 1919.

52. Report, "The American Committee," Feb. 17, 1919, box 1, Matthews Papers; Matthews, "The American Committee," *Sermonettes*, 1919.

53. *Seattle Post-Intelligencer*, Sept. 15, 1919.

54. *Seattle Post-Intelligencer*, Sept. 14–15, 1919.

55. Matthews, "The Future of Seattle," *Sermonettes*, 1919.

Chapter 9: Fundamentalism and Modernism

1. Ernest R. Sandeen, *The Roots of Fundamentalism: British and American Millenarianism, 1800-1930* (Chicago: University of Chicago Press, 1970), pp. 103-31; George M. Marsden, *Fundamentalism and American Culture* (New York: Oxford University Press, 1980); Joel A. Carpenter, *Revive Us Again: The Reawakening of American Fundamentalism* (New York: Oxford University Press, 1997); see also Marsden, "Defining Fundamentalism," *Christian Scholar's Review*, Vol. 1 (Winter 1971), 141-51; and Sandeen, "Defining Fundamentalism: A Reply to Professor Marsden," *Christian Scholar's Review*, Vol. 1 (Spring 1971), 227-32.

2. Marsden, "Fundamentalism," *Encyclopedia of the American Religious Experience: Studies of Traditions and Movements*, ed. Charles H. Lippy and Peter W. Williams, 3 vols. (New York: Scribners, 1988), pp. 947-62.

3. William R. Hutchison, *The Modernist Impulse in American Protestantism* (Cambridge: Harvard University Press, 1976), pp. 1-11; James D. Hunter, *American Evangelicalism, Conservative Religion, and the Quandary of Modernity* (New Brunswick, N.J.: Rutgers University Press, 1983), pp. 23-34.

4. Hunter, *American Evangelicalism*, p. 28.

5. Hutchison, *The Modernist Impulse in American Protestantism*, p. 79.

6. Matthews, "In Calvinism Is the Hope of the Future," *Sermonettes*, 1908.

7. Matthews, "Beware of Dogs," *Sermonettes*, Jan.–July 1910.

8. Sandeen, *Roots of Fundamentalism*, pp. 188-207; Ferenc Szasz, *The Divided Mind of Protestant America, 1880-1930* (Tuscaloosa: University of Alabama Press, 1982).

9. Matthews, "Beware of Dogs," *Sermonettes*, Jan.–July 1910.

10. Marsden, *Fundamentalism and American Culture*, p. 110.

11. *Ibid.*, p. 111.

12. *Ibid.*, pp. 109-18; Sandeen, *Roots of Fundamentalism*, p. 115.

13. Lefferts Loetscher, *The Broadening Church* (Philadelphia: University of Pennsylvania Press, 1957), pp. 98-99.

14. Matthews Scrapbook #15.

15. *Seattle Post-Intelligencer*, May 17, 1912.

16. Matthews Scrapbook #15; *The Continent*, May 23, 1912.

17. Matthews Scrapbook #15.

18. Giboney and Potter, *Life of Mark A. Matthews*, p. 37.

19. Matthews Scrapbook #15.

20. *Ibid.*

21. *Ibid.*

22. Matthews Scrapbook #16, p. 172.

23. Matthews Scrapbook #15.

Notes to Chapter 9

24. *Ibid.*

25. *Ibid.*

26. *Ibid.*

27. *Seattle Post-Intelligencer*, May 15, 1913; Matthews, "The Victories of Faith versus the Failures of Unbelief," *Sermonettes*, 1913.

28. *The Independent*, May 29, 1913; *Sermonettes*, 1913.

29. Loetscher, *Broadening Church*, p. 99.

30. Matthews to Francis Brown, Oct. 13, 1913, in *Sermonettes*, Jan.–July 1915.

31. *Ibid.*

32. W. M. Kingsley to Matthews, Nov. 11, 1913, in *Sermonettes*, Jan.–July 1915.

33. Rush Taggart to Matthews, Dec. 29, 1913; Matthews to Taggart, Jan. 3, 1914; Matthews to W. M. Kingsley, Feb. 20, 1914, all in *Sermonettes*, Jan.–July 1915.

34. Matthews, "Back to Fundamentals," *Sermonettes*, 1915.

35. *Continent*, April 29, 1915, in Matthews Scrapbook #17.

36. *Sunday School Times*, May 15, 1915, in Matthews Scrapbook #17.

37. *Presbyterian Banner*, April 22 and 29, 1915, in Matthews Scrapbook #17.

38. Matthews, "Report of the Special Committee," *Sermonettes*, Jan.–July 1915.

39. Matthews Scrapbook #16, p. 247.

40. *Ibid.*

41. Matthews, "Letter to the Editor of the *Oregonian*," *Sermonettes*, Jan.–July 1915.

42. Sandeen, *Roots of Fundamentalism*, pp. 62-69, 101-102.

43. Matthews, "Things to Be Accomplished before Christ's Second Coming," *Sermonettes*, Jan.–July 1909.

44. Matthews, "The Open Gate," *Sermonettes*, Jan.–July 1910.

45. *Los Angeles Tribune*, Jan. 16, 1913; Matthews Scrapbook #16.

46. Sandeen, *Roots of Fundamentalism*, p. 222.

47. Marsden, *Fundamentalism in American Culture*, p. 51.

48. Matthews, "The Reign of the Righteous through the Millennium Period," *Sermonettes*, 1916.

49. Matthews, "The Great Tribulation," *Sermonettes*, 1916.

50. Matthews, "The Church vs. the Tribulation," *Sermonettes*, 1917.

51. Matthews, *The Second Coming of Christ* (Grand Rapids, Mich.: Zondervan Publishing House, 1918). Ernest Sandeen provides a good account of the 1918 prophetic conference in Philadelphia; see his *Roots of Fundamentalism*, p. 237.

52. Matthews, "The Bible Institute in Seattle," *Sermonettes*, 1916.

53. Matthews, "The Bible and the Bible Institute," *Sermonettes*, 1917; Matthews, "Men's Club," *Sermonettes*, 1917.

54. Norman Furniss, *The Fundamentalist Controversy, 1918-1931* (New Haven, Conn.: Yale University Press, 1954), p. 130.

55. Matthews Scrapbook #17; Matthews, "Why the Interchurch Movement?" *Sermonettes*, 1920.

56. Matthews Scrapbook #16, p. 318; *New York Times*, May 18, 1920; Eldon G. Ernst, *Moment of Truth for Protestant America: Interchurch Campaigns Following World War One* (Missoula, Mont.: Scholars' Press, 1974), p. 148.

57. Furniss, *Fundamentalist Controversy*, pp. 130-31; Giboney and Potter, *Life of Mark A. Matthews*, pp. 85-86.

58. Robert E. Miller, *Harry Emerson Fosdick: Preacher, Pastor, Prophet* (New York: Oxford University Press, 1985).

59. Quoted in Loetscher, *Broadening Church*, pp. 109-10.

60. Quoted in *ibid.*, p.110.

61. *New York Times*, May 18, 1923.

62. *Minutes of the General Assembly of the Presbyterian Church in the U.S.A.*, 1923, p. 253.

63. *Ibid.*

64. Matthews quoted in Miller, *Harry Emerson Fosdick*, p. 126.

65. J. Gresham Machen, *Christianity and Liberalism* (New York, 1923; rpt., Grand Rapids, Mich.: William B. Eerdman's Publishing Company, 1946); Loetscher, *Broadening Church*, p. 116.

66. Machen quoted in Loetscher, *Broadening Church*, p. 116.

67. Charles Quirk, "Origins of the Auburn Affirmation," *Journal of Presbyterian History*, Vol. 53 (Summer 1975), 120-42; Loetscher, *Broadening Church*, p. 118.

68. Loetscher, *Broadening Church*, p. 119.

69. *Ibid.*, p. 121. Matthews was named to the Committee on Church Policy; see *Seattle Post-Intelligencer*, May 24, 1924.

70. Loetscher, *Broadening Church*, p. 122.

71. *Seattle Post-Intelligencer*, May 29, 1924.

72. Loetscher, *Broadening Church*, p. 123.

73. *Ibid.*

74. Matthews, "Victorious Facts," *Sermonettes*, 1924.

75. Matthews to J. Gresham Machen, Nov. 10, 1924, J. Gresham Machen Papers, Westminster Seminary, Philadelphia, Pa.

76. Machen to Matthews, May 5, 1925, Machen Papers.

77. Matthews to Machen, May 12, 1925, Machen Papers.

78. Machen to Matthews, May 26, 1925, Machen Papers.

79. Quoted in Loetscher, *Broadening Church*, p. 126.

80. *Ibid.*, p. 127.

81. *Ibid.*, p. 127-28; Sandeen, *Roots of Fundamentalism*, p. 255.

82. Sandeen, *Roots of Fundamentalism*, p. 255; Beau Weston, *Presbyterian Pluralism, Competition for a Protestant House* (Knoxville: University of Tennessee Press, 1997), pp. 72-74; Bradley Longfield, *The Presbyterian Controversy: Fundamentalists, Modernists, and Moderates* (New York: Oxford University Press, 1991), p. 156.

83. Charles Erdman, "The Special Commission of 1925," *Presbyterian Magazine*, Aug. 25, 1925, p. 405; Loetscher, *Broadening Church*, p. 128.

84. Loetscher, *Broadening Church*, p. 130.

85. Minutes of the Special Commission of 1925 of the General Assembly of the Presbyterian Church, U.S.A., March 11, 1926, p. 2, Presbyterian Historical Society, Philadelphia (cited hereafter as Commission Minutes).

86. Committee report cited in Weston, *Presbyterian Pluralism*, p. 80.

87. *Ibid.*

88. *Ibid.*

89. *Report of the Special Commission of 1925 to the General Assembly of the Presbyterian Church in the U.S.A.* (Philadelphia: Office of the General Assembly, 1927), pp. 4-13.

Notes to Chapter 9

90. Machen quoted in Loetscher, *Broadening Church*, pp. 132-33.

91. Weston, *Presbyterian Pluralism*, p. 81.

92. Matthews, "A Word of Assurance," *Sermonettes*, 1926.

93. *Ibid.*

94. Loetscher, *Broadening Church*, p. 135.

95. *Ibid.*

96. Mark Matthews, *Gospel Sword Thrusts* (New York, 1924).

97. Sandeen, *Roots of Fundamentalism*, p. 255.

98. Matthews, "The Only Thing Essential," *Sermonettes*, 1926.

99. Matthews, "Radio Address of Mark Matthews Re: Educational Institutions of the State of Washington," *Sermonettes*, 1926.

100. Loetscher, *Broadening Church*, pp. 140-41.

101. *Ibid.*, p. 141-42.

102. Matthews, "A Few Facts," *Sermonettes*, 1927.

103. *Ibid.*

104. Loetscher, *Broadening Church*, p. 146.

105. General Assembly Minutes, 1929, pp. 97-110.

106. Matthews Scrapbook #19.

107. *Ibid.*; Matthews, "The Watchman's Answer," *Sermonettes*, 1929.

108. Giboney and Potter, *Life of Mark A. Matthews*, pp. 87-88.

109. Bradley Longfield, *Presbyterian Controversy*, p. 178.

110. *Ibid.*, p. 180.

111. Russell, "Mark Allison Matthews," p. 452; Churchill, *Lest We Forget*, p. 134.

112. Sandeen, *Roots of Fundamentalism*, p. 255.

Chapter 10: Screenitis and the Radio

1. Sale, *Seattle Past to Present*, pp. 136-44. Murray Morgan speaks mainly of the influence of Dave Beck between the two world wars; Morgan, *Skid Road*, pp. 215-65.

2. Roderick Nash, *The Nervous Generation: American Thought, 1917-1930* (Chicago: University of Chicago Press, 1970); conservative themes and social anxiety in the decade are also stressed in Paul Carter, *The Twenties in America* (New York: Thomas Crowell Company, 1968); and David Shannon, *Between the Wars, 1919-1941* (Boston: Houghton Mifflin, 1965).

3. Joel Carpenter, *Revive Us Again*, pp. 39-41.

4. *Seattle Times* and *Seattle Post-Intelligencer*, March 25–April 10, 1919.

5. Matthews, "Report of the Special Committee to the Executive Committee of the Chamber of Commerce—Report B," *Sermonettes*, 1919.

6. *New York Times*, April 25, 1920; Matthews Scrapbook #17.

7. Matthews to Woodrow Wilson, March 22, 1920, box 5, Matthews Papers.

8. Matthews, "Interview in Re: Conference on Limitation of Armaments," *Sermonettes*, 1921.

9. Matthews, "America's Shame," *Sermonettes*, 1922.

10. *Ibid.*

11. Frederick Lewis Allen, *Only Yesterday* (New York: Harper and Row, 1931); William Leuchtenberg, *The Perils of Prosperity, 1914-1932* (Chicago: University of Chicago Press, 1958).

12. Matthews, "The Psychology of the Automobile," *Sermonettes*, Jan.–July 1910.

13. Matthews, "Three Black Spots," *Sermonettes*, 1922.

14. *Ibid.*

15. Matthews, "Three Black Spots," *Sermonettes*, 1922.

16. Matthews Scrapbook #17.

17. Matthews, "Amusement Mania," *Sermonettes*, 1922.

18. *Ibid.*

19. Matthews Scrapbook #17.

20. Norman Clark, *The Dry Years: Prohibition and Social Change in Washington* (Seattle: University of Washington Press, 1965), p. 179.

21. Matthews to Wesley Jones, Oct. 28, 1929, box 30, Wesley Jones Papers, University of Washington Libraries.

22. Wesley Jones to Matthews, Nov. 2, 1929, box 30, Wesley Jones Papers.

23. Matthews, "Law Enforcement," *Sermonettes*, 1929.

24. *Seattle Star*, Nov. 7, 1929; *Seattle Times*, Nov. 5, 1929, reported that scores of letters were in support of Matthews; *Seattle Post-Intelligencer*, Nov. 5, 1929, also editorialized against the Anti-Saloon League.

25. *Aberdeen Daily World*, Nov. 11, 1929; Matthews Scrapbook #17.

26. Matthews to Wesley Jones, Feb. 13, 1930, box 274, Wesley Jones Papers.

27. Wesley Jones to Matthews, Feb. 19, 1930, box 274, Wesley Jones Papers.

28. Clark, *Dry Years*, p. 209; the letter from Lyle to Jones, cited by Clark is currently missing from the Jones Papers.

29. *Ibid.*

30. Allen, *Only Yesterday*, p. 55.

31. *Ibid.*, p. 88.

32. Matthews, "The Featureless Flapper," *Sermonettes*, 1922.

33. R. Douglas Brackenridge, "Equality for Women? A Case Study in Presbyterian Polity, 1926-1930," *Journal of Presbyterian History*, Vol. 58, No. 2 (Summer 1980), 154.

34. Matthews, "Why Women in the Pulpit?" *The Presbyterian*, Jan. 16, 1930; Russell, "Mark Matthews," p. 460.

35. Lois A. Boyd and R. Douglas Brackenridge, *Presbyterian Women in America: Two Centuries of Quest for Status* (Westport, Conn.: Greenwood Press, 1996), p. 123.

36. Matthews to E. E. Phipps, July 13, 1922, and Feb. 9, 1923, box 2, Matthews Papers.

37. Matthews to William G. McAdoo, Feb. 16, 1923; McAdoo to Matthews, Feb. 24, 1923, both in box 2, Matthews Papers.

38. Matthews to Henry Wellcome, July 9, 1923, box 2, Matthews Papers.

39. Matthews Scrapbook #14.

40. James Ross to U.S. Commissioner of Navigation, April 13, 1922, box 72, Seattle Lighting Department Papers, University of Washington Libraries; Matthews to H. B. Fletcher, Sept. 19, 1922, in *Sermonettes*, 1922.

41. Matthews to H. B. Fletcher, Sept. 19, 1922, in *Sermonettes*, 1922.

42. *Boston Evening Transcript*, Dec. 9, 1922, clipping in Matthews Scrapbook #17.

43. J. T. Donegan to Matthews, Nov. 20, 1928, box 147, Seattle Lighting Department Papers.

44. Matthews to Ross, July 9, 1929, box 72, Seattle Lighting Department Papers.

45. Archie Taft to Matthews, April 26, 1929, box 147, Seattle Lighting Department Papers.

46. E. O. Holland to Matthews, Nov. 14, 1933, box 72, Seattle Lighting Department Papers.

47. Annual Reports, First Presbyterian Church of Seattle, 1920-1929, *Sermonettes*, 1920-1929; also see Giboney and Potter, *Life of Mark A. Matthews*, p. 76.

48. *Seattle Post-Intelligencer*, Jan. 26, 1925, and April 16, 1925.

49. Itinerary, box 2, Matthews Papers; interview with Gwladys Matthews Scott, Dec. 4, 1978.

50. Matthews to Mark Matthews, Jr., June 13, 1928, box 1, Matthews Papers.

51. Mark Matthews, Jr., to Matthews, April 12, 1925, box 1, Matthews Papers.

52. Matthews to Mark Matthews, Jr., June 13, 1928, box 1, Matthews Papers.

53. Matthews to Mark Matthews, Jr., June 28, 1924, box 1, Matthews Papers.

54. Interview with Glwadys Matthews Scott, Dec. 4, 1978; Rae Matthews to author, Oct. 20, 1979.

55. Interview with Gwladys Matthews Scott, Dec. 4, 1978.

56. Interview with Mrs. James Rice, Jan. 29, 1980; interview with Gwladys Matthews Scott, Dec. 4, 1978.

57. Interview with Gwladys Matthews Scott, Dec. 4, 1978; Giboney and Potter, *Life of Mark A. Matthews*, pp. 93-94.

58. Alfred O. Gray, *Not By Might* (Spokane: Whitworth College Press, 1965), p. 61.

59. *Ibid.*, p. 106.

60. G. Thomas Edwards, *The Triumph of Tradition: The Emergence of Whitman College, 1859-1924* (Walla Walla, Wash.: Whitman College, 1992) pp. 300, 406; Giboney and Potter, *Life of Mark A. Matthews*, p. 37.

61. *New York Times*, Dec. 22, 1924; Scrapbook #16, p. 275.

62. Matthews, "Ten Studies for Business Men," *Sermonettes*, 1923.

63. *Ibid.*

64. *A History of the Activities of the Thirty-Sixth Triennial Committee of the Knights Templar* (Seattle: Historical Committee, 1926), pp. 13-14, Northwest Collection, University of Washington Libraries.

65. *Ibid.*, pp. 41-42.

66. *Ibid.*, p. 44.

67. *Seattle Times* and *Seattle Post-Intelligencer*, July 25–31, 1925.

68. Matthews, "Managerial Form of Government," *Sermonettes*, 1925.

69. J. D. Ross to Matthews, Jan. 8, 1926, box 13, Seattle Lighting Department Papers.

70. *Seattle Post-Intelligencer*, March 10, 1926.

71. Lee Pendergrass, "Urban Reform and Voluntary Association," pp. 109-18; Richard C. Berner, *Seattle, 1921-1940: From Boom to Bust* (Seattle: Charles Press, 1992), pp. 80-84.

Notes to Chapter 10

72. *Seattle Times*, April 30, 1926.

73. *Seattle Times*, Oct. 30, 1926.

74. *Ibid.*

75. Matthews, "Managerial Form of Government," *Sermonettes*, 1925.

76. Interview with Dave Beck, Jan. 7, 1980.

77. William Short to Matthews, Oct. 3, 1925, box 5, Matthews Papers; interview with Dave Beck, Jan. 7, 1980.

78. Short to Matthews, Oct. 5, 1925; Dave Beck to Matthews, Oct. 6, 1925, both in box 5, Matthews Papers; see also Berner, *Seattle, 1921-1940*, p. 359.

79. Interview with Dave Beck, Jan. 7, 1980; Matthews to George Penny, Dec. 30, 1925, box 5, Matthews Papers.

80. *Ibid.*

81. Dave Beck to Matthews, Nov. 16, 1936, box 1, Matthews Papers; E. W. Scripps to Matthews, Feb. 7, 1938, box 3, Matthews Papers.

82. *Beginnings, Progress and Achievement in the Medical Work of King County, Washington* (Seattle, 1932), pp. 126-45, copy in box 3, Matthews Papers.

83. Alfred Schweppe to Matthews, Feb. 9 and 21, 1928, box 3, Matthews Papers. The University of Washington did decide to build its own hospital and medical school on the exact site that Matthews's group had located in the 1920s.

84. Matthews to the President of the General Education Board, March 31, 1928, box 3, Matthews Papers.

85. *Seattle Post-Intelligencer*, Nov. 7, 1928.

86. *Seattle Post-Intelligencer*, Feb. 28, 1931.

87. Berner, *Seattle, 1921-1940*, pp.134-37.

88. *Seattle Post-Intelligencer*, Oct. 6, 1926.

89. Matthews, "Radio Address of M. A. Matthews Re: Educational Institutions of the State of Washington," *Sermonettes*, 1926.

90. Matthews, "The Unwritten Story of Silent Places," *Sermonettes*, Jan.–July 1909.

91. Matthews, "Our Children's Kidnappers," *Sermonettes*, Jan.–June 1909.

92. Matthews Scrapbook #17.

93. *New York Sun*, May 19, 1924; Matthews Scrapbook #17.

Chapter 11: The Final Years

1. *Seattle Times*, July 9, 1937.

2. *Ibid.*

3. *Seattle Times*, Feb. 6, 1927.

4. *Seattle Post-Intelligencer*, April 16, 1929.

5. *Seattle Town-Crier*, April 20, 1929.

6. *Seattle Argus*, Dec. 26, 1931.

7. *Seattle Times* and *Seattle Post-Intelligencer*, June 24–25, 1932.

8. *Seattle Post-Intelligencer*, Dec. 21, 1934; George W. Scott, "The New Order of Cincinattus: Municipal Politics in Seattle during the 1930s," *Pacific Northwest Quarterly*, Vol. 64 (1973), 138.

9. *Seattle Post-Intelligencer*, Oct. 27, 1936; Matthews Scrapbook #19, p. 137

10. *Seattle Post-Intelligencer*, Oct. 27, 1936.

11. Peter Murray, *The Devil and Mr. Duncan: A History of the Two Metlakatlas* (Victoria, B.C.: Sono Nis Press, 1985), pp. 35-70.

12. *Ibid.*, pp. 174-221.

13. *Ibid.*, pp. 261-71.

14. *Ibid.*, pp. 277-91.

15. *Ibid.*, p. 189.

16. Matthews may have developed an interest in Duncan's work as early as 1908 when the *Seattle Times* ran an extensive article on the mission. See *Seattle Times*, Nov. 29, 1908.

17. Matthews to William Duncan, Oct. 5, 1917, box 2, Matthews Papers.

18. Matthews to Henry Wellcome, quoted in Murray, *Devil and Mr. Duncan,* pp. 312-13.

19. Murray, *Devil and Mr. Duncan,* p. 326.

20. Matthews to Ray Wilbur, May 14, 1929, box 2, Matthews Papers; see also Henry Wellcome to Matthews, July 30, 1929, box 186, Henry Wellcome Papers, National Archives and Records Administration—Pacific Alaska Region, Anchorage, Alaska; Herbert Hoover to Matthews, June 6, 1930, and Matthews to Wellcome, June 12, 1930, box 186, Wellcome Papers.

21. Matthews to Ray Wilbur, Secretary of the Interior, May 14, 1929, box 2, Matthews Papers.

22. Murray, *Devil and Mr. Duncan,* p. 327.

23. Matthews to Wilbur, May 14, 1929, box 2, Matthews Papers; U.S. Congress, Senate Committee on Indian Affairs, *Survey of Conditions of the Indians in the United States, Part 35: Metlakatla Indians, Alaska,* S.R. 230, 74th Cong., 2nd Sess., 1936, pp. 18541-19686; B. L. Myers to Matthews, Jan. 15, 1940, box 2, Matthews Papers.

24. Murray, *Devil and Mr. Duncan,* p. 327.

25. Giboney and Potter, *Life of Mark A. Matthews,* p. 28.

26. Matthews Scrapbook #19, p. 37.

27. *Seattle Post-Intelligencer,* July 11, 1928; Matthews, "Support Your President," *Sermonettes,* 1930.

28. Matthews, "In His Name," *Sermonettes,* 1931.

29. Matthews, "The World Crisis Calling Us into Action," *Sermonettes,* 1932.

30. Matthews, "The Condition vs. the Remedy," *Sermonettes,* 1933.

31. *Seattle Argus,* Aug. 20, 1921.

32. Matthews to J. D. Ross, July 21, 1931, Aug. 5, 1932, Nov. 17, 1933, box 72, Seattle Lighting Department Papers, University of Washington Libraries.

33. Mabel Loughead to F. L. Forbes, Oct. 10, 1938, and Matthews to Ross, Oct. 10, 1938, box 72, Seattle Lighting Department Papers.

34. Matthews, "Why and What," *Sermonettes,* 1932, Matthews to George Cotterill, Feb. 2, 1932, box 5, George Cotterill Papers, University of Washington Libraries.

35. Matthews, "Save America," *Sermonettes,* 1934.

36. Matthews to Burton Wheeler, April 16, 1937, in *Sermonettes,* 1937.

37. Homer Bone to Matthews, Feb. 8, 1934, box 1, Matthews Papers.

38. Lewis Schwellenbach to Matthews, March 18, 1939, and Homer Bone to Matthews, Jan. 27, 1939, box 1, Matthews Papers.

39. Matthews, untitled address, *Sermonettes,* 1937.

40. Matthews, "Statement on the Munich Compact," *Sermonettes*, 1938; Matthews to Stephen Chadwick, Sept. 30, 1938, box 12, Stephen Chadwick Papers, University of Washington Libraries.

41. Matthews to Neville Chamberlain, June 26, 1939, box 2, Matthews Papers.

42. Matthews to Franklin Roosevelt, Nov. 16, 1938, box 2, Matthews Papers.

43. Matthews, "Suspend Criticism," *Sermonettes*, 1939.

44. *Seattle Post-Intelligencer*, Oct. 10, 1939; Matthews, "Neutrality," *Sermonettes*, 1939.

45. Matthews, "Anarchy vs. Law," *Sermonettes*, 1938.

46. Matthews, "The Crooked Road of Fear and Cowardice," *Sermonettes*, 1938.

47. Matthews, "The Fury of Egypt," *The Presbyterian*, April 14, 1938, p. 3.

48. Carpenter, *Revive Us Again*, p. 99.

49. Matthews to Adolf Hitler, Oct. 28, 1939, in *Sermonettes*, 1939.

50. Carpenter, *Revive Us Again*, p. 103.

51. *Seattle Post-Intelligencer*, Feb. 15, 1935.

52. Matthews, "Whitman-Spalding 100th Anniversary," *Sermonettes*, 1936.

53. Matthews to John Reynolds, Aug. 25, 1936, box 147, Seattle Lighting Department Papers.

54. *Seattle Star*, Dec. 6, 1937; Matthews, "Purposes and Powers of Government," *The Presbyterian*, Dec. 29, 1938, p. 7.

55. Homer T. Cummings to Matthews, June 29, 1934, box 2, Matthews Papers.

56. Office of the Washington State Patrol to Matthews, July 23, 1934, box 5, Matthews Papers.

57. Matthews to Seattle Police Department, July 23, 1934, box 5, Matthews Papers.

58. J. Edgar Hoover to Matthews, July 30, 1936, Sept. 29, 1936, Aug. 23, 1937, July 7, 1939, Oct. 17, 1939, box 2, Matthews Papers.

59. Harry Chandler to Matthews, Dec. 13, 1937, and Matthews to Chandler, Dec. 21, 1937, box 1, Matthews Papers.

60. Matthews, "Ministerial Responsibility," *The Presbyterian*, Sept. 28, 1939, p. 6.

61. Ezra P. Giboney, "News from Seattle, Wash., and Vicinity," *The Presbyterian*, Nov. 17, 1938, p. 27.

62. Rachel K. McDowell, "Pacific Coast Presbyterianism As I Saw It (Part I)," *The Presbyterian*, Aug. 25, 1938, pp. 8-9.

63. Matthews to Austin Griffiths, Nov. 6, 1937, box 10, Austin Griffiths Papers, University of Washington Libraries.

64. Frank Smith to Matthews, Nov. 29, 1939, box 3, Matthews Papers; interview with James Rice, Jan. 31, 1980, and interview with Dr. Harold King, March 10, 1980.

65. Matthews to Frank Smith, Dec. 1, 1939, box 3, Matthews Papers.

66. Interview with Mark Koehler, Nov. 15, 1988.

67. Dr. B. L. Myers to Matthews, Jan. 15, 1940; Matthews in reply said of Duncan, "An unselfish, painstaking, altruistic, constructive missionary hero."

Matthews to Dr. B. L. Myers, Jan. 22, 1940, box 2, Matthews Papers.

68. Matthews, "The Growth of Christianity in the Northwest," *Sermonettes*, 1939.

69. *Seattle Times* and *Seattle Post-Intelligencer*, Jan. 31–Feb. 6, 1940.

70. *Seattle Times*, Feb. 5, 1940; The *Seattle Times* collected comments from around the state; Feb. 11, 1940.

71. *Seattle Post-Intelligencer*, Feb. 6, 1940.

72. Resolution, Seattle B'nai B'rith, Feb. 7, 1940, box 2, Matthews Papers.

73. *Seattle Post-Intelligencer* and *Seattle Times*, Feb. 8–9, 1940.

74. *Seattle Star*, Feb. 5–13, 1940.

Bibliography

Manuscripts

Erastus Brainerd Papers, University of Washington Libraries, Seattle
Thomas Burke Papers, University of Washington Libraries, Seattle
Stephen Chadwick Papers, University of Washington Libraries, Seattle
George Cotterill Papers, University of Washington Libraries, Seattle
Austin Griffiths Papers, University of Washington Libraries, Seattle
Wesley Jones Papers, University of Washington Libraries, Seattle
John Gresham Machen Papers, Montgomery Library, Westminster
    Theological Seminary, Philadelphia, Pennsylvania
Mark A. Matthews Papers, University of Washington Libraries, Seattle
Seattle Lighting Department Papers, University of Washington
    Libraries, Seattle
William Howard Taft Papers, Library of Congress, Washington, D.C.
Henry S. Wellcome Papers, National Archives—Pacific Northwest
    Region, Anchorage, Alaska
Woodrow Wilson Papers, Library of Congress, Washington, D.C.

Interviews with Author

Dave Beck, Jan. 7, 1980
Mrs. Rusty Callow, Nov. 15, 1979
Dr. Harold King, March 10, 1979
Dr. Mark Koehler, Nov. 15, 1988
Mrs. Mark A. Matthews, Jr., Dec. 5, 1978
James Priestley, Jr., Nov. 7, 1979
James Rice, Jan. 31, 1980
Wilmond Shearer, Nov. 15, 1979
Gwladys Matthews Scott, Dec. 4, 1978
Arthur Simon, July 23, 1980
Jane Ward, Jan. 29, 1980

Newspapers

Seattle Argus
Seattle Daily Times
Seattle Mail and Herald
Seattle Post-Intelligencer
Seattle Star
Seattle Sun
Seattle Town-Crier
Seattle Union Record
What's Doing (Tacoma)

Government Documents

United States Congress, Senate, Committee on Indian Affairs, *Survey of Conditions of the Indians of the United States, Part 35: Metlakahtla Indians, Alaska.* Hearings before a subcommittee of the Committee on Indian Affairs, S.R. 230, 74th Congress, Second Session, 1936.

Other Documents

A History of the Activities of the Thirty-Sixth Triennial Committee of the Knights Templar. Seattle: Historical Committee, 1926. Special Collections, University of Washington Libraries.

Griffiths, Austin. *"Great Faith: Autobiography of an English Immigrant Boy in America, 1863-1950."* Seattle, 1950 (typescript), Special Collections, University of Washington Libraries.

Prosch, Thomas. "A Chronological History of Seattle from 1850 to 1897." Seattle, 1900-1901 (typescript), Special Collections, University of Washington Libraries.

Jackson's Business: A Chronology of Business Enterprise in the Jackson Area of Western Tennessee, ed. Laurie Mercier and Clint Daniels (Jackson, Tenn.: Business History Project, Jackson/Madison County Library, 1981).

Red Cross News, Oct.-Nov. 1971, p. 3, Special Collections, University of Washington Libraries.

Report, *Program of the First Presbyterian Church Twenty-fifth Anniversary of Matthews' Seattle Pastorate* (Seattle: First Presbyterian Church Press, 1927), in First Presbyterian Church Archives, Seattle, Washington.

Alaska-Yukon-Pacific Exposition Scrapbooks, Special Collections, University of Washington Libraries.

Minutes of the General Assembly of the Presbyterian Church in the U.S.A., Philadelphia Office of the General Assembly.

Report of the Special Commission of 1925 to the General Assembly of the Presbyterian Church in the U.S.A. Philadelphia: Office of the General Assembly, 1927, in Presbyterian Historical Society, Philadelphia.

Minutes of the Special Commission of 1925 of the General Assembly of the Presbyterian Church, U.S.A., copy at Presbyterian Historical Society, Philadelphia.

Theses and Dissertations

Blackford, Mansel B. "Sources of Support for Reform Candidates and Issues in Seattle Politics, 1902-1926." M.A. thesis, University of Washington, 1967.

Dawson, Jan C. "A Social Gospel Portrait: The Life of Sydney Dix Strong, 1860-1938." M.A. thesis, University of Washington, 1972.

Donnen, James William. "Personality and Reform in the Progressive Era: An Interpretation of Five Washington State Careers." M.A. thesis, University of Washington, 1974.

Forth, William S. "Wesley L. Jones: A Political Biography." Ph.D. dissertation, University of Washington, 1962.

Krause, Mary Lou. "Prohibition and the Reform Tradition in the Washington State Senatorial Election of 1922." M.A. thesis, University of Washington, 1963.

Longfield, Bradley. "The Presbyterian Controversy, 1922-1936: Christianity, Culture, and Ecclesiastical Conflict." Ph.D. dissertation, Duke University, 1988.

McClintock, Thomas. "J. Allen Smith and the Progressive Movement: A Study in Intellectual History." Ph.D. dissertation, University of Washington, 1959.

Miller, Virginia. "The Development of Leisure Time Activities in Seattle, 1851-1910." M.A. thesis, University of Washington, 1980.

Pendergrass, Lee. "Urban Reform and Voluntary Association: A Case Study of the Seattle Municipal League, 1910-1929." Ph.D. dissertation, University of Washington, 1972.

Reiff, Jan. "Urbanization and the Social Structure: Seattle, Washington, 1852-1910." Ph.D. dissertation, University of Washington, 1981.

Saltvig, Robert. "The Progressive Movement in Washington." Ph.D. dissertation, University of Washington, 1966.

Sparks, William O. "J. D. Ross and Seattle City Light, 1917-1932." M.A. thesis, University of Washington, 1964.

Turner, Elizabeth Hayes. "Women's Culture and Community: Religion and Reform in Galveston, 1880-1920." Ph.D. dissertation, Rice University, 1990.

Books and Articles

———. *Today and Tomorrow Became Yesterday* (Sketch of Dalton History) (Dalton, Ga.: Bicentennial Commission, 1976).

———. "The First Presbyterian Church," *Whitfield-Murray Historical Quarterly*, Vol. 7 (April 1984), 7.

———. *Memoirs of Georgia*. Atlanta: Southern Historical Association, 1895.

Abell, Aaron Ignatius. *The Urban Impact on American Protestantism, 1865-1900.* Cambridge: Harvard University Press, 1943.

Abrams, Ray. *Preachers Present Arms.* Scottsdale, Pa.: Herald Press, 1933.

Ahlstrom, Sydney. "The Scottish Philosophy and American Theology,"

Bibliography

Church History, Vol. 24 (September 1955), 257-72.

Allen, Frederick Lewis. *Only Yesterday*. New York: Harper and Row, 1931.

Arnett, Alex. *The Populist Movement in Georgia*. New York: Columbia University Press, 1922.

Avery, Isaac Wheeler. *The History of the State of Georgia from 1850 to 1881*. New York: Brown and Derby, 1881.

Ayers, Edward L. *The Promise of the New South: Life after Reconstruction*. New York: Oxford University Press, 1992.

Bagley, Clarence. *The History of Seattle from the Earliest Settlement to the Present Time*. Vol. 2. Chicago: S. J. Clarke Publishing Company, 1916.

Bailey, Hugh C. *Liberalism in the New South: Southern Social Reformers and the Progressive Movement*. Coral Gables, Fla.: University of Miami Press, 1969.

Bailey, Hugh C. *Edgar Gardner Murphy: Gentle Progressive*. Coral Gables, Fla.: University of Miami Press, 1968.

Barrus, Ben, Milton Baughn, and Thomas Campbell. *A People Called Cumberland Presbyterians*. Memphis: Frontier Press, 1972.

Bederman, Gail. "'The Women Have Had Charge of the Church Work Long Enough': The Men and Religion Forward Movement of 1911-1912 and the Masculinization of Middle-Class Protestantism," *American Quarterly*, Vol. 41 (September 1989), 432-65.

Bell, Marion L. *Crusade in the City: Revivalism in Nineteenth-Century Philadelphia*. London: Associated University Presses, 1977.

Bellah, Robert. *Habits of the Heart: Individualism and Commitment in American Life*. New York: Harper and Row, 1986.

Berner, Richard C. *Seattle, 1900-1920: From Boomtown, Urban Turbulence, to Restoration*. Seattle: Charles Press, 1991.

_____. *Seattle, 1921-1940: From Boom to Bust*. Seattle: Charles Press, 1992.

Blackford, Mansel. "Reform in Seattle during the Progressive Era, 1902-1916," *Pacific Northwest Quarterly*, Vol. 59 (1968), 177-89.

Bledstein, Burton. *The Culture of Professionalism: The Middle Class and the Development of Higher Education in America*. New York: Norton, 1976.

Boswell, Sharon A., and Lorraine McConaghy. *Raise Hell and Sell Newspapers: Alden J. Blethen & The Seattle Times*. Pullman: Washington State University Press, 1996.

Boyd, Robert. *History of the Synod of Washington of the Presbyterian Church in the United States of America*. Seattle: Synod Office, 1909.

Boyd, Lois A., and R. Douglas Brackenridge. *Presbyterian Women in America: Two Centuries of a Quest for Status*. Westport, Conn.: Greenwood Press, 1996.

Boyer, Paul. *Urban Masses and Moral Order in America, 1820-1920*. Cambridge, Mass.: Harvard University Press, 1978.

Bozeman, Theodore Dwight. *Protestants in an Age of Science*. Chapel Hill: University of North Carolina Press, 1977.

Brackenridge, R. Douglas. "Equality for Women? A Case Study in Presbyterian Polity, 1926-1930," *Journal of Presbyterian History*, Vol. 58 (Summer 1980), 142-65.

Bryan, William Jennings. *The First Battle: A Story of the Campaign of 1896*. Chicago: Conkey Company, 1896.

Bibliography

Buerge, David M., and Junius Rochester. *Roots and Branches: The Religious Heritage of Washington State.* Seattle: Church Council of Greater Seattle, 1988.

Byler, Charles. "Austin E. Griffiths: Seattle Progressive Reformer," *Pacific Northwest Quarterly,* Vol. 75 (1985), 22-32.

Carpenter, Joel. *Revive Us Again: The Reawakening of American Fundamentalism.* New York: Oxford University Press, 1997.

Carter, Paul. *The Decline and Revival of the Social Gospel.* Ithaca, N.Y.: Cornell University Press, 1954.

_____. *The Twenties in America.* New York: Thomas Crowell Company, 1968.

Churchill, Robert. *Lest We Forget.* Philadelphia: The Committee for the Historian of the Orthodox Presbyterian Church, 1985.

Clark, Norman. *The Dry Years: Prohibition and Social Change in Washington.* Seattle: University of Washington Press, 1965.

_____. *Mill Town: A Social History of Everett, Washington, from Its Earliest Beginnings on the Shores of Puget Sound to the Tragic and Infamous Event Known as the Everett Massacre.* Seattle: University of Washington Press, 1970.

Commager, Henry Steele. *The American Mind: An Interpretation of American Thought and Character since the 1880s.* New Haven: Yale University Press, 1950.

Conway, Gregory, Jr. *A Presbytery Called Chattanooga: Tracing the History of Chattanooga Presbytery, Cumberland Presbyterian Church from 1842-1989.* Alpharetta, Ga.: W. H. Wolfe Associates, 1994.

Crunden, Robert. *Ministers of Reform: The Progressives' Achievement in American Civilization, 1889-1920.* New York: Basic Books, 1982.

Curtis, Susan. *A Consuming Faith: The Social Gospel and Modern American Culture.* Baltimore: The Johns Hopkins University Press, 1991.

DeWitt, Benjamin. *The Progressive Movement.* New York: Macmillan, 1915.

Dombrowski, James. *The Early Days of Christian Socialism in America.* New York: Columbia University Press, 1936.

Dorpat, Paul. *Seattle Now and Then.* Vol. 3. Seattle: Tartu Publications, 1989.

Douglass, Ann. *The Feminization of American Culture.* New York: Alfred Knopf, 1977.

Edwards, G. Thomas. *The Triumph of Tradition: The Emergence of Whitman College, 1859-1924.* Walla Walla, Wash.: Whitman College, 1992.

Eighmy, John Lee. *Churches in Cultural Captivity: A History of Social Attitudes of Southern Baptists.* Knoxville: University of Tennessee Press, 1972.

_____. "Religious Liberalism in the South during the Progressive Era," *Church History,* Vol. 38 (1969), 359-72.

Ernst, Eldon G. *Moment of Truth for Protestant America: Interchurch Campaigns Following World War One.* Missoula, Mont.: Scholars' Press, 1974.

Felton, Mrs. William H. *My Memoirs of Georgia Politics.* Atlanta: Index Printing Company, 1911.

Ficken, Robert E., and Charles LeWarne. *Washington: A Centennial History.* Seattle: University of Washington Press, 1989.

Foner, Philip. *A History of the Labor Movement in the United States.* 4 vols. New York: International Publishers, 1947-64.

Friedheim, Robert. *The Seattle General Strike.* Seattle: University of Washington Press, 1964.

Furniss, Norman. *The Fundamentalist Controversy, 1918-1931.* New Haven: Yale University Press, 1954.

Gates, Charles. *The First Century at the University of Washington, 1861-1961.* Seattle: University of Washington Press, 1961.

Giboney, Ezra P., and Agnes Potter. *The Life of Mark A. Matthews.* Grand Rapids, Mich.: William B. Eerdman's Publishing Company, 1948.

Glad, Paul. *The Trumpet Soundeth.* Lincoln: University of Nebraska Press, 1960.

Gould, Lewis. *Progressives and Prohibitionists.* Austin: University of Texas Press, 1973.

Gray, Alfred O. *Not by Might: The Story of Whitworth College, 1890-1965.* Spokane: Whitworth College, 1965.

Gusfield, Joseph. *Symbolic Crusade: Status Politics and the American Temperance Movement.* Urbana: University of Illinois Press, 1963.

Gutman, Herbert. *Work, Culture, and Society in Industrializing America: Essays in American Working Class and Social History.* New York: Alfred Knopf, 1976.

Hahn, Stephen. *The Roots of Southern Populism: Yeoman Farmers and the Transformation of the Georgia Upcountry, 1850-1890.* New York: Oxford University Press, 1983.

Hale, Edward Everett. *If Jesus Came to Boston.* Boston: J. S. Smith, 1894.

Hall, David D. "The Victorian Connection," in *Victorian America*, edited by Daniel W. Howe. Philadelphia: University of Pennsylvania Press, 1976.

Hardman, Keith. *Charles Grandison Finney, 1792-1875: Revivalist and Reformer.* Syracuse, N.Y.: Syracuse University Press, 1987.

Hart, Roger. *Redeemers, Bourbons, and Populists.* Baton Rouge: Louisiana State University Press, 1975.

Haskell, Thomas. *The Emergence of Professional Social Science.* Urbana: University of Illinois Press, 1977.

Hawley, Lowell S., and Ralph Bushnell Potts. *Counsel for the Damned.* New York: Lippincott, 1953.

Hays, Samuel P. *Conservation and the Gospel of Efficiency: The Progressive Conservative Movement, 1890-1920.* Cambridge: Harvard University Press, 1959.

Hendrick, Burton J. "The 'Recall' in Seattle," *McClure's*, Vol. 37 (October 1911), 660-63.

Herron, R. M., Sr. *Official History of Whitfield Country, Georgia.* Dalton, Ga.: A. J. Sholwater Company, 1936.

Hicks, John. *The Populist Revolt.* Minneapolis: University of Minnesota Press, 1931.

Higham, John. "The Reorientation of American Culture in the 1890s," in *Writing American History: Essays on Modern Scholarship.* Bloomington, Ind.: Indiana University Press, 1970.

Hodge, Charles. *Systematic Theology.* 3 vols. Grand Rapids, Mich.: William B. Eerdman's Publishing Company, 1871.

Hofstadter, Richard. *The Age of Reform: From Bryan to F.D.R.* New York: Alfred Knopf, 1955.

Holifield, E. Brooks. *The Gentlemen Theologians: American Theology in Southern Culture, 1795-1860*. Durham, N.C.: Duke University Press, 1978.

Hopkins, Charles H. *The Rise of the Social Gospel in American Protestantism, 1865-1915*. New Haven: Yale University Press, 1940.

Hunt, William R. *Front-Page Detective: William J. Burns and the Detective Profession, 1880-1930*. Bowling Green, Ky.: Bowling Green State University Popular Press, 1990.

Hunter, James D. *American Evangelicalism, Conservative Religion and the Quandary of Modernity*. New Brunswick, N.J.: Rutgers University Press, 1983.

Hutchison, William R. *The Modernist Impulse in American Protestantism*. Cambridge: Harvard University Press, 1976.

Hyman, Harold M. *Soldiers and Spruce: Origins of the Loyal Legion of Loggers and Lumbermen*. Los Angeles: Institute of Industrial Relations, 1963.

Kahlo, Dorothy Miller. *History of the Police and Fire Departments of the City of Seattle*. Seattle: Lumbermen's Printing Company, 1907.

Kolko, Gabriel. *The Triumph of Conservatism: A Reinterpretation of American History*. New York: Free Press of Glencoe, 1963.

LaFollette, Joan C. "Money and Power: Presbyterian Women's Organizations in the Twentieth Century," in *The Organizational Revolution: Presbyterians and American Denominationalism*, edited by Milton J. Coalter, John M. Mulder, and Louis B. Weeks. Louisville, Ky.: Westminster/John Knox Press, 1992.

Lears, T. J. Jackson. *No Place for Grace: Antimodernism and the Transformation of American Culture, 1880-1920*. New York: Pantheon Books, 1981.

Leuchtenberg, William. *The Perils of Prosperity, 1914-1932*. Chicago: University of Chicago Press, 1958.

Link, Arthur. "What Happened to the Progressive Movement in the 1920s?" *American Historical Review*, Vol. 64 (July 1959), 833-51.

Loetscher, Lefferts. *The Broadening Church*. Philadelphia: University of Pennsylvania Press, 1957.

_____. "Presbyterian Revivals since 1875," *Pennsylvania Magazine of History and Biography*," Vol. 68 (January 1944), 54-92.

Longfield, Bradley. *Presbyterian Controversy: Fundamentalists, Modernists, and Moderates*. New York: Oxford University Press, 1991.

McClintock, Thomas C. "J. Allen Smith, a Pacific Northwest Progressive," *Pacific Northwest Quarterly*, Vol. 53 (1962), 49-59.

McDowell, John. *The Social Gospel in the South: The Woman's Home Mission Movement in the Methodist Episcopal Church, South, 1886-1939*. Baton Rouge: Louisiana State University Press, 1982.

MacFarlane, Peter Clarke. "The Black-Maned Lion of Seattle," *Collier's Magazine*, Vol. 50 (December 28, 1912), 21-23.

Machen, J. Gresham. *Christianity and Liberalism*. New York: Macmillan, 1923.

McLoughlin, William G., Jr. *Modern Revivalism: Charles Grandison Finney to Billy Graham*. New York: Ronald Press, 1959.

McMath, Robert, Jr. *Populist Vanguard*. Chapel Hill: University of North Carolina Press, 1975.

Magnuson, Norris. *Salvation in the Slums: Evangelical Social Work, 1865-1920*. Metuchen, N.J.: Scarecrow Press, 1977.

Marsden, George. *The Evangelical Mind and the New School Presbyterian Experience*. New Haven: Yale University Press, 1970.

_____. *Fundamentalism and American Culture*. New York: Oxford University Press, 1980.

_____. "Defining Fundamentalism." *Christian Scholar's Review*, Vol. 1 (Winter 1971), 141-51.

Marty, Martin. *The Modern Schism*. New York: Harper and Row, 1969.

Matthews, Mark A. *The Second Coming of Christ*. Grand Rapids, Mich.: Zondervan Publishing House, 1918.

_____. *Gospel Sword Thrusts*. New York: Fleming H. Revell, 1924.

_____. *Building the Church*. New York: American Tract Society, 1940.

_____. "Racial Prejudice Un-American," *The Annals of the American Academy of Political and Social Science*, Vol. 93 (January 1921), 69-72.

May, Henry F. *Protestant Churches and Industrial America*. New York: Alfred Knopf, 1959.

Merz, Charles. *The Dry Decade*. Seattle: University of Washington Press, 1969.

Meyer, Donald. *The Protestant Search for Political Realism, 1919-1941*. Berkeley: University of California Press, 1960.

Miller, Robert E. *Harry Emerson Fosdick: Preacher, Pastor, Prophet*. New York: Oxford University Press, 1985.

Miller, Robert M. *American Protestantism and Social Issues, 1919-1939*. Chapel Hill: University of North Carolina Press, 1958.

Mitchell, Theodore. *Political Education in the Southern Farmers' Alliance, 1887-1900*. Madison: University of Wisconsin Press, 1987.

Morgan, Murray. *Skid Road*. New York: Viking Press, 1951.

Mowry, George E. "The California Progressive and His Rationale: A Study in Middle-Class Politics," *Mississippi Valley Historical Review*, Vol. 36 (September 1949), 239-50.

Murray, Peter. *The Devil and Mr. Duncan: A History of the Two Metlakatlas*. Victoria, B.C.: Sono Nis Press, 1985.

Murray, Robert. *Red Scare*. Minneapolis: University of Minnesota Press, 1955.

Nash, Roderick. *The Nervous Generation: American Thought, 1917-1930*. Chicago: University of Chicago Press, 1970.

Newell, Gordon, and Don Sherwood. *Totem Tales of Old Seattle*. New York: Ballantine Books, 1956.

O'Connor, Harvey. *Revolution in Seattle*. New York: Monthly Review Press, 1964.

Pendergrass, Lee. "The Formation of the Municipal Reform Movement," *Pacific Northwest Quarterly*, Vol. 66 (1975), 13-25.

Penney, Lura. "Dr. Mark A. Matthews," *Red Cross News*, October–November 1971, copy in Special Collections, University of Washington Libraries, Seattle.

Phillips, Paul T. *A Kingdom on Earth: Anglo-American Social Christianity, 1880-1940*. University Park: Pennsylvania State University Press, 1996.

Piper, John F., Jr. *American Churches in World War I*. Athens: Ohio State University Press, 1985.

Bibliography

Pitts, Lulie. *History of Gordon County, Georgia.* Calhoun, Ga.: Calhoun Times Press, 1933.

Pollack, Norman. *The Populist Response to Industrial America.* Cambridge: Harvard University Press, 1962.

Preston, William, Jr. *Aliens & Dissenters: Federal Suppression of Radicals, 1903-1933.* Urbana: University of Illinois Press, 1963.

Quirk, Charles. "Origins of the Auburn Affirmation," *Journal of Presbyterian History,* Vol. 53 (Summer 1975), 120-42.

Reeve, Jewell B. *Climb the Hills of Gordon.* Atlanta: L. A. Lee Publishing Company, 1962.

Reiff, Philip. *The Triumph of the Therapeutic.* New York: Harper, 1966.

Rodgers, Daniel T. "In Search of Progressivism," in *The Promise of American History Progress and Prospects,* edited by Stanley Kutler and Stanley Katz. Baltimore: The Johns Hopkins University Press, 1982.

Russell, C. Allyn. *Voices of American Fundamentalism.* Philadelphia: Westminster Press, 1976.

_____. "Mark Allison Matthews: Seattle Fundamentalist and Civic Reformer," *Journal of Presbyterian History,* Vol. 57 (Winter 1979), 446-66.

Sale, Roger. *Seattle Past to Present.* Seattle: University of Washington Press, 1976.

Sandeen, Ernest. *The Roots of Fundamentalism: British and American Millenarianism, 1800-1930.* Chicago: University of Chicago Press, 1970.

_____. "Defining Fundamentalism: A Reply to Professor Marsden," *Christian Scholar's Review,* Vol. 1 (Spring 1971), 227-32.

Schwantes, Carlos. *Radical Heritage: Labor, Socialism, and Reform in Washington and British Columbia, 1885-1917.* (Seattle: University of Washington Press, 1979).

Scott, Anne Firor. *The Southern Lady: From Pedestal to Politics, 1830-1930.* Chicago: University of Chicago Press, 1970.

Scott, George W. "The New Order of Cincinnatus: Municipal Politics in Seattle during the 1930s," *Pacific Northwest Quarterly,* Vol. 64 (1973), 137-46.

Shannon, David. *Between the Wars: America, 1919-1941.* Boston: Houghton Mifflin Company, 1965.

Sheldon, Charles M. *In His Steps: What Would Jesus Do?* New York: Hurst and Company, 1897.

Sherman, William T. *"War is Hell!" William T. Sherman's Personal Narrative of His March through Georgia,* edited by Mills Lane. Savannah: Beehive Press, 1974.

Smith, Gary. *The Seeds of Secularization: Calvinism, Culture, and Pluralism in America, 1870-1915.* Grand Rapids, Mich.: Christian University Press, 1985.

Smith, Timothy. *Revivalism and Social Reform: American Protestantism on the Eve of the Civil War.* New York: Abingdon Press, 1957.

Soden, Dale E. "Mark Allison Matthews: Seattle's Minister Rediscovered," *Pacific Northwest Quarterly,* Vol. 74 (1983), 50-58.

_____. "The Social Gospel in Tennessee: Mark Allison Matthews," *Tennessee Historical Quarterly,* Vol. 41 (Summer 1982), 159-170.

_____. "Northern Georgia: Fertile Ground for the Urban Ministry of Mark Matthews," *Georgia Historical Quarterly,* Vol. 69 (Spring 1985), 39-54.

_____. "Men and Mission: The Shifting Fortunes of Presbyterian Men's Organizations in the Twentieth Century," in *The Organizational Revolution: Presbyterians and American Denominationalism*, edited by Milton Coalter, John Mulder, and Louis Weeks. Louisville, Ky.: Westminster/John Knox Press, 1992.

_____. "In Quest of a 'City on a Hill'": Seattle Minister Mark Matthews and the Moral Leadership of the Middle Class," in *Religion and Society in the American West*, edited by Carl Guarneri and David Alvarez. New York: University Press of America, 1987.

_____. "Anatomy of Presbyterian Urban Revival: J. W. Chapman in the Pacific Northwest," *American Presbyterians: Journal of Presbyterian History*, Vol. 64 (Spring 1986), 49-57.

Stacy, James. *A History of the Presbyterian Church in Georgia*. Atlanta: Westminster Company, 1912.

Stanworth, Samuel. *History of First Presbyterian Church of Jackson, Tennessee*. Jackson, Tenn., ca. 1924.

Starr, Paul. *The Social Transformation of American Medicine*. New York: Basic Books, 1984.

Stead, W. T. *If Christ Came to Chicago*. Chicago: Laird and Lee, 1894.

Stelzle, Charles. *A Son of the Bowery*. New York: George Doran, 1926.

Stevenson, Louise L. *The Victorian Homefront: American Thought and Culture, 1860-1880*. New York: Twayne Publishers, 1991.

Susman, Warren. *Culture as History: The Transformation of American Society in the Twentieth Century*. New York: Pantheon Books, 1973.

Sweet, William Warren. *Revivalism in America*. New York: Abingdon Press, 1944.

Szasz, Ferenc. "The Progressive Clergymen," *Mid-America*, Vol. 55 (January 1973), 3-20.

_____. *The Divided Mind of Protestant America, 1880-1930*. Tuscaloosa: University of Alabama Press, 1982.

Talmage, Franklin C. *A Study of the Synod of Georgia*. Atlanta, 1961.

Thelen, David P. *The New Citizenship*. Columbia: University of Missouri Press, 1972.

Thompson, Ernest Trice. *Presbyterians in the South*. 3 vols. Richmond, Va.: John Knox Press, 1963.

Timberlake, James H. *Prohibition and the Progressive Movement, 1900-1920*. Cambridge: Harvard University Press, 1963.

Trollinger, William Vance, Jr. *God's Empire: William Bell Riley and Midwestern Fundamentalism*. Madison: University of Wisconsin Press, 1990.

Tuveson, Ernest. *Redeemer Nation*. Chicago: University of Chicago Press, 1968.

Weisberger, Bernard. *They Gathered at the River*. Boston: Little, Brown, and Company, 1958.

Weston, Beau. *Presbyterian Pluralism: Competition for a Protestant House*. Knoxville: University of Tennessee Press, 1997.

Wiebe, Robert H. *Businessmen and Reform: A Study of the Progressive Movement*. Cambridge: Harvard University Press, 1962.

_____. *The Search for Order, 1877-1920*. New York: Hill and Wang, 1967.

Bibliography

Williams, Emma Inman. *Historic Madison: The Story of Jackson and Madison County, Tennessee*. Jackson, Tenn.: Madison County Historical Society, 1946.

Willis-Watkins, David. "Systematic Theology," *American Presbyterians*, Vol. 66 (Winter 1988), 270-72.

Woodward, C. Vann. *Tom Watson: Agrarian Rebel*. New York: Macmillan Company, 1938.

_____. *Origins of the New South, 1877-1913*. Baton Rouge: Louisiana State University Press, 1951.

Index

Index

denominations, 28-29, 81; views on the poor, 31, 33-34, 215; views on health care, 21, 32, 77-78, 100, 204; views on race, 32-33, 78-80, 217; views on immigration, 89, 136-37; views of human nature, 96, 187, 214; views toward child welfare, 97-98; views toward monopolies, 98-99; views toward municipal government, 98, 108-109, 130-31, 200-201; views toward woman suffrage, 100-101

Matthews, Mark Jr., 63, 195-97, 222

Matthews, Mark Lafayette, 4, 26, 196-97

Matthews, Melinda Rebecca, 4, 26

McAdoo, William, 192

McGhee, Rev. Z. M., 72

McGraw, John, 66, 108-109

McKelway, Alexander, 25

Meany, Edmond, 142

Men and Religion Forward movement, 59

Metlakahtla affair, 210-14

Miller, John, 95, 109, 130

Moore, William, 95, 108, 109

Municipal Ownership League, 108, 200-202

Murphy, Edgar G., 25

Murphy, John, 117, 123, 128

New Era movement, 170

New Order of Cincinnatus, 209

Old School Presbyterianism, 9-11, 22, 161, 178, 180

Orthodox Presbyterian Church, 181

Palmer, A. Mitchell, 136, 149

Parkhurst, Rev. Charles, 93

Parry, William, 136

Populism, 14-15, 17

Postmillennialism, 71-72, 167

Powers, Mike, 134

Premillennialism, 157, 167

Presbyterian Church in the United States (PCUS) (Southern Presbyterianism), 9, 12, 163

Presbyterian Church U.S.A. (Northern Presbyterianism), 163, 181

Priestley, James, 193

Princeton Seminary Controversy, 180-81

Proctor, Robert, 135

Progressivism, 87-88; Matthews's views on, 36, 88-91, 97, 100

Protocols of Zion, 149

Rauschenbusch, Walter, 70, 90

Recall of 1910, 112-17

Red Cross, 77-78, 214

Red Scare, 149-50

Riley, William Bell, 217

Riplinger, John, 108-9

Rockefeller, John D., 64, 76, 98

Ronald, J. T., 117, 137

Roosevelt, Franklin, 216-17

Roosevelt, Theodore, 162

Ross, J. D., 66, 130-31, 193-95, 200-202, 215

Scopes Monkey Trial, 157, 179

Scottish common-sense realism, 10-11, 161

Seattle General Strike, 150-53

Seattle Ministerial Federation, 109, 125-26, 132, 141

Sedition Act of 1918, 150

Sheldon, Charles, 30, 70

Short, William, 135, 203

Sinclair, Upton, 69, 100

Smith, Al, 188

Smith, J. Allen, 108, 120

Social Gospel, 24-26, 76, 228

Special Commission of 1925, 175-77, 180

Spanish-American War, 35-36

Speer, Robert, 176-79

Stead, W. T., 69

Stelzle, Charles, 82-84, 99, 162

Strong, Anna Louise, 140, 153

Strong, Rev. Sydney, 140

Sunday, William Ashley (Billy), 57, 144

Suzzallo, Henry, 120, 204-205

Index   273